Jeremy Black is, according to Andrew Roberts, the most underrated historian in Britain. MBE and Professor of History at Exeter University, he is the author of over a hundred books and is one of the most respected military historians in the world. He is a former member of the Council of the Royal Historical Society.

Highlights from the series

A BRIEF HISTORY OF

SLAVERY

JEREMY BLACK

RUNNING PRESS
PHILADELPHIA · LONDON

ROBINSON

Constable & Robinson Ltd
3 The Lanchesters
162 Fulham Palace Road
London W6 9ER
www.constablerobinson.com

First published in the UK by Robinson,
an imprint of Constable & Robinson, 2011

A copy of the British Library Cataloguing in Publication Data is available
from the British Library

UK ISBN 978-1-84901-689-6

1 3 5 7 9 10 8 6 4 2

First published in the United States in 2011 by Running Press Book Publishers

9 8 7 6 5 4 3 2 1
Digit on the right indicates the number of this printing

US Library of Congress Control Number: 2010940978
US ISBN 978-0-7624-4277-5

Running Press Book Publishers
2300 Chestnut Street
Philadelphia, PA 19103-4371

Visit us on the web!
www.runningpress.com

Typeset by TW Typesetting, Plymouth, Devon

Printed and bound in the UK

For George Bernard

CONTENTS

ABBREVIATIONS

Add.	Additional Manuscripts
AE	Paris, Ministère des Rélations Extèrieures
Ang.	Angleterre
Bod.	Oxford, Bodleian Library
BL	London, British Library
CP	Correspondance Politique
FO	Foreign Office
NA	London, National Archives
SP	State Papers
ADM	Admiralty papers

PREFACE

Her Majesty was doubtless not amused by calls in 2007 that her anniversary visit to Jamestown in Virginia, to celebrate the founding of the first permanent English settlement in North America in 1607, should be the occasion for an act of contrition for the past treatment of both Native Americans and Africans, but the vexed subject of slavery continues to trouble public memory and private consciences. For example, the letters page of the Fredericksburg, Virginia, paper *The Free Lance-Star* for 18 April 2010 included a letter describing New England's role in the slave trade and complaining that only the South was being blamed for this evil.[1] The following month, the Texan Board of Education approved a new history and social studies curriculum that downplayed the role of slavery, arguing that the American Civil War was fought principally over states' rights. The new curriculum has already proved highly divisive, and, given the role of Texas as a major market for text books, this decision was nationally significant.

This issue is not simply one of public memory. Indeed, as this book hopes to show, slavery is not only a matter of the past but also has echoes to this day, not least with such practices as debt bondage, penal labour, sexual slavery, human trafficking and girls sold by dowry into marriages that are little better than servitude. The disproportionately black group of convicts working on a railtrack escorted by gun-holding white guards on horseback, whom I saw at Augusta, Georgia in the early 1990s were not slaves in the sense of those, including possibly their ancestors, sold at harboursides in the eighteenth century, but nor were the Mamluk slave soldiers of medieval Egypt. As Lord Mansfield noted in his ruling in the Somerset case in 1772 'the power of the master over his slave has been extremely different in different countries'. Coerced labour is a central theme of slavey, but the range of this work is broad. Tursun Beg, an Ottoman surveyor, noted of the successful campaign in the Morea (Peloponnese) in Greece in 1455, 'After these conquests . . . every tent had the appearance of a slave market with pretty young girls and boys thronging the entrances.'[2]

Slavery is a subject that has a long history and a broad geographical scope. The breadth of the story encompasses the ancient and the modern world, Atlantic and Islamic trades, and it is scarcely surprising that slavery does not have a single meaning, nor a uniform context. This diversity is important not only to understanding slavery in the past but also how it can be seen today. In particular, by raising the question of public or state slavery, I seek to advance a narrative and analysis that is different in its emphasis to the standard one, and this difference is relevant to the question of present-day legacies and apologies. Slavery is one of the most emotive issues in history, and I indeed have found this a distressing book to write as the subject involves so much hardship, misuse and cruelty. At every stage, it is important to appreciate in what follows that abstractions dissolved under scrutiny into real people and that these people felt and suffered.

In working on this topic, I have benefited greatly from holding a Mellon Visiting Professorship at Stillman College in

1992, and from being invited by the Division of Continuing Education of the University of Virginia to speak at a conference held in 2000 on Jefferson and Slavery, by Don Yerxa to speak on another held in 2007 on Abolitionism and Progress in History, by Carol Seigel to speak at Burgh House (Hampstead Museum) in 2007, and by Ahmed Banyn and Darryl Thomas to speak at the Department of African and African American studies at Pennsylvania State University in 2010. I have profited greatly from the comments of Bill Gibson, Leo Hollis and Joe Miller on an earlier draft, and of David Brion Davis, Keith Hamilton, David Northrup, Thomas Otte and John Thornton on sections of an earlier draft, and from discussing the subject with Charles Aldington, Kristofer Allerfeldt, Tonio Andrade, Nick Baron, Michael Bennett, Troy Bickham, Pita Burt, James Chapman, Karel David, Martin Dusinberre, Arthur Eckstein, Olavi Fält, Peter Fleming, Ron Fritze, Peter Garretson, Robert Gerwarth, Chris Gill, Derek Gore, Anthony Harding, Janet Hartley, Susan Hayward, Richard Hitchcock, Rudi Matthee, James Onley, Michael Prestwich, Geoff Rice, Peter Robb, Richard Scrivener, Claude Sintes, Jouko Vahtola, Eugene Vansickle, and Everett Wheeler. None is responsible for any of the errors that remain. It is a great pleasure to dedicate this book to George Bernard, an old friend and fellow historian, and, in doing so, to mark thirty years of friendship.

INTRODUCTION

Hadijatou Mani was sold into slavery at the age of twelve, and subsequently beaten, raped, and, indeed, imprisoned for bigamy for marrying a man other than her 'master'. This case was not one from the sixteenth or eighteenth century, but one that came before the Court of Justice of the Economic Community of West African States in 2008. The government of the state of Niger was convicted for failing to protect Ms Mani and was fined accordingly. In a reminder of the continuation of mistreatment, Ms Mani announced that a reason for her action was to secure the freedom of her children in a society where, despite the government's formal opposition to slavery, customary courts support the practice whereby the children of slaves become the property of their masters.[1] Slavery indeed is far from past, and this is a key theme of this book. Niger, one of the world's poorest countries, was ranked bottom by the United Nations in 2006 of the world's states in terms of 'human development'. Slavery was not one of the criteria, but Niger shows that it is still the condition of many.

The mournful, underground dungeons at Cape Coast Castle and other bases on the low, watery coastline of West Africa where African slaves were held from the fifteenth to the nineteenth centuries prior to shipment to the New World are a potent memory of the vile cruelty of slavery, and notably of the approximately 12.5 million Africans forced into this trade and transported on about 35,000 transatlantic voyages, yet these dungeons are not alone and should not crowd out other landscapes where slavery was carried on and the slave trade conducted.[2] Nicholas de Nicolay's mid-sixteenth-century account of slave dealers parading their captives naked to show that they had no physical defects, and so that they could be examined as if they were horses, with particular reference to their teeth and feet, could have referred to the world of Atlantic slavery, but actually was written about Tripoli in modern Libya, where large numbers of Christians captured from Malta and Sicily by the Barbary pirates of North Africa were sold.[3]

Indeed, the landscapes of slavery span the world, and range from the Central Asian city of Khiva, where the bustle of the slave market can still be visualized in the narrow streets, to Venice, a major entrepôt for the slave trade of medieval Europe albeit not one noted by modern tourists. The range is also from Malacca in modern Malaysia, an important centre for the slave trade around the Indian Ocean, especially under the Muslim sultans but also, from 1511, under, first, their Portuguese and, then, their Dutch successors, to the few remains of the murderous system of labour that was part of the Nazis' genocidal treatment of the Jews. The variety of slavery in the past and across history stretched from the galleys of Imperial Rome to slave craftsmen in Central Asian cities, such as Bukhara, and from the mines of the New World to those working in spice plantations in East Africa. Public and private, governmental and free enterprise, slavery was a means of labour and a form of control.

The purpose of this book is to provide an account of the history of slavery and the slave trade that focuses on the last half-millennium but includes an earlier background. Slavery is like war. In one light, 'you know it when you see it' and enforced servitude, like large-scale, violent conflict, is easy to define; but, just as discussion of war frequently overlaps with other aspects of conflict and violence, so the same is true with slavery, with force and servitude being open to varying definitions. In 2000, the International Association Against Slavery included debt bondage, forced work, forced prostitution and forced marriage in the scope of slavery, and, if such an understanding is the case today, it is unclear why it should not also be extended to the past. As another instance of varied definitions and understandings of slavery, this time from an historical perspective, there is a contrast between slavery as the condition of a distinct, hereditary caste, and enslavement as an individual fate or punishment. Societies with large-scale slavery have very much differed as to whether the status is hereditary or not.

A central theme here is that slavery is the most distinctive, but by no means the only, form of coercive labour, and that the latter is far more important in the history of labour than is often appreciated. Indeed, in many respects coercive labour is the core type of labour, while free labour – like, for example, secularism – is a product only of particular environments, notably those with high liquidity in which the purchase of work by means of wages could be used as the means to secure labour. Moreover, the extent to which either free labour or secularism can be seen as a product, or even definition, of modernization and modernity is less obvious than would have been the case twenty years ago.

The relationship between slavery and coercive labour does not offer a precise definition. For example, the International Convention with the Object of Securing the Abolition of Slavery and the Slave Trade ratified by the members of the League of Nations in 1926 defined slavery as 'the status or condition of a person over whom any or all of the powers attaching to the right of ownership are exercised', but, far from being readily agreed, that definition emerged only from political bargaining that led to the exclusion of forced labour and concubinage. An understanding of such bargaining subverts an attempt to present this, or any other, definition as of universal use. To turn to recent years, about 17,000 slaves were freed in the state of Niger in 2005, but they were described as 'bondage workers'.[4] Indeed, instead of clear definitions, there are overlaps[5] between slavery, convict labour, serfdom, debt servitude, indentured service, the idea that entire nations, such as modern North Korea, are slave societies, and so on.

As an instance of the problem of definitions, there was a legal and linguistic distinction between serfdom and slavery in Russia. *Kholopstvo* is slavery and a slave was known as *kholop* or *rab*, and serfs were not slaves even if their life differed in few respects. Yet, the word *rab* or slave was sometimes used when referring to serfs; serfs could be bought and sold, and families could be split up or moved against their wish. The character of Russian serfdom was bitterly criticized in Alexander Radishchev's book *Journey from St. Petersburg to Moscow* (1790), which denounced arduous work, poor living conditions, and the right of lords to sell and to flog serfs. Moreover, serfs were outside the normal legal system for all but the most serious criminal offences until the 1860s, while the distinction between the *robot* work regime of Polish serfs and the work done by Russian slaves was limited. A similar point might be made about the slaves and Cretan peasants alike forced by the Ottomans (Turks) to dig trenches to support the siege of the Venetian-held fortress of Candia in Crete from 1645 to 1669.

Furthermore, it is not necessary to draw attention to the modern term 'wage slave', in order to note that many who are not formally seen as slaves have had little or no choice about work and its character and context, not least in terms of subservience, emuneration and lack of labour mobility. Travelling from Füssen in Bavaria to Innsbruck in Austria in

1787, Adam Walker wrote of the women he saw, 'I sincerely pity them, they are such slaves as I have heard the Negroes in the West Indies described. No uncommon sight to see them threshing corn, driving wagons, hoeing turnips, mending the highways'.[6]

In the nineteenth century, comparisons were drawn by Southerners between the black slaves in the American South and the workers in many Northern company towns, who were tied there not least by payment in tokens that could be used only in company shops. This highly contentious issue was fought out in print on both sides of the Atlantic. Thus, in 1863, as men fought to decide the future of the United States, Edward Yates in Britain addressed *A Letter to the Women on Slavery in the Southern States of America* in which he agreed that there were 'white slaves' in the Northern states, as well as in Britain, but also established a clear difference with only black people in the South robbed of their right to their own labour, women robbed of children and men of wives, and all subject to the torture of the lash.[7]

Similar points were made about the condition of the poor in Britain, but, again, the argument came from both sides. Thus, *A Letter to those Ladies who Met at Stafford House in Particular, and to the Women of England in General, on Slavery at Home* (1853) by an 'Englishwoman', declared:

> there is a class of *English* slaves who deserve your pity as much as the bondmen of the United States . . . women . . . who are left to starve, or what is worse, to gain a livelihood with the wages of sin and infamy . . . Day after day, night after night, while life exists, do these our countrywomen toil at their needle, until either their eyesight fails, or else disease, consequent on close sitting and cramped limbs, calls them to a quieter home, the only resting place for them. Is it not slavery to work for fourpence-farthing a day, or rather day and night . . . Is it not slavery to live year after year dependent on the hard masters in many of the most fashionable shops in our great metropolis . . .

human beings herd together until the very air is loaded with
death ... [in England] on many thousands the curse of slavery
rests ... those hordes of half-savage beings who exist in
London and in many of our great manufacturing towns.[8]

This pamphlet, directed against 'great ladies' active in Abolitionism, captured the plasticity of the concept of slavery, the
extent to which it was employed in a critical factor but also
could be used to define hypocrisy. The use of the language of
slavery to discuss harsh working and living conditions at home
was to be extended by feminists to depict the female
condition, although their criticism in the late nineteenth
century largely rested on the absence of freedoms, particularly
the right to vote.

However, the classic Western assumption, which in part
draws on Karl Marx and in part on interest in the history of
the West, locates slavery as an aspect of labour control and use
(the two are closely related, but different) in capitalist
societies, most evidently the plantation economies of the New
World from c.1500 to c.1890. A key element here is the
removal of the labourer from their original society, which
helps lead to a defining isolation and vulnerability. In the case
of the New World, slaving indeed served to build up a labour
force based on fungible human collateral for the credit that
supported an Atlantic trading system that grew through very
heavy borrowing from Europe.[9] This, however, is far too
narrow an account of slavery, for it omits totally the
significance of public slavery: slavery in the service of the
state, which is a key strand from antiquity to the present, most
famously with the public construction projects of Ancient
Egypt and Classical Rome or the convict labour that powered
the opening up of Siberia under Stalin; convict generally only
in the sense of political crimes.

Slavery, therefore, is a state with different meanings in
particular contexts, but with a fundamental element of an
absence of freedom. This last element puts a focus on the

political dimension as well as the more customary economic one, and thus underlines the extent to which slavery is the collective experience of those who lack freedom as well as a personal one. Slavery as the condition of being without freedom is different to those of labour without payment to the worker, or of coerced labour, let alone to slavery as whatever is legally defined as such, but is also a valid definition of slavery. Coercive work entails a denial of personal freedom, but such a denial does not necessarily centre on coercive work. Indeed, far from seeing sale, purchase and sellability as key elements of slavery, they were, and are, particular means of exchange within one of the two central forms of slave society, with governmental power providing the other element. Moreover, the classic Atlantic slave trade depended on both capitalist exchange and government power, as African polities produced slaves through warfare, just as polities for much of history supported slave markets by these means. This point is also valid for slavery in, for example, Classical Rome, medieval India, and early-modern (c.1500–c.1800) Central Asia, as most of the slaves in these civilizations derived directly or indirectly from those seized in warfare.

Across the world, the slave trade might seem to open up an important distinction between slavery and serfdom, that of compulsory movement for work, but the category of those who were not apparently slaves still included many people subject to such movement. These people included serfs moved against their will, transported convicts, others sent to colonies or on internal exile against their will, and even, in one light, the indentured servants and others travelling for economic opportunity within a system in which their choices were limited or non-existent.[10] The use of child labour from workhouses and other sources in eighteenth-century Britain enabled the *Independent* of 2 August 2010 to run a piece on the Industrial Revolution being dependent on slavery.

In advancing a typology of slavery, it is possible to differentiate between societies with slaves, in which slavery was largely a domestic institution within the household, and slave societies, in which slavery was the mode of production on which the dominant group depended for its position.[11] It is also possible to focus on two types of the latter: slavery at the service of the state, and slavery within a private enterprise system. Slavery at the service of the state tends to receive the least attention, but state slaves of various types were important in many pre-modern states. In some cases, indeed, they were key elements in the governmental system, most obviously with the janissary units in the Ottoman (Turkish) Army, who played a crucial role in the army and the politics of the state until the 1820s, but also with the Scythian archers used as a police force in Classical Athens.

Moreover, certain modern governments, such as North Korea, can be seen to claim so much authority and to wield so much power that, whatever the legal and constitutional situation, their entire population can be regarded as slaves. This may be seen as a rhetorical device, but it is difficult to see how slavery at the service of the state can be discussed historically and the term not employed to describe such a contemporary society. Less dramatically, public ownership of the means of production underlines the problem of excluding some societies from the discussion of slavery, as such ownership can leave the individual with scant freedom to decide how and where to work. Thus, the focus on work in discussion of the private, capitalist type of slavery can be replicated for this type of public slavery even if the ideology about work and citizenship that is deployed is totally different.

The use of slavery to describe such modern societies may appear overblown, but the rhetorical use of slavery as a critical designation is longstanding and not confined to antiquity. Turning from the emphasis on work, European political rhetoric in the early-modern period also echoed the Classical fears of enslavement[12] and employed the juxtaposition of liberty and slavery, typecasting the subjects of political systems judged unacceptable as slaves. Thus, in England, the opposition in 1297 claimed that, by means of arbitrary taxation, Edward I was reducing them to a state of servitude, which was a potent rhetorical argument. Such claims became more insistent in the early-modern period. The British Whig journalist James Baker linked slavery to ignorance and reiterated Classical Greek themes about Persia when he wrote in 1723,

> There is not a trick in religion, nor a piece of villainy in politics, but what owe their rise and growth to ignorance. Keep the people in the dark and you may lead them where you will … hence slavery and superstition have overrun the eastern monarchies, from the beginning to this day; and for their sins, these evils rage now and ravage in too many western nations.[13]

In 1740, James Thomson offered a vision of national destiny in these terms:

> When Britain first, at heaven's command
> Arose from out the azure main,
> This was the charter of the land,
> And guardian angels sung this strain:
> 'Rule, Britannia, rule the waves;
> Britons never will be slaves'.[14]

William Cowper added in 1785:

> Slaves cannot breathe in England, if their lungs
> Receive our air, that moment they are free;
> They touch our country, and their shackles fall.[15]

This argument was used by the British against the Spaniards and the French in the eighteenth century, and was also to be employed by the American Patriots against the British at the time of the American Revolution. Protestant polemicists defined Catholicism in terms of enslavement to a false image and practice of Christianity. These arguments were not only made in print but were also seen in private correspondence, as when John Tucker MP wrote to his brother in 1748 about the 'inevitable slavery' threatened by a failing resistance to French expansionism.[16]

The contrast with the reality of slave labour was readily apparent while there was no racial component to these arguments, but they were important in keeping slavery alive in the minds of commentators as a signifier of what was totally unacceptable. Indeed, this use of the terminology of slavery was important to the subsequent traction of Abolitionist arguments in Britain. At the same time, alongside this rhetorical usage, the discussion of politics as slavery testified to an anxiety that aspects of the latter could spread and were not limited by current signifiers of race and location.

Yet, although there were slaves in Christian Europe during the Middle Ages, and, in the shape of galley slaves, they continued to exist throughout the early-modern period, with Mediterranean galley fleets ending only in 1816, a characteristic of Western slavery from the sixteenth century was that it was predominantly part of the commercial economy and generally practised in colonies outside Europe. Slavery in the Western world was a system of servitude driven essentially by free enterprise, and this situation also provided the crucial context for the slave trade in this world: it was a response to economic need, and a product of the search for economic opportunity.

Western slavery represented an aspect of the commodification of human beings for reasons of labour that is central to economic activity. However, focusing modern concerns, it also reflected particular socio-cultural assumptions and practices in which nationhood, ethnicity and religion all played important, although varying, roles. Historically, there was no necessary relationship between slavery and racism. Indeed, enslavement was frequently a penalty for illegal behaviour. There were the white slaves of white states, most obviously those who manned the oars of the large numbers of Christian galleys that contested the Ottoman advance in the Mediterranean.[17] In sub-Saharan Africa and Ancient Rome, where owners and slaves were often of the same colour, manumission, the freeing of slaves, was common, and in Africa women and children were enslaved for lineage incorporation as well as labour.

Despite this, there was a deeper identity of racialism and slavery, for enslavement was frequently the response to the 'other': to other peoples (irrespective of their skin colour), and other creatures. This treatment extended to Europeans, especially with the large numbers enslaved by Muslim powers, notably the Barbary pirates of North Africa. Treating conquered peoples and their offspring as slaves seemed as logical to many as treating animals such as horses as slaves. The latter, beasts of burden, were also the creation of God, and therefore part of the divine plan, but the fact that they could be readily subordinated and trained for service to humans apparently demonstrated a natural and necessary fate. The contrast in the sixteenth to nineteenth centuries between white workers sent to the Americas as indentured labour, not slaves, and Africans moved as slaves, not indentured labour, reflected more than racism; but racism was a core component of the slave trade and slavery, both the Western-run one and its Arab equivalent, and this racism was an aspect of its vileness. There was no voluntary emigration from Africa to the New World.

At the same time, racism was more varied than is suggested by a stress on the Atlantic slave trade. For example, Native American (American Indian) ownership of slaves in the United States was pervasive until Emancipation – which scarcely conforms to the standard image. Moreover, there was large-scale slavery within Africa itself, and also in areas not usually associated with the history of slavery and the slave trade, such as India. Thus, the history of slavery was a more central and dynamic feature of the history of the world than it is comfortable for us to acknowledge.

I

PRE-1500

The ballad tells the story of a mother who sets out to retrieve her only child, seized by a slaver. When crossing a river, she sees a group of people under some willow trees and the boatman tells her that a boy, abandoned by slavers as too weak to continue its journey, has died. The boy was her son. The ballad, *Sumidagawa*, is a work of medieval Japan,[1] not usually noted as a centre of slavery, but, like Ancient Japan, a slave-owning society. It is a testimony to the global range of slavery.

An important part of human history, slavery has no starting point, but it seems to have played a major role from early times. When slavery began in the prehistoric world is a matter of supposition, since there is no written evidence, and interpreting either artefacts or picture is a subjective exercise. Slavery probably played a particular role in the treatment of those from other groups: in this respect, other humans were treated as animals, and indeed there was an important overlap. One form was that of ritual sacrifice, with both animals and humans captured to that end, a reminder that slavery had short-term as well as long-term purposes. In some societies, notably Egypt from the third millennium BCE and steppe societies, moreover, the servants and household of a ruler were consigned to the grave on his death.[2] The ceremonial sacrifice of slaves continued in Dahomey in West Africa until slavery was abolished there.

The development of agricultural systems was a crucial instance of the long-term purposes of slavery, as irrigation had large-scale needs. Slavery was certainly common in Bronze Age Egypt and the Ancient Near East, probably from the third millennium BCE, and in the Eastern Mediterranean from the second millennium BCE. Much of the agricultural labour, however, was provided by the peasantry, and slaves were frequently required for other purposes that were non-agrarian, notably as mine workers, palace and temple servants, and soldiers, the last being a frequent fate for those captured in war. The status of slaves is unclear. For example, in the Linear B documents of Minoan Crete of about 1600 BCE, *doeros* and *doera* were mentioned at Knossos in Crete and the Mycenaean site of Pylos in the Peloponnese (Morea), but it is unclear whether these terms meant male and female slaves or bondsmen and bondswomen. Moreover, some were referred to as the property of living individuals, but others, especially at Pylos, as belonging to a god or goddess, and the latter had a status different to that of other slaves, as they could have leases on land and they appear to have lived similarly to ordinary free persons. The children of parents of whom only one was a slave were also slaves, which was unlike the situation later in Classical Greece.[3]

Slavery in the Classical World
Slavery was a central element of the Classical world and the world known to it. Slavery was significant in the Babylonian laws of Eshnunna of about 1900 BCE and the Code of Hammurabi of about 1750 BCE,[4] while Egypt obtained slaves

from Nubia in the north of modern Sudan to the south, frequent wars providing large numbers of captives. Thus, Khakāura Senusret III (c.1870–1831 BCE) campaigned at least four times in Nubia, killing men and enslaving women and children. From at least the Fifth Dynasty (2494–2345 BCE), trading missions were sent to Punt to obtain products including slaves, Punt probably being in eastern Sudan or Eritrea.[5] With time, the sources of slaves for Egypt expanded to include further and more varied lands, notably the Levant, a process that was taken still further once Egypt was absorbed into, first, the Hellenistic (332 BCE) and, then, the Roman (30 BCE) worlds, not least with slaves coming from markets in Anatolia. Moreover, slavery was accepted as a fact of life in the Old Testament and practised in Israel, a point made by the defenders of slavery in the American South in the nineteenth century. Slavery was also seen across Bronze Age Europe. For example, slaves appear on the engraved stelae, or stone slabs, of south-west Spain of about 850 BCE that show warriors surrounded by their chattels.[6]

The idea of a slave as a human, legally owned and used as if a domestic animal, was widespread even if the legal treatment and anthropological context might vary. There was also a sense of the naturalness of slavery, and Greek thinkers proved able to rationalize the practice as an important instance of human development. In particular, they advanced the idea of such development as occurring in stages, an idea that was also to be central to European thought at the time the slave trade was at its height in the eighteenth century. These stages were seen as creating differences between societies, and the more advanced ones therefore naturally benefited from the others.

The major Greek philosopher, Aristotle (384–322 BCE), in his influential *Politics*, notably presented slavery as part of a developmental model, with development in terms both of the use of human slaves rather than animals and of stratified political organizations. In Book One of his *Politics* he argued that people who were inferior because, due to a defective rational faculty, they could only use their body, were by nature slaves.[7] To Aristotle, the simple village was a community in which the ox was the slave of the poor man, whereas the more advanced and benign Greek *polis* offered a city state where the pursuit of public culture and virtue was possible because of a socio-political stratification that was in part feasible due to slavery and partly its cause. This *polis* included farmers able to rely in part on the slaves obtained by war,[8] although Aristotle criticized the practice of Greeks enslaving conquered Greeks. Aristotle also distinguished between the *polis* and 'barbarian' states that, he suggested, were the equivalent to a 'community of slaves', although that did not preclude these states' enslavement of others.[9] In such states, the key distinction in practice was not that between free and slave but between those in the ruler's household and the rest; and this distinction was also seen within the Greek world, for example in the earlier Mycenaean civilization of Crete.

The presentation of the uncivilized as inherently enslaved, both to their own base wants and, whether or not formally slaves, in the polities of barbarian uncivilization, was one that was advanced in antiquity and that had a long life. The Greek historian Herodotus (c.485–425 BCE) portrayed Achaemenid Persian troops being whipped to press forward an attack, as if they were slaves, although this was probably Greek propaganda pushing the standard theme of the clash between Greek freedom and Oriental despotism.[10] Racial difference informs some of this account, but was not inherent to it. What was more significant was that a sense of slavery as natural, and thus of enslavement as appropriate, was frequently the response to the 'other', to other peoples (irrespective of their skin colour) and other creatures. This enslavement was a matter not only of the fact of slavery, but also of the psychological designation of the condition of these peoples as inherently that of slaves. This condition meant that these people were regarded as deserving, and/or being readily conducive to, subordination and being trained for service. This Aristotelian concept of natural slavery was to be used by jurists and writers, such as Juan Ginés de Sepúlveda, to justify the subjugation of the Native Americans by the Spaniards in the sixteenth century.

In a fictional form, this treatment of the 'other' was captured in William Shakespeare's play *The Tempest* (1611) which, in part, drew on accounts of English transoceanic exploration and colonization. In the story, Caliban, the sole inhabitant of the island, has an accursed parentage with his father being the Devil and his mother a witch. He is enslaved first by Prospero, a wise but exiled Italian monarch, and then, in response to his exposure to alcohol, by two drunken Italians. Called 'thou poisonous slave' and 'abhorred slave', Caliban is a coerced worker ordered to fetch in wood.

Gender was also an aspect of slavery. Thus, in the Homeric world, the slaves described in the *Iliad* and the *Odyssey* were mainly women, generally spoils of war, and used as servants and concubines.[11]

The role of slavery in antiquity was to be deployed by its subsequent defenders to argue that the practice was not only compatible with civilization and progress, both of those associated with Classical Greece and Rome, but even necessary to them. Reflecting the potent role of Greece and Rome as exemplars of appropriate behaviour, this argument was to be made with considerable force by American Southerners in the nineteenth century. Indeed, the imaginative weight of antiquity played an important role in the debate about slavery, one that has receded over the last century as this weight has diminished.[12] As with most such ahistorical parallels, the use of the analogy by American Southerners said more about the values and issues of those making it than about their subject or evidence, but it was certainly the case that slavery was significant to the economics, societies, politics and culture of the polities of antiquity, whether these were city states or great empires.

The role of slavery in antiquity is often underplayed. It is instructive to note tourists visiting the major slave marts of antiquity, such as the Aegean island of Delos, without expressing opprobrium or any equivalent to the critical catharsis expected of those who visit the West African equivalents of the later transatlantic slave trade. In 2010, I expressed surprise at the Musée Gallo-Romain in Vienne (France) at the absence of any discussion of slavery. Thus, the site includes the remains of a c.2 CE *fullonica* (fulling mill) without a discussion of the labour force. The staff I spoke to responded that the museum was concerned about daily life, which further led to my sense that slavery was being written out of the past, but the same was true of the Musée Départemental Arles Antique, which, for example, displayed a map about trade in the Roman empire without any mention of the slave trade. In the case of the latter museum, the lack of archaeological discoveries relating to slaves affected the finds that could be displayed.[13]

The scale of slavery in antiquity was considerable, fuelled as it was by the determination to use victory in order to drive home the point of triumph, the example of submission, and for profit. Delos was made a free port in 166 BCE, and, according to the geographer Strabo (c.64 BCE–23 CE), 10,000 slaves could be sold in a single day. Ironically, the capture of Delos in 88 BCE by Menophaneses, a general of Mithradates VI, King of Pontus, was followed by the killing of many and the enslavement of its surviving population. A pirate attack in 69 BCE led to the enslavement of much of the remaining population and the island was then left nearly uninhabited. Slaves in the Greek world were also the product of debt enslavement, piracy, banditry and slave trading, especially from the Black Sea, Thrace and Anatolia (Asia Minor, Asian Turkey).

In antiquity, as is already clear from the arguments of Aristotle, slavery was not an 'other' associated only with less-developed societies, but was seen as an aspect of the differentiation that made internal development possible. Indeed, slavery developed in part alongside the democracy of the *polis*,[14] with citizenship clearly distinguished from slavery in Classical Greece and Rome. Given the arduous physical nature of much work in societies lacking the resources of mechanization, this use of slavery also allowed a politics in which there were slaves at the bottom of the ladder. Non-slaves who lacked social status could be differentiated from the slave population, a process that made it possible for them to enjoy privileges, notably citizenship, which in some polities led to a measure of democracy.[15] This situation prefigured that in later slave societies, such as the American South, in giving those who lacked status a sense of superiority that lessened social tension and aided inclusion and cohesion at the cost of the exclusion of others.

Prefiguring George Orwell's comment on the 'stone-like cruelty of the ancient world', there was scant criticism of slavery which indeed was common across antiquity, with all but the poorest Greek households having at least one slave. Some thinkers, such as Aristotle, saw slavery as good discipline for those who were natural slaves and weak. He claimed:

> the slave is a part of the master – he is, as it were, a part of the body, alive but yet separated from it; hence there is a certain community of interest and friendship between slave and master in cases when they have been qualified by nature for these positions, although when they do not hold them in that way but by law and by constraint of force the opposite is the case.

Thus, Aristotle saw slavery as entailing an important psychological element. He also wrote of 'the just acquiring of slaves, which is akin to the art of war or that of the chase'.[16]

Slavery existed even in the ideal cities discussed by Plato (c.428–347 BCE). Other thinkers, such as Thucydides (c.460–c.400 BCE), more critically thought of slavery as just the exploitation of the weak by the strong. Slavery as necessary but only, of course, appropriate for others emerged in the work of Polybius (c.200–c.120 BCE), who, in his *History of*

Rome, presented slaves as simply one of the requirements of a gentleman's life, but praised those free men who killed themselves rather than be enslaved, for example the people of the city state of Abydus, which was captured in 200 BCE by Philip V of Macedon (r.221–179 BCE). Polybius recorded the criticism of free people being made into slaves when the citizens of a *polis* which had surrendered to Philip V on promise of good treatment were enslaved anyway because he needed the money.[17] Philip was to be defeated by the Romans at Cynoscephalae in 197 BCE.

This criticism of slavery was very specific and has to be set alongside a willingness to boast of making slaves, as when Julius Caesar (c.101–44 BCE) wrote in his *Gallic Wars* of selling tens of thousands of Transalpine Celts into slavery on a single day. Lucius Aemilius Paulus, victor over the Macedonians at Pydna (168 BCE), was ordered by the Senate to divide Macedon and ravage Epirus in order to affirm Roman control. He reportedly sold 150,000 of the population of the latter into slavery, and was awarded a triumph in Rome and the honorific 'Macedonicus'. There are also tombstones of slave merchants which depicted them conveying slaves in chains.[18] Yet, Scipio Africanus (236–183 BCE) is presented by Polybius, who was a protégé of his grandson Scipio Aemilianus, as accepting limits. Thus, in the Second Punic War with Carthage, when Scipio captured New Carthage in Spain in 209 BCE, 'he told the working men that for the time being they were public slaves of Rome, but if they showed goodwill and industry in their several crafts he promised them freedom upon the war against Carthage terminating successfully.' The strongest of the prisoners became galley slaves on the same basis.[19] Scipio's restraint was to be praised in his unwillingness to accept women for concubinage after his defeat of Hannibal at Zama in 202 BCE, a subject often celebrated by Renaissance painters.

The work done by slaves varied greatly depending on environmental and political contexts. In the region of Attica, the part of Greece near Athens, the mines, notably the great

silver mines at Laurium, contained maybe 35,000 slaves in
about 340 BCE, mostly from Anatolia and Thrace. Conditions
were harsh. The slaves worked in small tunnels 300 feet (100
metres) underground, the cramped conditions forcing them to
crawl and kneel, with guards at the mine entrance to maintain
control. Many of the slaves were children. One of the leading
slave gangs belonged to Nicias (?–413 BCE), a prominent
politician and general.

More generally, in the Classical world, because it lacked the
technological strength provided in the nineteenth century by
high explosives and machine power, mining – with the vast
labour force it required – was a major centre of a form of
capitalism linked to slavery. This point serves as a reminder of
the need to consider slavery not only as an anachronistic and
limiting element in labour markets but also, potentially, as an
aspect of economic dynamism. However, the emphasis in
Attica was on independent small farms with maybe a few
slaves. In Thessaly, in contrast, there was more social
stratification and, with it, much serfdom, a system that was
open to large-scale slavery. Such slavery became more common
in Greece under the Hellenistic regimes of the third and second
centuries BCE, when agriculture was less intensive.[20]

More generally, a lack of liquidity encouraged slavery as the
means to provide substantial labour forces and these, in turn,
produced wealth. In the Roman empire, slavery was particularly associated with agricultural regions with large-scale
estates producing, often with the aid of irrigation, crops for
movement to Rome, for example grain, wine and olive oil
from Africa (Tunisia), and wine and olive oil from Baetica
(southern Spain). These estates contained substantial slave
labour forces and these regions contrasted with areas with
fewer large estates, and less production for distant markets, for
example northern Spain and west England. Yet, there were
also substantial slave forces in mining areas, which included
northern Spain. Work in the mines was one of the harshest
forms of slave work. The most important marble quarries

belonged to the emperor and were worked by convicts condemned to forced labour.

The varied sources of slaves in the Greek and Roman worlds reflected the need for large numbers of them. The key requirements for slaves were for public functions, household service, agricultural tasks – for example as shepherds in Apulia – mining and as craftsmen. The range of sources of slaves arose in part from the extent to which slavery was a ready measure of social difference. Some slaves were born to existing slaves, a major source that underlined the value of slave women and that also ensured that, for many, the experience of slavery was from cradle to grave. Slave status was also created as punishment for offences, individual or collective, or as a result of impoverished individuals choosing to become slaves in order to ensure their livelihood or selling their children for that reason in times of debt or famine. Slaves were also acquired through force, with, war, conquest, and the suppression of rebellions all yielding large numbers, the sale of whom was very profitable. Slave raiding was linked to this practice and overlapped with the purchase of slaves from other societies.

Among the large numbers of slaves, those born to slavery were often brought up in a situation of some stability, and habituated to what they were to experience. Many others, however, were outsiders, for whom the process of enslavement was exacerbated by the need to respond to a society which they did not know and where any process of adaptation was mediated through their subordinate status and often brutal exploitation as a commodity. To this extent, the argument that slaves were the world's first 'modern' people, uprooted from their context, outsiders who remained marginal and vulnerable, and thus the first exemplars of the migratory labour and confused identities of the modern world, can be challenged. The terms on which slaves took part in their world involved, on the whole, a greater role for coercion than modern outsiders, while their condition was frequently more alone, and thus vulnerable. As in the modern world with migrant labour, the slave condition was frequently ameliorated by being part of a community of slaves of similar origin, but the capacity of slaves to ensure this outcome was minimal, and thus contrasted with the situation for modern migrants.

The complexity of the position of slaves was captured by the situation in the Roman Army, the largest force of men under arms in European history until the seventeenth century. Maybe up to a quarter of a million Italians were in the Roman Army in 31 BCE, nearly a quarter of the men of military age, but the Romans did not turn to slaves to fill the ranks. The exception to this was in the manpower shortage after the severe and bloody defeat by Hannibal in the Second Punic War at Cannae in 216 BCE, which led to the enrolling of two legions of slaves. But this expedient was an anomaly not repeated and these slave soldiers were later discharged with freedman status. Paradoxically, the obligations of military duty hit the Roman yeomanry as part of a crisis of the viability of the agrarian economy of this yeomanry, a crisis linked to the economic competition posed by the rise of large estates reliant on slave labour.[21]

The Roman stigma against the use of slaves as troops reflected prudential concerns, based on the danger of arming them and on the problems posed by enlisting important productive capacity,[22] but also ideological, cultural, political and social beliefs focused on the links between citizenship and military service. Slaves, even freed slaves, were prohibited by law from service in the Roman Army, and this stipulation was preserved even in the Late Roman period when the empire was under savage pressure from 'barbarian' attacks. The army remained a privileged class, and, although barbarian prisoners of war could be recruited, Late Roman law codes sought to weed out runaway slaves who had managed to enter the ranks. Even the use of slaves as rowers in the galleys of the Roman Imperial fleets has been exaggerated, although privately owned ships were another matter. Contests for imperial power and provincial revolts both led to claims that the other side or the rebels armed slaves, claims which are instructive as they cast a social stigma on the accused party. The stigmatiz-ation of slavery scarcely prevented the practice, but, as the Roman Army showed, it limited the extent of slavery. Officers and some soldiers had personal slaves, but that was very different to the reliance on a slave army, and this contrast was seen in antiquity, certainly by the Greeks and Romans, as a proof of their civilization. Leaving aside the validity of that argument, it is instructive to note how far, and with what consequences, this 'placing' of slavery varied between civiliza-tions.

The role of coercion and force in the provision of slave populations encouraged violent opposition to enslavement, although those who rebelled or sought escape were not solely slaves obtained in that way. There were frequent slave revolts, the most famous today being that of the Thracian-born Spartacus, who was enslaved for desertion from the army and became a gladiator before leading a major uprising in 73 BCE. He built up a large army, possibly 90,000 strong, and, advancing along the length of the Italian peninsula and devastating the great estates, vanquished a number of Roman forces before being defeated and killed in 71 BCE at the battle of Luciania by the Praetor, Marcus Lincinius Crassus. As an instance of the exemplary punishment the Romans sought, large numbers of Spartacus' followers were crucified and their bodies left hanging along the Appian Way.

This rebellion is very important to modern views on slavery in the ancient world. Spartacus became a key figure in the late-twentieth-century depiction of the Roman empire, no-tably as a result of Stanley Kubrick's film *Spartacus* (1960). Slave rebellions served both the Communists as an example of the continuity of resistance to social oppression that they claimed to exemplify in the modern world, and also Western writers and filmmakers seeking a way to make Rome dramatically accessible. From their perspective, slavery was a crucial depiction of the wrongness of a political system that also crucified Christ. Thus, America could be seen as the modern descendant of the linked opposition to slavery, imperialism and paganism, and there was a clear Cold War subtext with Roman/Soviet oppression opposed to Christianity/American democracy. Similar assumptions and values were advanced in other films, such as Ben Hur (1924 and 1959), Demetrius and the Gladiators (1954), and, more recently, Gladiator (2000).[23] In 2010, Spartacus was the subject of Spartacus: Blood and Sand, a television series by the American cable channel Starz that was strong on violence and sex, rather than any exploration of the nature of slavery.

Other slave revolts also challenged the Roman world. That led by Eunus the Syrian, began in 139 BCE and involved about 60,000–70,000 slaves, mostly on Sicily but also on the Italian mainland. This revolt led to a fall in the grain shipments that kept the Roman population quiescent, and the anger of the Romans was shown in the slaughter of the last 20,000 of the rebel slaves when they surrendered in 132 BCE.[24] Nevertheless, there were other revolts on Sicily, notably in 104–100 BCE, that, in turn, were also crushed.[25] More generally, the murder of masters by slaves helped lead to a fear of slaves, resulting in the controversial law that in such cases all the household slaves should be executed.

The far-flung nature of the Roman slave trade extended beyond the bounds of Rome's conquests, which produced slaves for example from Gaul, Germany and Dacia (Romania), to interact with the movement of slaves further afield. Slaves were an important source of imports into the Roman empire, coming from a range of areas including sub-Saharan Africa, Yemen, and the Caucasus. The Romans drew on networks that moved slaves from West Africa across the Sahara to North Africa, from the Ethiopian Highlands and Yemen down the Red Sea to Egypt, and from southern Russia via the Black Sea; although these networks did not only move slaves towards the

Roman empire. The relative difficulty and distance of routes across the Sahara helped underline the importance of the maritime route provided by the Red Sea. There was no equivalent to the later European trade along the Atlantic coast of Africa. Trade along the Red Sea involved the cooperation of the kingdom of Axum, in what is now Eritrea, with Rome, just as the slave trade from the Upper Nile required the cooperation of the kingdom of Cush with Rome.[26]

The importance of the slave trade from outside the territories controlled by Rome declined with time, as the slave population was increasingly maintained by reproduction among the slave population. In turn, attacks on the Roman empire by 'barbarians' saw raiders and invaders seizing large numbers for slavery.

Slavery in the East pre-1500

Slavery was also found elsewhere in the world, although complex issues of definition emerge. For example, the China of the Shang dynasty (1766–1122 BCE) has been called a slave society, but it has been argued that this is misleading as most of the population were not bought nor sold nor deprived of their personal freedom, although they were subject to coercive work.[27] The situation appears to have varied by dynasty. In Han China (206 BCE–25 CE) about 5 per cent of the population was enslaved, while slavery was important in the legal code of the T'ang dynasty in the seventh century. Agricultural slaves continued to exist in China, for example under the Ming in the fifteenth, sixteenth and seventeenth centuries CE, but the availability of plentiful cheap labour lessened the need to turn to slavery. Concubinage was also frequent. In neighbouring Korea, there was large-scale slavery, as there was in Japan, where, aside from enslavement in wars within Japan and kidnapping, there was also the selling of children by debtors and the indigent, and the use of criminals as slaves.[28]

Slavery in the Americas and New Zealand pre-1500

Coercive work can be seen with New World cultures such as the Moche (c.1–c.600 CE) of coastal Peru, an expansionist, sun-worshipping culture that organized large labour forces to take part in public works. The Moche were to be succeeded by the more extensive Huari empire (c.500–c.800 CE) which used a labour tax to carry out public works such as very extensive road building. A reliance on irrigation also encouraged patterns of labour control. The far more extensive Inca empire (1438–1532 CE), based on the Andean chain, also relied on forced labour, which provided troops, agricultural workers, transport porters and men for public works such as mining and building. The extraction of forced labour from subject peoples was a key aspect of power relationships in South and Central America. Slavery in pre-Columbian America was personal, rather than hereditary, and slaves derived from war, tributary status, debt and punishment.

As an instance of this personal quality, the slaves of Aztec Mesoamerica, an empire in central Mexico from the mid-fourteenth century to 1521, could purchase their liberty or obtain it if they could show that they had been mistreated. Slavery in Mesoamerica prior to the Spanish arrival in the early sixteenth century arose not only from capture in war, but also from purchase, including from relatives, debt bondage and punishment. Slaveholding was widespread, and slaves performed a range of tasks, including household service.

In New Zealand, the Maori practised slavery in conjunction with cannibalism. Slaves were taken in war to increase a tribe's labour force for food production, but the chiefs had power of life and death over the slaves, and could order them to be killed and cooked for a feast. Warriors, especially chiefs, thus preferred death to capture.

Slavery in the Islamic world pre-1500

The social relations of much of the Classical world were
challenged by religious movements, providing a new context
for slavery, but also greatly influenced those relations.
Christianity and Islam proved particularly important. Christianity
was generally presented by later Christians as being
opposed to slavery, with Christ's message being equally given
to all.[29] Some Christian leaders certainly called for fair
treatment for slaves and the latter were allowed to participate
in the liturgy. However, in practice, both Islam and Christianity
adapted to the widespread slavery of the societies in
which they established themselves, and there was a considerable
overlap, notably in the idea that slavery was part of the
divine plan.[30] Although Joseph being sold into slavery by his
bothers was scarcely a good example, slavery was endorsed by
the Old Testament and was accepted as a fact of life in the
New Testament with Jesus saying little on the subject because
in his social milieu no one owned any slaves. Coming from a
different background, St Paul addressed the issue, arguing that
slaves had to accept their station; he referred to conversion to
Christianity as being a transition from being a slave to sin to
becoming a slave to righteousness. The Canon Law of the
Church accepted slavery, which seemed irrelevant to the more
significant possibility of salvation after death. Eventually,
however, Christian teaching also contributed to a degree of
liberalization, with the theologian St Gregory of Nyssa
(c.331–95) criticizing slavery.[31] To guard against the risk of
proselytism or a refusal to permit Christian worship, Jews
were forbidden to own Christian slaves, while the Code of
Justinian, the major sixth-century codification of the laws of
the Eastern Roman empire, altered the definition of a slave
from a thing to a person.[32] Cruel owners were deprived of
their slaves. However, although he was opposed to the
ownership of humans, St Augustine (354–430), Bishop of
Hippo from 396, the leading Latin Father of the Church, saw
slavery as a product of the Fall of Man and therefore as a

condition that had to be borne. Christianity was established as the official imperial creed by the Edict of Milan (313) issued by Constantine I (r.307–37) who also established a new capital at Constantinople in 300. The Byzantine (Eastern Roman) empire based, from 395, on Constantinople took part in extensive warfare with its neighbours, the wars with the Sassanians and, from the 630s, Muslims to the east, yielding slaves – as did those in the Balkans. The slaves from Sassanian and Arab cities were particularly valued as skilled craftsmen and commanded higher prices.[33]

The Islamic world, created by the Arabs and their Muslim converts by conquest in the century from the 620s CE, stretched from Spain to the Indus river and was very much organized in terms of its original subjugation. In the 620s, as Muhammad developed his position in the Hejaz, the Quraiza tribe of Jews in Medina were destroyed in 627, with the men killed and the women and children enslaved. The following year, the Jews of the nearby oasis of Khaibar were defeated and enslaved. The large numbers of slaves produced by Muslim conquests were important to political and social status, as well as for more functional reasons. There was also the basic demographic fact that the Arabs and their supporters were a minority in the lands they conquered, and that slavery helped structure the resulting social, political and religious relationships. Only non-Muslims could be enslaved, although slaves who converted to Islam kept their servile status. There is an interesting contrast with the fears of Caribbean slave-owners who tried to exclude missionaries in the eighteenth century for fear that conversion to Christianity might lead to pressure for freedom.

Islamic law was far from monolithic, with different schools providing competing accounts. Nevertheless, it was agreed that non-Muslims living under non-Muslim rule could readily be enslaved by Muslims, and their status was heritable, although owners could free as well as bequeath, sell and give slaves. However, although, even among orthodox Muslims, the notion that slaves were properly secured by conquest alone was very far from being observed, non-Muslims living under Muslim rule were protected from enslavement, Christians and Jews being regarded as Peoples of the Book, and thus related to Muslims, and enjoying religious freedom on payment of a poll tax. Thus, for the purposes of ensuring slave labour, Muslim societies were not able to draw on the bulk of the population under their control and had to rely on the slave trade.[34] In India, Islamic rulers, such as the sultans of the Delhi sultanate (1206–1526), used enslavement as a form both of extracting revenues and of punishment, not least for not paying taxes. Fiscal factors were to the fore and territorial expansion was in part financed by the sale of slaves.[35]

In the Islamic world, slave labour was significant to the economies both of households and of production, for example making the Shatt al-'Arab in southern Iraq – the marshlands alongside the lower Tigris and Euphrates rivers – cultivatable and a major centre of sugar production in the ninth century.[36] There were also large numbers of construction slaves, while skilled slaves working in pottery and textiles were much in demand and commanded a premium. Their seizure was a desirable product of conquests, as when the Uzbek conqueror Timur (Tamerlane) seized Delhi in 1402. Christians seized and sold into slavery in North Africa in the seventeenth century worked in a range of activities including rope-making, and at the slave market calluses were seen as evidence of experience of labour, which was regarded as desirable.[37]

Moreover, the extensive sexual economy included slaves in harems and as eunuchs. The castration of eunuchs reflected the power of masters and the extent to which the aggregate strength of the slave system was replicated in individual households and, in turn, was confirmed by their arrangements. The emphasis was on personal service, and the Islamic law of slavery was patriarchal and belonged more to the law of family than to that of property.[38]

The public side of slavery was also significant, in so far as such a concept has separate meaning when the ruler often adopted a patrimonial approach to his position and people. In the Islamic world, the notion of service encompassed soldiers and bureaucrats, and each group were frequently slaves, albeit favoured slaves. The legal category of 'licensed slaves' made it possible for slaves to represent their owners in transactions, which ensured that slaves could become trusted figures. This position helped make slaves prominent in elite households, as did their dependence on their masters, and the role of slaves in government was an aspect of this situation as government was very much organized on a household basis. So also was military service, as the elite force was the bodyguard of the ruler and such palace bodyguards had a slave status.

Thus, private and public usage overlapped, although the governmental, public, side of slavery in both administration and military service stretched to include many who were not personally members of the household. From at least the time of the early Abbasid caliphate of Baghdad in the eighth century, Muslim rulers used slave armies and slaves in government, rather than tribal Arabs, the basis of their original power, many of whom had proved politically unreliable. However, serious problems with Turkic slave soldiers in 836 led to the move of the Abbasid capital for a time. Muslim armies took a variety of forms, but a key component in some were professional slave soldiers. For example, slave troops were used by al-Hakam I (r.796–822), the Umayyad Emir of al-Andalus (Islamic Spain), who established a bodyguard that included slaves of Eastern or Northern European origin, a bodyguard expanded by his son, Abd al-Rahman II (r.822–52) and used as a key force to increase control over the state. In turn, greater control ensured more taxation which permitted further territorial expansion. This process was taken further by al-Mansur, the chief minister of al-Andalus in the late tenth century, who recruited large numbers of slave soldiers as well as Berber mercenaries from North Africa, and was able to launch regular attacks into the Christian territories of northern Spain from which loot and slaves were obtained. Some of these slaves were then sold on to Islamic markets across the Mediterranean. In the Middle East, Saladin (1138–93), a Kurdish general who became ruler of Egypt, Palestine and Syria, had large numbers of military slaves who played a major role in his campaigns, to the north-west the Seljuk Turks of Rum in Anatolia in the thirteenth century used slaves for both government and troops, including as military commanders, and even established a school of Konya for their education. By the time of the Ottomans, who became a major force in Anatolia and the Balkans in the fourteenth century, recruitment into Ottoman service was often as a slave.[39] There were also numerous slave soldiers in the armies of the Islamic states in sub-Saharan Africa.

The number of favoured slaves reflected the extent to which in the Islamic world, as in other slave societies, there was a stratification by owner, privilege and task, a process that was part of the integration of the slave world with that of the non-slaves, and one that greatly lessened any sense of unity among the slaves. Membership of an elite household brought an elevated position for slaves and this situation had a military edge as slave soldiers could be used to control other slaves and even to suppress opposition.

The pace of conquest produced large numbers of slaves for the Islamic world in its first century and, thereafter, a certain number of new slaves came by birth from the existing slave population, although castrations reduced the potential number. However, there was also demand for additional slaves, not least due to the widespread practice of freeing slaves after a number of years, a practice that looked back to the Old Testament stipulation of freedom for Hebrew slaves after six years. This demand encouraged both slave raiding and slave trading, although frequently the same individuals were involved in both. Raiding was practised across the borders of Islam as well as against subject populations. It was seen for example in the Horn of Africa, especially against Ethiopia, and in the steppes of Russia, in each case being important to the

economy of frontier regions, with the large numbers seized
mostly being sold on to the slave marts providing for more
settled Islamic societies, especially urban ones such as Alexandria and Baghdad. As such, the slave raiding was an aspect of
the stadial relationships already referred to. In Europe, there
was slave raiding against Christian communities, with sea-
borne raiders being particularly important. For example, such
raiders established a position at Fraxinetum in Provence in 890
from which, until its fall in 972, they raided southern France,
notably the Rhone valley, and northern Italy. Similarly, the
Adriatic was raided from the base at Bari between 841 and 871.
Rome itself was raided from Tunis in 846.

The continued dynamism of successive Islamic societies
produced fresh bouts of conquest that led to new sources of
slaves. Thus, on the eastern end of the Islamic world, Mahmud
of Ghazni, south-west of Kabul (r.971–1030), whose empire
stretched from the River Oxus to the River Indus, launched
numerous raids into northern India from the 990s, annexing
the Hindu state of Sahi to the east by 1021. Religious factors
played a role in his attacks, which in 1022 extended far down
the Ganges valley and in 1026 into Gujarat. Chroniclers
claimed that his campaign of 1024 yielded over 100,000 slaves.
Such numbers fed a major slave trade into Central Asia, Persia
and Iraq, as well as bringing wealth to the army. The Delhi
sultanate (1206–1526), established by Qutb-ud-din Aybak,
who had been a military slave of the Churid Sultan Muizz
u-Din, so that it is sometimes referred to as the Slave Dynasty,
in turn, used Turkic slave soldiers from Central Asia as well
as local Hindu soldiers.[40] This sultanate took part in large-
scale slave raiding in India.

Additional examples of Islamic societies producing fresh
episodes of conquests and more slaves were provided by the
successes of the Seljuk Turks, Almoravids, Mamluks and
Ottoman Turks. The Almoravids, Berbers from North Africa,
made significant gains in southern Iberia in the late eleventh
and early twelfth centuries and also advanced south of the

Sahara conquering, in 1076 the polity, sometimes described as the state of Ghana, which was oriented towards the upper Senegal river. In the same period, the Seljuk Turks, newly converted to Islam, conquered most of Anatolia.

The Mamluks were largely Circassians from the Caucasus, captured in childhood, enslaved, and trained as slave soldiers. In 1250 they seized power in Egypt from the Ayyubid sultanate, and rapidly conquered both Muslim territories in Syria and the Hejaz, and the Christian territory in the Levant, culminating with the seizure of Acre in 1291. The Mamluks also proved able to defeat the Mongols in Syria in 1260 and held Egypt until they were conquered by the Ottoman Turks in 1517.[41] This period of Mamluk rule was roughly equivalent in length to that of slavery in what became the USA, and it is an interesting sign of relative concerns that the attention devoted to slavery in the Mamluk empire and the USA is as a drop of water compared to the ocean.

The idea of slavery in the service of Islam and of mankind as the slaves of God is kept alive in the popular name 'Abdullah, which means slave of Allah: the Arabic word for slave is 'Abd. The Ottoman Turks, who began a major series of Balkan conquests from the fourteenth century, developed the janissaries, the sultan's household infantry, first from captives in warfare. They supplemented this source by a levy of slaves from among their Christian subjects, the *devshirme* or collection, which, although illegal under Islamic law as non-Muslim subjects were protected infidels, became the practice during the fourteenth century. The standard rate of collection was described in the fifteenth century as one boy from every forty households. Timur (1336–1405), who created a short-lived empire based at Samarkand in Transoxiana, extending from northern India to Syria and the Aegean, preferred to persuade cities to surrender and then pay ransom, but when they resisted, as for example Isfahan did, he erected pyramids from the skulls of the slaughtered and marched the rest away into slavery to Transoxiana. Many died on the way.

Alongside raiding there was slave trading, which was greatly encouraged by the strong demand for slaves in Islamic society. The directions of trade shifted in what was an often complex pattern of slave movements as, by the end of the eighth century, there were Islamic centres from northern India to Spain and from Central Asia to the Sahara. Furthermore, Islam continued to expand, for example into the *sahel* belt to the south of the Sahara Desert and into Sumatra, both by 1300. In the ninth and tenth centuries, the Abbasid caliphate of Baghdad, the centre of the Islamic world, was the focus of a wide-ranging slave trade, receiving, in particular, Turkic slaves from Central Asia, Slavs from Eastern Europe, and Western European slaves via traders in Prague, Venice and Marseilles. Thus, Muslim merchants purchased slaves in Prague in the late tenth century. There were also slaves from Africa, some crossing the Red Sea to Jedda and then coming overland to Baghdad. Others came via the Persian Gulf. The Zendj, who worked in the Shatt al-'Arab and rebelled in 869, came from the lands to the south of Ethiopia via the great slave market at Basra. They overran much of lower Iraq, but the Abbasid reconquest, launched in 880, was finally victorious in 883. Balkan slaves were also sold to Islamic societies in North Africa and southern Spain, a situation that reflected the lack of a strong Balkan power and the linked openness of the Balkans to raiding.

The interaction between the movements of slaves to and in the Islamic world and those in Christian Europe was to be significant to the eventual development of the slave trade of the latter. Yet, the slave movements to the Islamic world often had little to do with Christendom, as with the movement into Central Asia of Hindu slaves from India, of non-Sunnis from Afghanistan, and of Buddhist Oirats from Mongolia. Moreover, Arab slave traders benefited from the development of major polities in the *sahel* belt, for example Mali from the early thirteenth century, as well as from the related warfare in sub-Saharan Africa that produced slaves. The southward expansion of Islam in Africa, such that it became well-established south of the Sahara, also encouraged the development of trans-Saharan trade routes along which slaves were moved. There was an important movement of slaves from West Africa across the Sahara via entrepôts such as Sijilmassa, Taourit, Ghat, Murzuk and Kharga to North African and Spanish markets, for example Marrakech, Tlemcen, Tunis, Kairouan and Tripoli in North Africa. This movement led to a longstanding concern by the Muslim rulers of al-Andalus with control over North Africa, as in the tenth century when the Umayyad caliphs drove the Fatimids from the Maghreb. Further east, the Mamluks maintained the traditional import of slaves into Egypt from Nubia. In the Nile valley in the thirteenth and fourteen centuries there were vulnerable small states between the Mamluk empire and the state of Alwa at the junction of the White Nile and the Blue Nile, and their vulnerability helped in the provision of slaves. The town of Sennar on the Blue Nile was a major entrepôt, providing slaves both for Egypt and also, via the Red Sea ports of Suakin and Jedda, for Mecca. In the Indian Ocean, the sources of slaves for the Islamic world extended to northern Madagascar by the tenth century, but there were also continued supplies from raiding into India.

Slavery in Christian Europe, pre-1500

Slaves were important in early medieval Christian Europe, although there were significant regional differences which contribute to the degree to which, as far as popular views are generally concerned, slavery has, in part or whole, been written out of the history of the period. Slavery was certainly frequent in large areas of Europe until the twelfth century when it declined because of shifting practices of labour control as well as the influence of Christian opposition to the enslavement of fellow Christians. Prior to that, there had been slave raiding and trading within Christian Europe, and enslaving of non-Christian captives, notably in Spain and

Eastern Europe. For example, just as Irish raiders captured people then sold as slaves in Ireland – in the fifth century the future St Patrick was one of these – so there was slave trading from Ireland in Anglo-Saxon England. Anticipating the town's prominent role in the African slave trade, many of these slaves were brought ashore at Bristol. Patrick later attacked Coroticus, the slaver who carried off his Irish converts to Britain as slaves, for having 'stained his hands with the blood of the children of God' by failing to accept the converts' Christian character.[42]

In the centuries after the fall of the Western Roman Empire, with polities originally established on a tribal basis, such as those of the Franks or Saxons, subordination in Christian Europe was linked with non-membership of the tribe and this, as well as warfare, could lead to slavery. In 694, Egica, the Visigothic King of Spain, decreed that the Jews of Spain who refused to convert be consigned to slavery as a punishment for alleged conspiracy, although it is unclear that this happened in full. Slavery was certainly important to the Visigoths, who ruled Spain from the fifth century to the Moorish conquest from 711, and the Visigoths faced slave revolts. Some slaves were recruited into the Visigoth army: some of whom may have been born into slavery; they were not necessarily recruited during slave raiding. More generally, the enslavement of outsiders helped explain that of Muslims and Jewish Khazars in Hungary, and of Roma (Gypsies) and Tatar prisoners in Moldavia and Wallachia.[43]

Christendom also suffered from slave raiding from non-Christians. Muslim attacks were a prime issue but were not alone. The Vikings were much dreaded. Slaves played a prominent role in Viking society, not least providing farm labour, and were captured for use in Viking society and for sale elsewhere, including to the Islamic world.[44] For example, the Vikings based in Dublin from the late ninth century took 2,000 prisoners from Anglesey for sale as slaves in Ireland in 987. Those Vikings who established themselves in Kievan Rus played a prominent role as slave traders, as their trading routes reached from the Baltic to the Caspian and Black Seas in the tenth century. As an instance of far-reaching networks, Vikings took Slav slaves to Denmark, from where they were taken to Spain and North Africa. In the Baltic, Finland was subject to the Viking slave trade. In addition, Finnish epic folklore indicates that the Finnish elite, certainly in the period 800–1050, owned slaves.

The second wave of 'barbarian' attacks on Christendom also included pagans from western Asia, notably Magyars and Bulgarians, and both of these took part in raiding in which people were part of the booty. Settling in the Danube basin from 896, the Magyars with their mounted archers raided far into Europe, particularly Germany, but also into Italy, Spain, France and the Balkans, with especially far-ranging raids in 938 (into France) and 942 (into Spain). A crushing defeat by Otto I of the East Frankish kingdom (later Germany) and his heavy cavalry at the Lechfeld in 955 helped transform the situation, and the Magyars were Christianized soon after.

In turn, slavery declined across much, but not all, of Christian Europe, especially Western Europe, because of a reduction in the availability of enslavable people and related developments in the direction and influence of Christian teachings, notably because the norms of war did not come to allow for the enslavement of captives in legitimate warfare between Christian states. Anticipating the role of Christianity in Abolitionism, St Wulfstan, Bishop of Worcester in England from 1062 to 1095 made a major effort in preaching visits to Bristol to persuade the people there to end the slave trade, and his efforts helped William I in his suppression of the trade. Moreover, Church reformers challenged traditional patterns of male violence that had found honour in terms of slave raiding and, in particular, in the brutal sexual exploitation of enslaved women. By treating such behaviour as dishonorable, sinful and associated with uncivilized societies, the clerics helped discredit slavery.[45]

Changing patterns of land use, particularly an increase in rented land, were also significant. It was more economic to give slaves smallholdings so that they became servile tenants, a change which was often linked with a transition from slaves as single people to servile families, as on the smallholdings it was easier to organize a family economy (in which different members fulfilled particular tasks) and thus support families. This shift ensured that the labour force reproduced itself, which was more useful for the landlord than purchasing slaves, although the cost of feeding young children lessened this advantage. In England, the number of slaves probably declined from the early tenth century, although they still formed a substantial group in the Domesday survey of 1086. By the early twelfth century, slavery, as an institution, was a pale shadow of its former self, although Peterborough Abbey still reported slaves on its estates in the 1120s.[46]

Slavery continued in medieval Europe, especially Eastern Europe, but serfdom became the key form of labour control in both Western and Central Europe and Byzantium (the Eastern Roman Empire), which is an instructive reminder of the extent to which slavery was but one alternative among a number of forms of labour control. Like slavery, serfdom varied in its character, notably its legal basis, practical implications and context, but, in essence, it was a system of forced labour based on hereditary bondage to the land. Serfs were thus bought and sold with the land. Serfdom was used to provide the mass labour force necessary for agriculture, and was intended to ensure a fixed labour force at a time when, in a largely unmonetarized and low-efficiency agrarian economy that was short of labour, 'free-market' incentives to that end were not practicable. The legal essence of serfdom was a form of personal service to a lord in exchange for the right to cultivate the soil, a form of (inegalitarian) contractualism that was not present for slavery, and this situation was readily compatible with Christian teachings.

Yet, serfdom entailed restrictions on personal freedom that, in their severe form, were akin to slavery, and it has been argued that 'many aspects of medieval serfdom were very like slavery'[47] a point that is also worth considering for subsequent centuries. Serfs were subject to a variety of obligations, principally labour services, and owed dues on a variety of occasions, including marriage and death, and could be sold. Adam Smith, the famous eighteenth-century Scottish economist and author of *The Wealth of Nations* (1776), was to describe serfdom as a 'milder kind' of slavery.[48]

Slavery continued in areas of Europe that were as yet not Christianized, for example Finland. Expeditions and eventually crusades against pagans yielded slaves, and some of these were then moved considerable distances. In the tenth century, the Lombards imposed a 10 per cent duty on slaves and other products entering Italy from northern Europe.[49] In turn, the patterns and language of labour control changed with Christianization, which occurred in Finland in the twelfth century. There was also a major tranche of Christendom where slavery was practised: essentially Mediterranean Christendom, and more particularly southern Portugal and Italy, southern and eastern Spain, the islands of Crete and Cyprus and the Balearic Islands. In these territories, as a consequence of the combined legacy of Classical slavery, the experience of conquest from Islam and the availability of new slaves as a result of privateering and other attacks on the Islamic world, slavery was ubiquitous and provided labour for agriculture, industry, mining, transport and household service.[50]

This slave world was fed from a number of sources. Enslavement as a penalty for illegal behaviour remained an option in late medieval Christendom. Subjugating Sardinia in the fourteenth century, the Aragonese enslaved large numbers of Christian Sards. More significantly, there was the enslavement of non-Christians captured in war and raiding, for example in Spain in the late twelfth century. A large number of Spanish Muslims remained after the conquest to till the soil, while, seen as a security threat, others were expelled or allowed to emigrate, but many Muslims were forced into slavery. Thus, the conquest of Minorca and Ibiza in 1287 by Alfonso III of Aragon was followed by much of the Muslim population being sold into slavery, which produced both money for their captors and land for settlement. The supply of slaves from lands captured in the *reconquista* was supplemented by raiding, especially into North Africa.

The slave trade from outside Christendom was notably to markets in the Mediterranean as the practice of slavery retained a stronger grip there than further north in Europe where, in contrast, serfdom was more important. Catalan merchants imported slaves from North Africa to Spain, where Barcelona, Valencia, Cartagena, Cadiz and Seville were major markets, but the key sources of supply to the Christian Mediterranean were further east, especially the Balkans, the Black Sea and Anatolia. These sources expanded and became more profitable as a result of the overthrow and despoilation of the Byzantine (Eastern Roman) Empire by the Fourth Crusade in 1204. The Crusade led to the establishment of a Latin Empire in the East which provided a new colonial-style political control, and also resulted in Italian participation in the existing slave-trading economy based on the Black Sea. Within the extensive sphere of protection and influence provided by the Italian merchant republics, notably Genoa and Venice, this participation helped ensure expanding opportunities for this economy, and slaves from the Black Sea region, notably from the Caucasus, but also from Russia down the valleys of the Volga and Dnieper, were exported to the Mediterranean with Kaffa and Trebizond being big entrepôts.

The markets in the Mediterranean for the slaves from the Black Sea encompassed both Muslim areas, notably Egypt and Syria, and also Christian ones, including Crete, Cyprus, Sicily and eastern Spain, each of which contained a form of hybrid Christian-Muslim society, reflecting the legacy of Muslim rule before these territories were conquered by Christian powers. This slave trade, which was of 'whites', was the principal source of slaves for Christian Europe and it continued after the fall of the Latin Empire (Constantinople was recaptured in 1261), as the revived Byzantine Empire looked to the Venetians and Genoese, each of which had a base in Constantinople, for much of their foreign trade and naval protection. Unlike their Ottoman opponents, the Byzantine armies did not use slaves.

The Caucasus–Black Sea–Mediterranean slave route was separate to, but also an outlier of, the movement of slaves across much of Eurasia that reflected the far-flung Mongol conquests of the thirteenth century which stretched from China to the Black Sea. The Mongols obtained many slaves from the cities they sacked. To give a glimpse of the range of Mongol activity, these cities included Zhongdu in China in 1215, Bukhara in 1219, Samarkand in 1220, Kaesong in Korea in 1231, Ryazan and Vladimir in the campaign into Muscovy in 1237–8, Kiev in 1240, Cracow and Pest (Budapest) in 1241, Baghdad in 1258, and Aleppo in 1259. Having captured the cities, Mongol armies rode on with the slaves following them. The appearance of the Manluk state in 1250 was dependent on the Mongols as their invasions ensured the availability of large numbers of slaves who were shipped to Egypt.

Karakorum (in modern Mongolia), which became the Mongol capital in 1235, was a leading centre of slave trading, and the Mongols also sold slaves in the Volga valley, where New Sarai became their major base and the centre of the khanate of the Golden Horde, one of the successor states to the Mongol empire. This khanate pressed on the Russian principalities, such as Kiev, Vladimir and Galich, its raiding producing large numbers of slaves that were then moved to the Black Sea via the lower Volga and the Crimea, both of which were part of the khanate. In turn, Timur sacked New Sarai in 1395, gaining new slaves there.

The slave trade from the Black Sea did not satisfy the total demand across the Mediterranean. In Iberia there was an already well-established pattern by the Christian states of obtaining Moorish slaves by raiding as-yet unconquered Arab lands in the south, with Andalusia raided before it was conquered in the thirteenth century and Granada before it was finally conquered in 1492. This pattern developed in the fourteenth and fifteenth centuries in another iteration of the Iberian expansion that by then had become far more than the Christian *reconquista* of lands there seized by the Arabs in the eighth century. Conflict spilled over into North Africa, with raiding followed by the establishment of bases in Morocco, Ceuta being captured by the Portuguese in 1415, followed by Alcacer (1458), and Arzila, Larache and Tangier, all in 1471, while the Castilians (from modern Spain) conquered Melilla in 1497.

In addition, there was expansion into the Atlantic. From 1341, Castilians began to colonize the Canary Islands, seizing the native Guanches, whom they regarded as inferiors, as slaves; but they also encountered a vigorous resistance. With its strong maritime interests, Portugal proved the key player, although Portuguese expeditions along the Africa coast were motivated largely by a search for gold, not slaves. In a world of metal-based currencies, gold was a source of power, and the illustrations on the African portion of the *Catalan Atlas* of 1375 included a depiction of Mansa Munsa, the fabled ruler of Mali in the West African interior, the text reading, 'So abundant is the gold in this country that the lord is the richest and noblest king of all the land.' The Portuguese wished to sail along the coast of West Africa in order to be able to trade for gold in the West African interior without any intermediary role for the North African Muslims, who took Saharan salt south by camel in order to exchange it for gold. Although the Portuguese found it difficult to gain entry into the gold trade, they did so, and this entry was linked to a developing slave trade, because slaves became useful as a commodity to sell in exchange for gold,[51] rather as the British were later to use opium from India as a way to open the China trade. The Portuguese first met black Africans in Senegambia, the region from the mouth of the River Senegal to that of the River Gambia, and from there came their first slaves from sub-Saharan Africa.

Alongside the use of slaves for trade in Africa, the Portuguese also exploited them as a labour force in Portugal and its Atlantic island colony of Madeira, the sale of slaves from Africa from 1441 feeding into the pattern already established for Moors. Between 140,000 and 170,000 slaves were exported to Portugal or Madeira from 1441 to 1505, most working in domestic service in Portugal, on the pattern seen in Islamic societies, or on the developing sugar plantations of Madeira.[52]

The supply of African slaves also became more significant in the Mediterranean, because the Ottoman conquest of Constantinople in 1453 was followed by the overthrow of Italian trade networks from the Black Sea, the Genoese base of Kaffa in the Crimea falling to the Ottoman ally, the khan of the Crimean Tatars, in 1475. The Ottomans focused Black Sea and Balkan slave sources on their new capital, Constantinople, and the importance of this challenge to the earlier pattern of supply for the Mediterranean slave trade was enhanced by the resumption of Ottoman expansion in the Balkans. In the sixteenth century, moreover, the Ottomans gained control, direct or indirect, over many of the leading Islamic slave markets including Cairo, Mecca, Basra, Algiers, Tripoli and Tunis, although others to the east, such as Bukhara and Malacca, were not in the Ottoman world and tapped into very different slave trade networks.

The disruption to the supply of slaves from the Black Sea to Italy further enhanced the importance to Christian Europe of slaves from sub-Saharan Africa. Part of the demand was satisfied by the Arab slave trade across the Sahara, with slaves moved on from there to Europe via entrepôts on the southern shores of the Mediterranean. Prior to 1450 there were already many African slaves at the major Sicilian slave market of Palermo, obtained from Bornu, in sub-Saharan Africa via the slave entrepôts of Tunis and Tripoli. This route, however, posed a severe challenge to the slaves, not only due to the distance that had to be covered but also because of the differences in food, climate and disease that they faced from sub-Saharan Africa, across the Sahara, and into the Mediterranean world, differences that could be deadly.

Portugal proved another source for slaves for Europe, encouraging the Italian commercial and financial interests that had been significant for the Black Sea trade to transfer their expertise and capital to the new Portuguese-controlled African slave trade. Like the Black Sea trade, the new one involved permanent overseas protected bases for trade, long-range shipment by sea, and the ability to invest capital for distant returns, the last a situation captured in Shakespeare's *Merchant of Venice* (c.1596) where the plot rested on the problems of the merchant, Antonio. The role of Italian intermediaries was shown when, in 1470, Bartolomeo Marchionni, the agent for a Florentine family involved in the Black Sea slave trade, moved to Lisbon from where he developed sugar plantations in Madeira and gained from the Crown a privileged position in the slave trade on the Guinea coast.

Sources of Slaves

The Western European words for slaves reflected the original importance of slave movements within Europe as they all derived from the word Slav, the term used to describe the inhabitants of Eastern Europe. However, by the end of the fifteenth century, black slaves were more significant in the Christian Mediterranean, although not only there. Henry VII of England (r.1485–1509) was one of many prominent Europeans who kept some black domestic servants. However, the lack of evidence of many others would suggest that black slaves were not at all common in England. The few exceptions were probably gifts and not sold on. English merchants based in lower Andalusia in Spain at the end of the century were to be important to the development of English slavery linked to sub-Saharan Africa, with William de la Founte in 1490 proving to be the earliest documented English slaveholder there.

Other sources of slaves still existed. There are indications of a market in Bristol and on the east coast of England for children brought from and/or bought in Iceland. During the fifteenth century English trade with Iceland rose considerably as a result of English entrepreneurship and Icelandic isolation within the Danish-Norwegian empire. The imports included human labour, mainly children and youths, labour that was in demand given the decline and then stagnation in England's population after the Black Death, the bubonic plague epidemic, of 1346–9. Some did not come voluntarily and were kidnapped or sold by their parents.[51] The latter possibly belong in some intermediary category between chattel slaves and deserted children who were put into service. Such children long proved a significant source of dependent labour, and they remain very important to the modern sex trade.

However, black slavery became more important, and this change affected the European perception of all sub-Saharan Africans. 'Blackness' had proved a slippery concept for Europeans, who tended to see some of their own number as dark-skinned, but, as a result of the slave trade, 'black skin came to embody much of the interpretative apparatus that Europeans engaged in when looking at and understanding Africans', black Africans were stereotyped and many African cultural practices were misunderstood and recast in a negative light. Denigration of them as inferior and uncivilized was related to associating Africans with occupations linked to physical prowess, and thus to slavery.[54] This situation contributed to the justification by European thinkers of African slavery in natural law, a justification that had the authority of Classical writers, notably Aristotle, an authority that was important to Renaissance thinkers.

Colour was not only an issue for the Christian Europeans, but was also of importance in the Islamic world which, in the fifteenth century, came more often into contact with black people than the Christian Europeans did. Whereas the offspring of a black mother and white father was admitted to full equality, 'the full-blooded Negro generally remained an outsider in Muslim society', and prejudice was an issue although the barrier did not exclude black people from high office.[55] Ethnic differences were more broadly an issue in the Islamic world. For example, in India, they interacted with those between Hindu subjects and Muslim rulers, notably the Lodi sultans of Delhi, their Mughal successors from 1526, and the Deccan sultanates, notably Bijapur and Golconda; this interaction influenced attitudes to enslavement.

In both Christendom and Islam, social identities and fault-lines were religious and ethnic as much as class based, and thus these factors were routinely involved in the character of social control. If slavery was one instance so also was control over serfs, and when religious and/or ethnic differences were combined with social dominance, the latter was generally harsher. Pejorative attitudes toward Africans were stark but can also be compared with the severe treatment in Europe of the poor, whose lot was frequent moral intimidation. The able-bodied unemployed were regarded as lazy or greedy, being presented as bestial or semi-bestial in print, and they were treated cruelly as rogues and vagabonds, for example in the English Poor Laws of the sixteenth century.

Physical prowess was a key element in the assessment of slaves by the Portuguese. This criteria was important because the spread of sugar cultivation, an arduous task, became a leading prompt to the slave trade thanks to the establishment of plantation slavery on the Atlantic island of Madeira, where Portuguese settlement began in 1424. Madeira became the leading producer of sugar in the Portuguese world, and this success fed the demand for slaves, in contrast to the Canary Islands, where the Spaniards relied initially on the conquered Guanches as slaves on the sugar plantations, rather than on importing slaves.

At first, the Portuguese tried to obtain slaves from West Africa by seizing them in raids, a method they were later to use in Brazil, but it was abandoned in the late 1440s because the rulers of Upper Guinea south of the River Senegal were too strong.[56] This point about African strength is crucial to an understanding of the power politics and economics of the Atlantic slave trade as it helps account for the crucial role of the Africans themselves in the trade. This strength emerges clearly if the military history of the period is understood not, as is conventionally the case, in terms of a military revolution centred on gunpowder weaponry, related tactical and organizational developments, and a consequent growth in European strength. Instead, it is necessary to note the limitations in, and stemming from, these developments, and to appreciate the consequences for the slave trade.[57] In particular, it was a case of Portuguese power on the coast of Africa, and not vice versa; nevertheless, once arrived, Portuguese capabilities were limited. For example, African coastal vessels, powered by men using paddles and carrying archers and javelin men, were able to challenge Portuguese raiders on the West African coast, and, although it was difficult for them to storm the larger, deeper-draught, and higher-sided Portuguese ships, these coastal vessels were too fast and too small to present easy targets for the Portuguese cannon. In contrast, the Portuguese were to be more successful in slave raiding on the coasts of the Bay of Bengal in the seventeenth century because they used shallow-draught *galias* there and had the cooperation of local Magh pirates and the support of the rulers of nearby Arakan.

The African environment posed a formidable challenge for the Portuguese. Prevailing wind and ocean conditions limited access to the African coast south of the Gulf of Guinea, while the extensive coastal lagoons and swamps of West Africa made approaching the coastline difficult, notably so for deep-draught ships. Penetration inland was variously hindered by tropical rainforest and, to the north and south, on the coasts of modern Mauritania and Namibia, by deserts that reached to the coast. Once ashore in West and East Africa, the Europeans encountered deadly diseases with high death rates.

As a consequence of these problems, slaves were obtained by trade, the business conducted either from onboard slave ships anchored in estuaries or on the coast, with the latter method leading to the establishment of permanent bases. This Atlantic slave trade was a new variant on the longstanding pattern of slavery and slave trade within Africa, with the possibilities of the Atlantic trade encouraging new ways of exploiting existing trade networks and political and social systems. Slave-owning and hierarchical monarchies did not originate at the time of the Atlantic slave trade, but were in evidence in parts of Africa, for example the western Sudan (the region of modern Mali), from the eleventh century when the kingdom of Ghana was at its height, if not considerably earlier. This, however, might suggest not indigenous origins for such monarchies but, instead, the impact of the slave trade across the Sahara to North Africa. It is unclear how far labour shortages in Africa, a continent that was short of manpower, and where land only took on value if it was farmed, encouraged enslavement as a means of securing labour, rather like serfdom was developed in Europe, and, then, how far this system helped provide slaves to European traders. Because manpower was a form of wealth, both its source and its symbol, Africans could readily commodify slaves for use in barter and as money. Aside from holding slaves, African societies developed slave law and had rules about who could and could not be enslaved.

Rule over much of Africa, especially West Africa, was segmented and most polities were not far-flung. This segmentation helped encourage the conflict within the continent that fed the slave trade, for the majority of Africans who were sold as slaves were captured in warfare, with some seized in wars largely waged in order to capture people. Some Africans were enslaved as a result of (violent) seizures for debt. Those who were captured lost their tribal identity, an aspect of slavery also seen in other societies, for example the Maori of New Zealand and in North America, where Native American slaves interbred with African slaves, so that many African Americans by the 1860s would have had a mixture of African, European and Native American ancestry.

Trade therefore provided the Portuguese with major opportunities, and its profits helped to finance further expansion. The profits from the trading base of São Jorge da Mina (Elmina) on the Gold Coast, founded in 1482, financed later voyages along the African coast, such as those of Diogo Cão and Bartholomeu Dias. A logistical achievement, prefabricated with stores, timbers and tiles all prepared in Portugal, the base was followed by others including Axim (1495) and, off the coast, Fernando Po (1483).[58] The infrastructure included the establishment, in 1486, of the Casa dos Escravos de Lisboa, the Lisbon Slave House.

The Portuguese were leaders in the African coastal slave trade, not least because Castile, the principal Spanish kingdom, which had conquered the Canaries and traded from West Africa from 1453, ceased to trade there in 1479, surrendering its claims to trading rights in Guinea and the Gold Coast to Portugal by the Treaty of Alcáçovas. This agreement was a reflection of the longstanding Spanish willingness to purchase slaves from others and looked toward the papal-sanctioned division of the Atlantic world between Spanish and Portuguese zones by the Treaty of Tordesillas of 1494, a division that awarded Africa and Brazil to Portugal. Moreover, unlike the Castilians, the Portuguese had developed the expertise, infrastructure and financing to make a success of the slave trade and, with Madeira, had a key offshore market.

The Portuguese also benefited from the experience gained in long-distance, deep-sea commerce and voyaging, and from significant improvements in the capability of shipping, which gave the Europeans a powerful comparative advantage over non-European societies. Late fourteenth-and fifteenth-century developments in ship construction and navigation included the fusion of Atlantic and Mediterranean techniques of hull construction and lateen-and square-rigging, the spread of the sternpost rudder and advances in location-finding at sea. Carvel building (in which hull planks are fitted flush together over a frame), which spread from the Mediterranean to the Atlantic from the late fifteenth century, replaced the clinker method of shipbuilding using overlapping planks, and contributed significantly to the development of the stronger and larger hulls necessary for trade across the Atlantic. The increase in the number of masts on large ships expanded the range of choices for rigging and provided a crucial margin of safety in the event of damage to one mast. Developments in rigging, including an increase in the number of sails per mast and in the variety of sail shapes, permitted greater speed, a better ability to sail close to the wind and improved manoeuvrability.[59]

Navigational expertise also increased. Thanks to the use of the magnetic compass, the spread from the Mediterranean to Atlantic Europe of astrolabes, cross-staffs and quadrants (which made it possible to assess the angle in the sky of heavenly bodies), and other developments in navigation, such as the solution in 1484 to the problem of measuring latitude south of the Equator, it became possible to chart the Atlantic Ocean and to assemble knowledge about it. This was an important prelude to the further development of the slave trade, not least because better charts helped reduce the risk of voyaging, and thus the hazards of sailing. By the end of the fifteenth century, the basis was therefore well laid for the expansion of the European slave trade to new colonies across the Atlantic, where the plantation system was to be transferred to Hispaniola (today divided between Haiti and Dominican Republic) in 1503 and to Brazil in the 1530s.[60] Yet, as the beginning of the next chapter shows, the long-term significance of this development should not distract attention from other important strands of slavery and the slave trade.

2

THE AGE OF CONQUEST, 1500–1600

They buy several hundred men and women and take them aboard their black ships. They place chains on their hands and feet and throw them into the holds of their ships. Their torments are worse than those in hell ... It is said that hell has been made manifest on earth. We hear that the local Japanese have learned their ways by imitating them and sell their own children, parents, wives and daughters.[1]

The spread of slavery

This Japanese account of Portuguese slave trading in the 1580s reflected both the ubiquity of the practice and the extent to which it developed during the sixteenth century as new trade links were created around the world. Moreover, control over large parts of the world's surface changed hands over this century, not least as empires were destroyed, notably the Aztec (Central American), Inca (Andean), Mamluk (Egyptian), Songhay (West African) and Lodi (North Indian) empires, while others expanded or were created, particularly the Ottoman (Turkish), Spanish Habsburg, Safavid (Iranian) and Mughal (North Indian) empires. These conquests, which produced many slaves, were matched by the subjugation of indigenous peoples, from Siberians at the hands of expanding Russian power, to Caribbean Arawaks at those of Spain.

The spread to the New World of slave plantations, and the transatlantic slave trade, were part of this process of expropriation and imperial control, but the relationship was complex, and it would be misleading to automatically put European activity first. This was the case even in Africa, which remained the prime source of slaves for the European-controlled slave trade despite the wider projection of European power in this period, including into the Indian Ocean. Instead of putting European activity first, the domestic slave trade within Africa remained crucial, while the Arabs continued to be key slavers in Africa, and, indeed, trans-Saharan slave raiding and trading by Arabs into sub-Saharan Africa became more prominent.

An important instance of relative external power was provided by Morocco. In 1578, a Moroccan army smashed a Portuguese invading force at Alcazarquivir, killing the king, Sebastian, and opening the way for the Spanish takeover of Portugal in 1580. The battle totally ended the longstanding Portuguese attempt to establish a dominant position in Morocco, as well as consigning Portuguese captives to slavery as part of a standard procedure in both the Muslim and African worlds by which captives became slaves. After this, the Moroccans went on to send an expeditionary force, partly composed of Christian renegades, across the Sahara where, at Tondibi in 1591, it won a victory that overthrew the Songhay empire. In its place, the Moroccans created a pashalik of Timbuktu, and its links with Morocco itself strengthened one of the major axes for the trans-Saharan slave trade.

Further east, another instance of Islamic pressure on sub-Saharan Africa linked to the slave trade was provided by Idris Aloma, from 1569 to about 1600 *mai* (ruler) of Bornu, an Islamic state based in the region of Lake Chad. Bornu captured slaves by raiding and, as well as making full use of them itself, transported some of them north, across the Sahara, to the well-established slave markets of North Africa, notably Ghadames and Tripoli. Bornu was later undermined by the Tuareg of the Sahara, but, to its east between Lake Chad and the Nile valley, three other states developed in the *sahel* (savannah) belt between the Sahara and the forests further south: Bagirmi, Wadai and, in what is now west Sudan, Darfur. These states used their military strength to acquire slaves, whom, aside from their own uses, they also sent to North Africa.

East Africa was another major source of slaves, who were bought or seized in the interior of East Africa and brought to ports such as Sofala, Mozambique, Kilwa, Zanzibar, Pemba, Mombasa and Malindi, from where they were moved north along the coast to Mogadishu. Other slaves were brought by boat from Madagascar to these East African slave ports. The slaves were then traded across the Red Sea and Gulf of Aden via the ports of Jedda and Aden, and, further south, across the Indian Ocean. The slaves were sent to markets in the Middle East, especially in the Arabian peninsula, for example Chutar on the south coast, but also to Aleppo, Damascus and Cairo. There was also a movement of slaves from Mogadishu across the Indian Ocean to India, notably to the port of Daybul south of Bombay (Mumbai), and on to South-East Asia, especially Malacca. Thus, the movement of slaves by sea was part of the Indian Ocean world as well as its Atlantic counterpart. India was also a source of slaves, for example with girls taken to Afghanistan and the Middle East and, from the mid-seventeenth century, forced labour moved to plantations in the Dutch-ruled coastlands of Sri Lanka.

Economic advantage was linked to conquest and Islamic proselytism, notably with Ahmad ibn Ibrihim al-Ghazi of Adal in the 1520s to 1540s whose *jihad* against Christian Ethiopia involved slaving, part of a long pattern of activity. Conversely, defeats for Islam also affected the slave world, notably the Portuguese capture in 1511 of Malacca in modern

Malaya, the capital of a sultanate that had been a major centre of the slave trade in South-East Asia. The trade there drew on piracy, the many people captured by pirates and sold as slaves as was common in the waters of the East Indies, as well as on slaves produced by war and by debt. Religious factors played a role, with non-Muslim peoples such as the Moklen being particularly subject to enslavement, while the island of Bali in the East Indies (Indonesia) was a source of Hindu slaves for the Muslim world.[2]

Other major aspects of the movement of slaves into the Islamic world included the continuing raiding for slaves from the Islamic khanates in southern Russia north against non-Islamic peoples, especially the Grand Duchy of Muscovy. Thus, there was a major raid by the Crimean Tatars in 1571 in which large numbers of slaves were obtained, including from Moscow. Slave raiding became less serious with the expansion of Muscovite power, especially under Tsar Ivan IV, Ivan the Terrible, who conquered the khanates of Kazan (the most northerly Islamic state) and Astrakhan in 1552 and 1556 respectively, but in 1633 another raid on Muscovy by the Tatars led to the capture of large numbers of slaves. The development of frontier defence lines by the Russians helped limit such raids. The Abatis Line, built from Ryazan to the Seversk region in the sixteenth century was followed in 1635–53 by the thousand-kilometre Belgorod Line.

The expansion of Ottoman naval power in the Mediterranean and the reversal of earlier Hispanic success in the Maghreb were followed by the revival of raiding on Christian coasts. Khair-ed-Din, known to Westerners as Barbarossa, who dominated Algiers from 1529 and, in 1533, was appointed admiral by the Ottoman ruler, Suleiman the Magnificent, led repeated attacks, for example raiding Catalonia in 1542 and harrying the Italian coast in 1544.

The slave trades across the Sahara and from East Africa were different from those across the Atlantic for a number of reasons, including the role of Islam. Whereas the prime

European demand in the Americas was for male labour, which, as a result, ensured a serious sexual imbalance in those African societies serving the trade;[3] in the case of these other trades, the demand was primarily for women, particularly as domestic servants and sex slaves. This was because there were few equivalents in the Islamic world to the large labour-hungry plantation economy of the European New World, while concubinage was an important feature of Islamic society. In Egypt, Ethiopian females, who were greatly prized for their beauty, were more highly valued than males.[4] Lack of sources makes it harder to estimate the number of Africans traded across the Sahara, the Red Sea and the Indian Ocean than across the Atlantic, but it was probably as many – and indeed there are suggestions that it was greater.[5]

These are well-established comparisons, but, although the number of slaves is even more uncertain, enslavement more generally arose from other episodes of conquest across the world during the century. For example, in the Indonesian archipelago, the capture of prisoners for slavery was important to conflict, although, as a reminder of the varied character of conflict and forms of domination, so also was headhunting which was a more immediate proof of control and newfound status.[6] Moreover, the nature of conquest varied, with the incorporation of local elites into the conquerors' political world proving an important means by which power was extended, for example by the Ottomans into Wallachia and Moldavia (in modern Romania) in 1393 and 1504 respectively, and by the Mughals into Rajasthan. Thus, conquest did not automatically equate with enslavement.

Types of slave and slave work
Slave soldiers proved important to the very armies carrying out these conquests, whether the janissary infantry of the Ottomans or the *ghulams* of the army of the Safavid Shah Abbas I of Persia. The Moroccans developed a similar army in the seventeenth century, and the Muslim sultanates of the

Deccan in India also had slave units. The treatment of the boys conscripted in the Ottoman empire was described in *The Laws of the Janissaries*, which was written in the early seventeenth century. Boys were regarded as easier to train and subdue than men. The best-looking were allocated to the palace to receive an education in the palace schools and serve the person of the sultan, while the physically strong were chosen to work in the palace gardens, but most were destined for the elite janissary corps. First, however, they were assigned to Turkish farmers in Anatolia in order to accustom the boys to hardship and physical labour, and to teach them some basics of Islam and, more significantly, Turkish, which was the language of the corps and the imperial elite. Recalled after about seven or eight years, and based in the barracks of the novices near the palace entrance, the novices were used for palace and imperial tasks, such as transporting firewood to the palace or manning troop ferries, or working as palace laundrymen and apprentices in the naval dockyards and on construction projects. The circumcision of the boys when they arrived for the first time at Constantinople was designed to assert their Muslim future and was a clear instance of symbolic power over the slave soldiers-to-be.[7]

The role of slave forces, for which the slave rowers of Mediterranean galleys were a pale imitation in Christian Europe, serves as a reminder of the problems of advancing a single account of slavery in terms of economic advantage and related labour needs. Moreover, these forces underline the conditional nature of slave service in certain circumstances, a conditional nature that was to be demonstrated by large-scale janissary mutinies in the seventeenth century, for example in 1621 and 1622.

Alongside the variety of non-Western slavery, and the extent to which expansionism could involve political dominance and labour control without the formal processes of slavery, similar points can be made about the Western world. For example, the native population of Spanish America was controlled and exploited by means of tied labour and forced migration that represented a de facto slavery that, however, was seen by the colonial administrators as different to the slavery experienced by Africans brought across the Atlantic. Such de facto slavery was widespread, both in Spanish America and more generally, as it ensured that labour and land were linked without the cost, disruption and responsibilities attendant on moving and controlling slaves to provide labour. In short, the protection and opportunity costs of de facto slavery were lower than those involved in the transatlantic slave trade.

Similar points can be made about serfdom, which became more intense and comprehensive across parts of Europe (while it declined in others) at the same time that Western-controlled slavery spread in the Atlantic world. Paralleling the role of plantation exports from the New World, the heavy labour services of this peasant serfdom in Eastern Europe were a response to the commercial opportunities offered by early-modern grain exports to other parts of Europe, in short a European version of Atlantic-scale globalization. Serfdom appears also to have been at least prefigured by fifteenth-century changes, as lords who had gained private possession of public jurisdictions responded to the economic problems of the late medieval period, especially fixed cash incomes and labour shortages.[8] In the fifteenth century the sale of slaves was prohibited in Poland. Paralleling the role of landlords in the New World, the attitudes and powers of landlords in Eastern Europe, not least the character of their seigneurial jurisdiction, were crucial to the spread of serfdom. The state stood aside or stepped back, and peasant rights were lessened, for example in the Russian Ulozhenie (legal code) of 1649, a code that devoted much space to regulating the legal status of bondage and also to categorizing the different types of slaves.[9] In another parallel with New World slavery, ethnic divisions in Eastern Europe, for example between German landlords and Polish or Livonian peasants, or Polish landlords and

Ruthenian peasants, exacerbated social differences in some areas.

Serfs were subject to a variety of obligations, most significantly *robot* (forced labour), usually assessed in terms of number of days although sometimes made more onerous by setting a daily norm of achievement that was impossible to accomplish and then making the serfs work additional days. Other burdens could also be heavy: all Bohemian serfs in what is now the Czech Republic were obliged to seek their lord's permission, which was generally granted only in return for payment, before migrating, marrying, or having their children educated or apprenticed outside the manor, which was in effect buying their freedom. Limitations on personal mobility reduced the serfs' bargaining power within the labour market, while rulers made few attempts to see that serfs' rights were observed. In much of Eastern Europe, serfs were routinely beaten for real or alleged misdemeanours, while landlords' torture chambers were not unknown.

Serfdom was not the only form of forced labour, nor Eastern Europe the sole sphere for it. For example in Spain, Roma were consigned as forced labour to the mercury mine at Almadén as well as to the galleys.[10] Their use in both was part of the system of penal servitude[11] and reflected the needs of the state, as mercury, aside from being poisonous, was used in the production of silver. Similarly, in Wallachia and Moldavia, slaves, including Roma, were made to work in the salt mines, again a major source of revenue. The use of slaves in such mines provided a link across time, back to the Classical world and forward to the *gulags* of the Soviet Union.

Penal servitude more generally served in the sixteenth century as a source of labour and settlers. This system also provided a way to deal with convicts and those judged unwelcome, such as the Jewish children transported from Portugal to the island of São Tomé off the coast of West Africa, an island where the transported convicts were used as a militia to control the African slaves on the sugar plantations.[12] In 1524, 300 African slaves were transported from the island to Hispaniola.

Slavery in Europe and European colonies off the coast of Africa, however, was increasingly to be cast into the shade by the spread of slavery alongside European power across the Atlantic. This spread was both as an aspect of the labour control necessary for profitable economic activity, which can be treated as a modernizing force, and also a product of more traditional practices of conquest and control. The key difference in the case of the New World was that large numbers of slaves were to be brought across the ocean, but this was not the initial intention. Instead, the history of New World slavery indicated the importance of particular circumstances within the more general context of European transoceanic expansion. The latter, indeed, was not to be the automatic motor of the development of European-controlled slavery, nor did it require a slave trade to sustain it. Instead, European expansion also involved the establishment of bases and colonies in a number of areas, from Newfoundland to Java, in which slavery did not become the pattern.

This variety underlines the degree to which European commercial expansion, like labour exploitation, was not co-terminous with slavery. However, as with Eastern European serfdom, enforced labour which can be seen as akin to slavery could still be central to economic activity, as with the Dutch production of spices on plantations in Java, Ambon and elsewhere in the East Indies from the seventeenth century. As an instance of another, and different, form of exploitation of native peoples, which did not involve plantations, the Russian treatment of the conquered peoples of Siberia was also harsh, especially the seizure and trading of local women and *iasak*, the forced tribute in furs. In Russia, pagan tribespeople were obliged to pay *iasak*, and were treated in effect like children without full responsibility before the law, a context which helps explain the ability to buy them.

Compared to East and South Asia, Africa was short of

people, but it was not so compared to the New World after
the initial European impact on the latter. Disease, especially
smallpox, proved the key element in the New World,
weakening potential resistance and acting like enslavement in
disrupting social structures and household and communal
economies, leading to famine. Disease also had a savage effect
on the potential labour force, greatly lessening both its size
and the possibility of replenishment by the native population.
The impact of disease was exacerbated by the herding together
of enslaved peoples in order to satisfy labour needs, as, in the
1510s, with Arawaks brought from the Bahamas by the
Spaniards to work the gold mines of Hispaniola, an island
whose population was decimated by smallpox.[13] Aside from
disease, Hispanic colonial policies and practices, including the
violent suppression of native religious rituals, limited the
possibility of post-epidemic population recovery, and induced
a degree of social breakdown. For example, the Taínos of the
Caribbean ceased to be a culturally distinct social and ethnic
group.

The potential labour force available to exploit the new
colonies was also limited by native resistance, as had already
happened in the Canaries.[14] After the initial conquest stage on
the American mainland in the first half of the sixteenth
century, Spanish and Portuguese territorial expansion in the
Americas slowed down, with major implications for the
labour supply; as with other empires, conquest was a matter
of the use of one type of manpower to acquire another type.
Natives who were willing to supply goods to the Europeans
by barter were not prepared to provide continuous labour on
plantations, which encouraged the Europeans to resort to
raiding into unconquered areas, a practice that continued for
centuries and of which there are echoes today.[15] Thus, in
Central America, the Spaniards took part in large-scale slaving
both among native peoples in Honduras, to satisfy demand in
the Caribbean, and in Nicaragua, mainly to provide labour for
Peru, but also for Panama and the Caribbean. The conse-

quences were devastating, with areas of Nicaragua under Spanish control losing more than half of their population.

Raiding, however, faced many military and economic difficulties. In an illustration of the degree to which the slave trade and slavery were, at least in part, shaped by the responses of non-Europeans, the native peoples either fled before the raiders or resisted them, and there was a major rebellion in the leading Brazilian sugar-producing area in 1567. Moreover, some of the areas into which raids were conducted, for example the interior of Brazil, were distant from the coastal centres of agriculture. As a result, native slaves were most important in frontier regions distant from the points of arrival of African slaves, such as Amazonia and northern Mexico.

Alongside labour supply problems, ideology played a major role as control over native labour within the area of Spanish sway was affected by royal legislation which sought to address clerical pressure to treat the aboriginal people as subjects ready for Christianization rather than as slaves. This pressure was a result of the intention that Christianity should be a world religion open to all, rather than the religion of an ethnic group, and, from this perspective, transoceanic expansion represented both an opportunity and a problem. The linkage of Church and state ensured that opportunity and problem became a subject for royal action. Following the precedent of the 1477 decision by Queen Isabella of Castile to order the freedom of those natives peoples from the Canaries who had been sold as slave in Castile, the New Laws for the Good Treatment and Preservation of the Indians issued in 1542 banned their future enslavement and ordered the freeing of slaves whose owners could not prove legal ownership. Under Spanish rule, the Portuguese government followed with legislation in 1609.[16] In a crucial distinction, freedom was seen as an opportunity for proselytism, rather than simply as a reward for becoming Christian.

Although most slaves in areas under close governmental supervision had been freed by 1560, the implementation of edicts elsewhere took time and was frequently ignored by landowners and by officials concerned about their views. Similarly, the churches adapted to colonial circumstances, displaying little interest in the training of native ministries. Moreover, in frontier territories such as Chile and New Mexico, where the Spaniards regarded themselves as waging a just war, the taking of captives for slavery was permitted.[17] More generally, what was permitted to landowners by Spanish officials represented de facto slavery, notably the *encomienda*, a system of tied labour under which land and native families were allocated to colonists, and the *repartimiento*, under which a part of the male population had to work away from home. Making service an element of debt repayment was also a means of ensuring labour control. These methods contributed to a caste system based on ethnicity that became hard-wired into the society and politics of Latin America.[18]

These systems of tied labour were useful, especially in and near where the native population was numerous, such as over much of Mexico, but they involved costs and did not provide sufficient numbers of malleable workers for the colonizers' needs across the new conquests. Initially, the resulting response to labour needs was highly varied. Moors captured in the conflicts that were so frequent in the fifteenth and sixteenth centuries were an important source of labour, but eventual Portuguese and Spanish failure in North Africa in the sixteenth century[19] largely closed this source. Portuguese peasants were moved to Brazil, but this movement also proved a limited resource, and one not suited for the arduous labour regime in the sugar plantations. The enslavement of part of the native population was, as already discussed, another resource and, at the outset, the Spaniards satisfied their labour needs largely by this means.

Indeed, at first, the spread of African slavery was not primarily to do with the needs of agricultural labour. As it was initially more expensive to supply Spanish America with slaves who had to be purchased in Africa and brought across the Atlantic than with native slaves, the Africans were often used as house slaves, a form of high-value slavery that indicated their cost as well as a continuation of a pattern also seen in Europe. As a reminder, moreover, of the variety of roles that Africans were to take in the Americas, a few fought as *conquistadors*,[20] although such activity undercut racial typecasting far less than it should have done. Initially, Africans were shipped to Spanish America via Spain as early as 1501, but, in 1518, *asientos* (licences) were granted for the import of slaves direct from Africa to Spanish America. Three years later, one of the earliest revolts of African slaves in the New World occurred near the city of Santo Domingo on Hispaniola. Thanks largely to sugar plantations, Hispaniola had about 15,000 African slaves in the 1540s and 25,000 by the 1550s.[21] From the mid-century, the trend in transatlantic slave shipments was upwards, reflecting demand from both Spanish and Portuguese colonies and, rather than providing a marginal part of the labour force, Africa was becoming steadily more important, not least because, although more expensive, it was believed that African slaves were physically stronger than the native inhabitants.

African slaves were used for a variety of tasks across Spanish America, prefiguring the situation later in British America and the USA and also reflecting a general characteristic of slave economies. In some areas, agricultural work was important, usually for cash crops as profits from these crops covered the cost of purchasing slaves. Sugar in the valleys of northern Peru and near Veracruz, cocoa in Costa Rica, and wine on the Peruvian coast were key instances. Africans were judged more suited to the heat and humidity of the coastal valleys than Native Americans, who were generally used in the higher and drier terrain and colder climes with which they were more familiar. There were relatively few slaves in the Andes. Thus, the slave trade was part of the process by which the Europeans responded to the geography and demographics of the areas they conquered. The coastlands, however, were more dangerous as infectious disease was a major problem there.

The economic importance of slaves in Spanish America was also seen in their use to produce food destined to be sold to the cities and to the mining towns. The most important was the great silver-producing centre of Potosí in modern Bolivia, founded by the Spaniards in the Andes in 1545 – a crucial source of bullion for the Spanish empire and its numerous wars, and for the European trading system. This use of slaves reflected, first, the extent to which this trading system, like earlier large-scale ones, such as the Roman empire, created new economic spaces and links, indeed can be defined by these, and, secondly, that these spaces required the provision of labour from new sources. In Spanish America, mine towns were an area of employment for slaves, although the prime labour supply was Native American. Africans, instead, as a reflection of their higher value, tended to be used in refining and as overseers. The African slaves suffered like the native workers from the dangers and diseases of mining, such as silicosis.

Similarly, in the cities of Latin America, such as Cartagena and Veracruz, the major mainland ports for landing slaves, Lima, Mexico City and Havana, slaves were employed in various roles, including as craftsmen, servants and labourers. Slaves played a major role in Mexico's large textile industry, where the hot, humid and noxious conditions were hard. They were also prominent in Lima's building industry. The presence of Crown slaves indicated that state slavery also played a role. Thus, in Havana, the Crown had slaves for the construction and maintenance of fortifications, and they could also be rented out.[22] The availability of native labour and, possibly, the lack of Spanish bases from which African slaves could be obtained, helped ensure that black people remained a smaller group than Native Americans across most of Spanish America, but where disease had really ravaged the native population, for example in Puerto Rico and Hispaniola, the black population by 1600 was greater than that of the surviving

Taínos. Intermarriage, however, led to a lessening of the value of these racial categories.

In coastal Brazil, which was then Portuguese America, the situation was different to that in Spanish America, not least because of the major demands posed by sugar production and the limited size of the surviving native population. Brazil rapidly supplanted the island of São Tomé as the leading producer of sugar in the Portuguese world, enjoying as it did an advantage due to slave labour, as well as a lengthy harvest season, comparatively mild weather, and relatively fresh soil in plentiful quantities.[23] The number of sugar mills in Brazil rose from 60 in 1570 to 192 in around 1600. The initial emphasis in Brazil was on the use of native labour, and slave raiding into the interior remained important, but, aside from resistance, the native slave population of Portuguese Brazil was hit hard by a smallpox epidemic in 1560–3 and measles in 1563. As a result of a shortage of labour, the Portuguese turned to importing slaves from West Africa and Angola. North-east Brazil, the centre of sugar production, and its ports, such as Recife and Bahia, were close to Africa, which serves as a reminder of how oceans could link rather than separate and of how the European practice of dividing the globe into continents is misleading.[24]

Relatively short slaving voyages were particularly valuable because they reduced the need for credit in bridging the period between the purchase and sale of slaves, while death rates among the slaves were generally lower on shorter voyages. In the 1570s, the number of Africans among the slaves in north-east Brazil increased so that, by the mid-1580s, about one-third of slaves there were Africans, and, by 1620, they were in a majority. In the last quarter of the sixteenth century, about 40,000 African slaves entered Brazil in a trade that provided revenues to the Crown, as, aside from slaves moved on the royal account, private slave traders were taxed.

The Portuguese slave world was far-flung. Established in the Indian Ocean, from East Africa via Muscat and Hormuz, to India and Sri Lanka, and then on via Malacca to the East Indies, Macao in China and Nagasaki in Japan, the Portuguese also shipped slaves to the new Spanish colony of the Philippines, moving there those they had enslaved from East and South Asia as well as some Africans. In turn, some of the slaves they brought to the Philippines were shipped on in the seventeenth century across the Pacific to deal with labour needs in Mexico, a trade that continued until 1700.[25]

The Portuguese obtained some of their slaves in the sixteenth century from Japan which was then gravely weakened by civil war, providing captives for enslavement, as well as by the pattern of weak and precarious local powers that were not well placed to resist external encouragement, if not pressure, to trade in slaves. However, unification in Japan brought this trade to an end with a key role taken by Toyotomi Hideyoshi (1537–98). Scarcely a William Wilberforce character, Hideyoshi was a successful warlord who had defeated his rivals by 1590, with his conquest of Kyushu in 1587 proving a key step and one that led him to condemn the slave raiding and trading practiced there on behalf of the Portuguese. In 1592, Hideyoshi began an initially successful invasion of Korea that was followed by the enslavement of captives, although in 1598 the enterprise was finally abandoned.[26]

Portugal and Spain were not alone in the Americas. The English made an attempt, from the 1550s, to break into Portugal's trade with West Africa and the profitable slave trade from there to the Spanish New World. Plymouth-born John Hawkins obtained his slaves in West Africa on the coast of modern Sierra Leone by raiding, rather than through purchase, losing men in the process to poison arrows and other hazards, as well as by piracy against Portuguese ships. He then shipped the slaves across the Atlantic and sold them to the Spaniards at considerable profit, which was a means of gaining access to the Spanish-controlled bullion of the New World. Thus, the slaves were not sold to England, where indeed there were increasing numbers of free black people.[27]

In 1568, however, at San Juan de Ulúa near Veracruz, on Hawkins' third slaving voyage, the presence of the viceroy of New Spain led to a Spanish attack on what was, in the official view, an unwelcome interloper. Only two English ships survived the attack and the venture made a large loss.[28] Subsequently, Hawkins played a major role in the development of the Royal Navy that was to defeat the Spanish Armada in 1588.

England, nevertheless, did not go to war with Spain until 1585, and, until then, the unwillingness of Elizabeth I (r.1558–1603) in the early years of her reign to confront directly the imperial interests of Portugal and Spain encouraged a reliance on unofficial or semi-official action, such as privateering, rather than attempting to establish bases in areas claimed by Portugal or Spain, let alone to seize their bases. In 1580, Philip II of Spain became also Philip I of Portugal and the crowns were thus joined until 1640. Throughout that period, Portuguese slave traders held the *asiento*, the monopoly on the slave trade to Spanish America, although their willingness to grant concessions breached the monopoly. As a result of the union of the crowns, anyone challenging Portuguese interests risked conflict with Spain, but it was possible for those at war with Spain – such as the Dutch rebels, and the English from 1585 – to breach Portuguese monopoly trade rights or attack Portuguese positions without fear of admonition from their home governments. This situation encouraged greater English and Dutch interest in West Africa.

In the late sixteenth century, the English commitment to the slave trade was far less than it was to be a century later as most English voyages to West Africa were for pepper, hides, wax and ivory, and in search of gold rather than of slaves, on whom English trade with West Africa did not focus until the mid-seventeenth century. No English fort was built in the region in the late sixteenth century.[29]

The Dutch initially also played only a modest role as they were primarily concerned with the war for independence and the naval struggle in home waters. However, Philip II banned Dutch trade with Lisbon in 1594, encouraging them to look further afield. French attempts to found bases in Brazil in the 1550s and Florida in the 1560s proved short-lived in the face of vigorous Portuguese and Spanish opposition, and French energies thereafter focused on the (civil) Wars of Religion which lasted until 1598. Had their attempts succeeded, then the French would have moved into slavery and the slave trade earlier than was to be the case.

The sixteenth century thus left a new Atlantic world of transoceanic links under Hispanic control and with Africans as the principal victims. The high death rate and low fertility rate of African slaves once they arrived in the New World, rates which reflected the cruel hardships of enslavement, transport and labour as well as the profound dislocation of slave life, ensured that it was necessary to import fresh slaves in order to sustain the numbers required. This situation was mirrored in slave movements into the Islamic world, where slavery continued to be a matter of public and private ownership and use different to that in the Christian world. Yet, the seeds of the vast expansion of the transatlantic slave trade had now been planted, a trade that was to come to dominate later attention.

3

THE SPREAD OF CAPITALIST SLAVERY, 1600–1700

Slavery appeared benign in the scenes of life in Dutch Brazil that were included in the map made by the order of Count John Maurice of Nassau, the Governor-General of Dutch Brazil. Those working the sugar mill are not under control or coercion,[1] a depiction which scarcely captured the reality of a brutal work regime that crushed men as well as sugar cane.

This Atlantic world is the subject of much of this chapter, but it is important to put the spread of Western capitalist slavery in its global context and to appreciate that slavery and the slave trade were also important outside the Atlantic economy. Far from being an anachronism associated with hordes of medieval cavalry, slavery as a public institution remained highly significant in the seventeenth century.

Beyond the Atlantic trade

The Islamic world not only maintained traditional slave forces, but also witnessed the creation of new ones that appeared to offer the means for central command and the changes that this could lead to. Important examples occurred at the beginning and end of the century. Abbas I of Persia (r.1587–1629), one of the most vigorous rulers of the period, sought to develop a strong, centrally controlled force based on *ghulams*, a variant on the Mamluk phenomenon: the *ghulams* were outsiders, slaves from the Caucasus, the region whence the medieval Black Sea traders had derived most of their slaves. Most *ghulams* were Armenians, Circassians or Georgians. This force included a 12,000-strong corps of artillerymen with about 500 cannon, although most of the *ghulams* fought with traditional weapons. By increasing the land under his control, Abbas was able to fund this system, rather than having to rely on feudal and tribal levies, and his *ghulams* contributed to a string of successes, including the capture of the city of Herat from the Uzbeks in 1598, of Kandahar from the Mughals and Hormuz from the Portuguese in 1622, and of Tabriz and Baghdad from the Ottomans in 1603 and 1623 respectively.

The *ghulams* had an impact similar to the Ottoman janissaries except that they did not develop a comparable *esprit de corps* and political influence. *Ghulams* were also brought in to serve in administrative positions, while the women were sent to the harems of the elite. Aside from this slave service focused on the ruler and his entourage, there was much slavery across Persian society, mostly within the household. Slaves were brought in from East Africa in particular, but also from India, and Indian slaves were put to work in mines. The campaigns in India of the Mughals and the Deccan sultanates produced many Hindu slaves, some of whom were sold on to Central Asia and Persia. As an aspect of the longstanding Muslim interest in slavery as a source of concubines, there was also a lively trade in women into Persia from neighbouring Sunni Muslim lands such as Uzbekistan and Daghestan, with slave markets in towns like Shamakhi in Shirvan. Little is known about this type of slavery as the Persian-language sources say very little about it while few Westerners had insight into it. Yet, the animosity between Sunni and Shi'ia appears to have been important to this slavery, encouraging and easing the enslavement of those judged heretics. Thus, Shi'ia Persians were often available in the major slave market of Bukhara in Uzbekistan, while frequent conflicts between Persia and the Ottoman empire, notably between 1603 and 1639, led to the enslavement of prisoners of war and others seized on campaign, each side treating the other as heretics.

Moreover, conflict with non-Muslims did not only produce more slaves from India: the Ottomans seized large numbers when they attacked Austria, including in 1663 and 1683, and other opponents, such as Poland, which was attacked in 1620 and 1671.

Slavery also increased in China as a result of the Manchu conquest of the Ming empire in the seventeenth century. Slavery was already established in Manchu society (north of China) prior to this conquest, with Manchu commanders by the late sixteenth century having both household and agricultural slaves on the Mongol pattern. In the early years of the Manchu conquest, up to 1624, the Chinese who were overrun were generally enslaved; not only prisoners of war were enslaved but also civilians, landowners and peasants. Thus, in the 1640s, when much of northern China was conquered, large slave-worked estates were established, with the slaves harshly treated by their Manchu overseers. They were also bought and sold. Slavery was not only seen in the workforce, but also in the army, and the Manchu took forward the Mongol practice of servitude where soldiers were considered slaves of the ruler.[2] The Manchu imperial court established in Beijing in 1644 had a system of home slaves in the Imperial Household Department which was important to the administration as well as to providing an imperial bodyguard.[3] With permission, these slaves could enslave other slaves.

Europeans, far from dominating the world of slavery, were irrelevant to the situation in China. In the Indian Ocean,

European interests were affected by the expansion of Islamic powers active in slavery as the Portuguese bases of Hormuz and Muscat both fell, in 1622 to the Persians and 1650 to the Omani Arabs respectively. The Omani Arabs, who were much engaged in slave trading and raiding, sacking the Portuguese Indian base of Diu in 1668 and 1676, and pillaging Mozambique in 1670, pressed on to capture, after a long siege, Fort Jesus in Mombasa in 1698. The fall of the major Portuguese position on the Swahili coast of East Africa was a testimony to the military dynamism of this slave-trading state.

In India, the Mughals enslaved rebels and those deemed rebels, for example, Hindus who rejected attempts at proselytism, as at Benares in 1632. Those captured in Mughal campaigns were often given to the troops for their use or for them to sell. Enslavement was also the fate of peasants who could not meet their taxes and rents, with men, women and children often sold to Muslim lords as a consequence. Further south in India, enslavement was used by the Deccan sultanates, notably Bijapur and Golconda, in suppressing opposition. These major Muslim states campaigned extensively into southern India and enslaved Buddhists, Hindus and others. Thus, in the 1640s, Golconda seized much of the state of Vijayahagara and Bijapur that of Mysore. However, the Mughal conquest of the Deccan sultanates of Bijapur and Golconda in the 1680s led to the end of military slavery there.

The Islamic world and Barbary slave raids

The vitality of the Islamic slave world was also displayed in Morocco, where Sultan Mawlay Ismai'il (r.1672–1727) developed a corps of black soldier slaves, attached by religious ties to the Sultan, who wished to be free of local political pressure. Slave children were trained in horsemanship and the use of firearms and spears, and then married to slave girls to produce more slaves, while slave raids were also mounted south into the Sahara. This force contributed greatly to the largely successful military pressure on the remaining European bases on the Moroccan coast. The Spaniards were driven from La Mamora (1681), Larache (1689), and Arzila (1691), although they held onto Ceuta despite a lengthy siege from 1694 to 1720. Charles II of England had acquired Tangier as part of the dowry with his Portuguese wife, Catherine of Braganza, and slavery was practised there, the Royal Navy bringing in slaves captured in the Mediterranean from North African ships to man a galley and then to help build the harbour breakwater.[4] However, Moroccan pressure led to the English abandonment of Tangier in 1684, after a major effort to retain the base; although it proved possible for the English to keep control of Bombay, the other gain from the marriage.

The public uses of slavery in the Islamic world serve as a reminder that the Atlantic world of capitalist slavery remained only one of its forms. Moreover, the slave trade into the Islamic world continued to be an important form of capitalist slavery. Nevertheless, this trade has received far less attention than the Atlantic sphere, in part because of the weight of scholarship and political reasons, but also because the slave trade across the Atlantic changed greatly in scale in the seventeenth century and led to far-reaching demographic and economic developments.

The slave trade into the Islamic world that has received most attention is that from Europe, rather than those in and from Africa, Central and South Asia and the Indian Ocean, which each involved more slaves. Raiding, an activity conducted by Muslims in the Mediterranean from the eighth century, was dominated in the sixteenth and seventeenth centuries by the 'Barbary' pirates of North Africa, especially Algiers, who sought loot and captives, both as slaves and for ransom; the last always being important to the economics of piracy, with slavery proving the fate of those who were not ransomed. Maybe one million Christians were seized as slaves in the sixteenth and seventeenth centuries, although the demographic impact was slight compared to the movement of African slaves to the New World.[5]

The 'Barbary' attacks focused on the Mediterranean, for example that of 1638 in which the coast of Calabria was devastated, but were also more wide-ranging. For example, the Newfoundland fishery was a victim of 'Barbary' attacks and there were also raids in British waters, especially off south-west England in 1625–6. In response, in 1620, a fleet of James I's warships was sent to Algiers, but, in 1621, it failed to force Algiers to acceptable terms. Unsuccessful attacks from 1625 were bad for the reputation of Charles I.[6] Barbary slaving led to widespread redemption activity in Christian Europe, with religious and governmental efforts to free captives, efforts encouraged by sermons and captivity accounts.[7] Money was collected in order to redeem captives.

The European transoceanic slave trade in the South Atlantic

The Barbary slave raids greatly affected the coastlands of Spain and Italy and posed a significant problem for the Mediterranean economy, but they did not have the economic impact of the major growth in the European-run Atlantic slave trade in the seventeenth century. This trade was to be driven by the expansion of New World exports to Europe, and the particular labour demands of individual crops and trades ensured that this growth in the slave trade was linked to the expansion of plantation crops, especially sugar, tobacco and coffee, but not, for example, of the important cod exports from Newfoundland. Moreover, the export from the Americas of plantation crops, and the export of European manufactured goods to the Americas and Africa that it helped finance, played a major role, alongside the problems of the Mediterranean economy, in restructuring much of the European economy. This restructuring powerfully developed and accentuated the role of Europe's Atlantic seaboard, and crucially the importance of port cities, particularly Lisbon and Seville, Bordeaux and Bristol, Liverpool and Nantes. The import of plantation crops also greatly affected the material culture of

Europeans, and their diet and health. By supplying new products, or providing existing ones at a more attractive price or in new forms, this trade both satisfied and stimulated consumer demand.

Transoceanic trade provided Europeans with goods design-ed to stimulate taste, appetite and consumption: sugar, tobacco, and caffeine drinks – tea (from Asia), coffee and chocolate.[8] As none of these was 'necessary', the rise in demand was very much consumerism, and one linked to shifts in taste. Sugar had been a luxury, but came to be much more important to the response of many Europeans to food and drink, partly replacing honey as a sweetener in cooking and drinks. When, in 1603, James VI and I's daughter Elizabeth came south from Scotland with her father, she was presented with a sugar loaf at York. Demand for sugar, however, interacted with rapidly rising supply from the Americas, and, as a result, the average retail price of sugar fell considerably in Europe in the second half of the century. Greater demand led the trade to become more predictable, which encouraged more investment, and that, in turn, led to downward pressure on prices. The addition of sugar to drinks increased their popularity by making them easier on the European palate, while, as the consumption of caffeine drinks rose, so demand for sugar increased. Chocolate was altered by sugar, making it a sweet rather than a bitter drink, which made it more popular in Europe and encouraged the growth in the import of its main ingredient, cacao. Sugar was also added to jam, cakes, biscuits and medicine.

Much cacao was obtained by the Spaniards from the native population of the Americas, but this source was supplemented by plantation production. The French established cacao plantations on their colonies of Martinique and Guadeloupe in the West Indies in the early 1660s, the Portuguese following in Brazil in the late 1670s, and the Dutch in Surinam, and the English on Jamaica, but with limited success, in the 1680s. As the production of cacao increased, prices fell, and this fall encouraged consumption.[9]

As also with sugar and other plantation crops, the development of cacao production helped drive the slave trade. The sale of cacao from the Spanish-ruled Venezuelan coast began in the 1610s and encouraged the import of African slaves there, as the *encomienda* system and the use of the Native American population it offered was of limited use in satisfying the new labour demand. Much of this cacao was sold to Spanish markets in the Americas, which is a reminder of the variety of the Atlantic economy in which slavery played such a dynamic role and of the extent to which slave labour was not solely producing plantation goods for European markets. In the 1630s and 1640s, rising cacao sales helped finance larger slave imports and each adult slave earned on average each year about 40 per cent of their market value, which was a very high rate of return and one that made slaves valuable even if they died after only a few years' work. The slaves were initially provided by the Portuguese, but, from mid-century, the Dutch based on the nearby Caribbean island of Curaçao became more important. The mobility of the slave gangs helped expand the frontier of production and by 1744 there were over five million cacao trees in the Caracas province.[10]

Sugar was also profitable, particularly when special opportunities beckoned, opportunities that usually arose from interruptions in competing supplies caused by war involving rival producers. For example, in the 1650s, annual profits per slave on the English colony of Barbados were as much as 40 or 50 per cent, reflecting the impact of the lengthy mid-century war in Brazil between Portugal and the Dutch on competing Dutch and Portuguese sources of sugar imports into Europe.[11] Sugar cultivation also demanded slaves. Initially, settlers in the English West Indian colonies had largely been labourers provided by contracts of indenture, a practice of labour provision and control transplanted from England. Plantation work, however, was hard, meaning that labour availability and control were key issues; hacking down sugar cane – crucial to the production process – was backbreaking work. It also required a large labour force, and slavery provided this more effectively than indentured labour, which was not only less malleable but also less attuned to the environment in the West Indies, in particular the climate. The impact in the late 1640s of disease on the white settlers encouraged this process.[12] Captain William Freeman, who from 1670 developed a sugar plantation on the English colony of Montserrat in the West Indies, claimed that 'land without slaves is a dead stock'.[13]

All too often, the slave trade is seen in terms of the North Atlantic, but the South Atlantic trade was crucial[14] and came first. Sugar production developed at a major rate in Portugal's colony of Brazil from the 1570s, producing a 'white gold' economy based on slave labour, initially from Senegambia in West Africa, the part of sub-Saharan Africa where the Portuguese had first arrived, but increasingly linking Brazil to the Portuguese colony of Angola further south on the western coast of Africa. Sugar production helped ensure that Brazil received 42 per cent of the slaves imported into the Americas during the seventeenth century, by far the largest individual flow by colony. The number who arrived in Brazil exceeded that of white settlers. This flow was necessary because, on the sugar estates in Brazil, slaves had a life expectancy of less than eight years, a grim reality that reflected the arduous nature of the work there and the harshness of the conditions. Afro-Portuguese (Luso-African) slaving networks, rather than the government, provided the capital, dominated the supply and took the profit. These networks linked the African interior to the Atlantic coast where, in Angola in 1616, a new port was opened at Benguela in order to support the trade. It was to take second place to Luanda (founded in 1575) as the port for the Angolan slave trade, serving another part of the coast.[15]

The Dutch attempt to conquer Brazil from the 1620s as part of the war with Spain resumed in 1621, however, greatly disrupted sugar production there, not least because the Dutch focused on north-east Brazil, then part of the Spanish system as Philip IV of Spain was also ruler of Portugal. The Dutch captured the major centre of Recife in 1630, and this disruption led to a marked shift in sugar production to the West Indies, a process accentuated when Dutch failure in Brazil, which began in 1645, was followed in 1654 by the Portuguese recapture of Recife and the expulsion of Dutch and Jewish settlers from Brazil. They brought to the Caribbean their capital, mercantile contacts and expertise in sugar-mill technology. On the other side of the Atlantic, the Dutch had also captured the Portuguese slaving bases of Luanda, Benguela and São Tomé in 1641, affecting the availability of slaves. This attack on Portugal's bases encouraged slave hunting in the Brazilian interior as an alternative source of slaves. Similarly, the Dutch seizure of Portuguese positions in India and Sri Lanka from the 1630s to 1660s hit the slave trade between the Portuguese colonies, disrupting the Portuguese hold on the other colonies, and making them more vulnerable.

In 1640, a successful rebellion in Portugal led to the end of the Spanish link and was followed, after initial disruption, by greater energy. In 1648, a Portuguese fleet from Brazil recaptured the African positions lost to the Dutch in 1641,[16] although in West Africa the Dutch retained São Jorge da Mina, which they had captured in 1637 and renamed Elmina. The recapture of Luanda, Beneguela and São Tomé provided the basis for a marked revival of the integrated Portuguese slave and sugar economy in the South Atlantic, which was one of the most important aspects of Atlantic geopolitics. The profitability of Brazil, in turn, meant that the Portuguese Atlantic empire did not suffer from the lack of capital and relative uncompetitiveness seen in Portuguese Asia,[17] and this situation ensured that the slave trade could serve to accumulate capital and thus provide an opportunity for fresh investment in more slaves.

Dutch slave exports to Brazil were adversely affected by the Portuguese victory, which pushed the Dutch towards the market of Spanish America, using their Caribbean bases of Curaçao and St Eustatius as entrepôts. In 1648, Spain and the Dutch had negotiated an end to the war started in 1618, and they remained at peace with each other for the remainder of the century. The Dutch also supplied slaves to their colonies in the Guianas: Essequibo, Demerara, where New Amsterdam was founded in 1627, and Surinam, where Paramaribo was founded in 1613. They competed with England on this coast, especially in Essequibo and Surinam. Further east, Cayenne, the basis of French Guiana, was founded as a colony in 1635, although French efforts to control the coast to the east failed. In 1558 and 1612, the French made unsuccessful attempts to colonize São Luís to the east of the Amazon, and until the late 1690s they claimed much of the coastline, finally abandoning the claim in order to win Portuguese support in European power politics.[18] The Dutch were also very active in the Indian Ocean slave trade. Their presence there was different but similar to that of the Portuguese in that, in addition to seizing Portuguese bases in Sri Lanka and at Malacca, the Dutch had their own colonies in the East Indies and Africa.[19]

France, England and the Dutch, moreover, all acquired bases further north in the Americas. As well as Cayenne, the French settled a number of islands in the West Indies – St Christopher (St Kitts, 1625), Martinique (1635), Guadeloupe (1635), Dominica (1635), Grenada (1650), and Saint-Domingue (now Haiti, 1660) – as well as Louisiana. Claimed by La Salle in 1682, the latter had its first French base at Fort Maurepas in Biloxi Bay on the Gulf of Mexico coast of the modern state of Mississippi in 1699. The French also established positions on the coast of West Africa: St Louis at the mouth of the River Senegal in 1638, Gorée near Cape Verde in 1677, and Assinie on the Ivory Coast in 1687 becoming bases for slavers.

The English began by establishing settlements on islands that the Spaniards had not colonized – St Lucia in 1605 and Grenada in 1609; although this was not an easy process.

Opposition from native Caribs helped lead to their failure, and provided a valuable instance of the folly of assuming an automatic Western military superiority with clear-cut consequences. Bermuda, an island in the Atlantic remote from other islands, was discovered in 1609, helping inspire Shakespeare's play *The Tempest*. Settled in 1612, it became a successful colony where tobacco cultivation was swiftly introduced. The first black slaves there arrived in 1616.

Bermuda was followed by the establishment of lasting English colonies in the West Indies: on Barbados in 1627, Nevis in 1628, and Antigua and Montserrat in 1632, while an attempt upon the Spaniards on Trinidad in 1626 failed. These colonies were no mere adjunct to the English possessions in North America; instead, they generated more wealth and, until the 1660s, attracted more settlers than the possessions on the North American mainland, Barbados proving the most popular destination.

Buccaneering and contraband trade remained important in the English colonies. Indeed on Jamaica, these activities provided much of the initial capital that financed plantation agriculture.[20] Once settled, the islands were rapidly converted for commercial agriculture. The labour-intensive nature of the resulting plantation economies led to a need for settlers. Slavery increased after the 1640s when tobacco, the price of which slumped, was replaced by sugar as the main crop. Tobacco was grown on smallholdings and its cultivation relied heavily on indentured labour, but sugar meant plantations and slaves. The labour regime in sugar and rice cultivation was particularly arduous and deadly; tobacco and cacao were less so. In 1678 on Montserrat, 40 per cent of the 4,500-strong population was non-white; but this grew to 80 per cent of the 7,200-strong population in 1729.[21] The same process occurred on other islands, such as Barbados which was hit by a falling supply of white servants. These servants were now attracted, instead, to South Carolina, Virginia and Maryland, which were healthier and offered greater opportunities for social mobility.[22]

This shift drove the slave trade to the English West Indies. Slaves suddenly appeared in Barbados' deeds in 1642 as a result of the first arrival of English slave ships there the previous year. Although prices of slaves thereafter fluctuated annually, they fell over time,[23] encouraging the trade and reflecting its more sophisticated organization, responsive to both sources and markets. Price was not the sole factor in encouraging the use of slaves, as they also ensured a longer labour availability than that provided by indentured servants.[24]

On Jamaica, an English colony from the 1650s, the black population rose to 42,000 in 1700, when there were only 7,300 whites. With this rise in the slave population, Jamaica switched from smallholdings to plantation monoculture. During this period, slave buying was widespread among the white community, but large purchasers dominated the market, which both reflected their access to credit and also accentuated social stratification. The slave market became more complex and controlled by specialized traders, with a growing resale market within Jamaica which further increased the instability of the slaves' lives.[25]

The numerical relationship between slaves and whites led to the need for garrisons, and the removal of troops for whatever reason alarmed the whites. The anxiety was communicated to European readers by publications such as *Great Newes from the Barbadoes, or, A True and Faithful Account of the Grand Conspiracy of the Negroes Against the English and the Happy Discovery of the Same* (1676). Government support was therefore much in demand, a situation that looked towards the contrasting response to the fiscal policies of the British government, of the Thirteen Colonies that rebelled in 1775 and those in the Caribbean that did not.

Significant as sugar plantations were, it is important not to see them as the inevitable economic and social pattern of the colonies in the West Indies. Sugar was not the sole plantation crop there in the late seventeenth century: on Jamaica, where there were 246 sugar plantations in 1684, the English also had cacao, cotton, ginger, indigo and pimento plantations. Moreover, a more mixed economic pattern that was less capital intensive was initially dominant, and it continued to be important even after sugar began to dominate the colony. Food crops and stock-rearing were each important.[26] Similarly, the use of slaves in Spanish American agriculture was not simply linked to export agriculture. In Cuba, alongside sugar and tobacco plantations, there was stock-rearing and food production.

The English presence in the West Indies was expanded by the settlement of Jamaica (the largest English colony there) and the Cayman Islands from 1655, the Virgin Islands from 1666 and the Bahamas from 1670; although much immigration, by both white migrants and slaves, was to already established colonies such as Barbados. Expansion took place within a system made dynamic by conflict. The value of plantation exports encouraged the European powers to try to seize each other's positions, although they were frequently unsuccessful. Thus, the English Western Design of 1654–5 against the Spanish colony of Hispaniola failed, England unsuccessfully attacked Guadeloupe in 1691 and Martinique in 1693, and failed to capture Saint-Domingue in 1695. Moreover, the Dutch failed to take Martinique from the French in 1674, and the French Curaçao from the Dutch in 1678.

Increased demand for slaves had meanwhile accentuated and refocused European interests in West Africa, but trade was not easy; for example, the Company of Adventurers of London Trading to the Parts of Africa (the Guinea Company), which was granted a monopoly by James I of England in 1618, only traded to the Gambia in 1618–21 before abandoning the unprofitable trade. A Scottish Guinea Company that operated on the Gold Coast was founded in 1634, but the Company, which in fact was largely London based, had only limited success.[27] The overthrow of Crown authority as a result of the English Civil War (1642–6) challenged the monopoly rights that rested on it, and the Guinea Company lost its monopoly. On that coast, English factories were established at Anomabu (1639) and Takoradi (1645), while interloping merchants who were not under the Company were active.

There were also struggles over control of trade from West Africa, a prize made profitable in particular (though not only) by the slave trade. In 1658, the Danish crown, then at war with Sweden, provided backing for the seizure of the Swedish bases in West Africa, including the fort at Anamabo, which was then sold to the Dutch West Africa Company. In 1661–4, there was a bitter conflict between the (English) Company of Royal Adventurers Trading into Africa, chartered in 1660, with the return of royal authority under Charles II, and the Dutch West Africa Company. In early 1661, the English Company sent out a small expedition using royal vessels under the command of the aggressive Captain Robert Holmes, a protégé of James, Duke of York, the Lord High Admiral, and later James II who was a stockholder in the Company. Holmes occupied two islands in the mouth of the Gambia and attacked nearby Dutch forts, but the Dutch reacted sharply, seizing English ships and in June 1663 captured the English base at Cape Coast Castle. That November, Holmes was sent to support the Company, and to maintain the rights of English subjects by force, and in early 1664 he seized the major Dutch settlements on the Gold Coast; Sir George Downing, the English envoy in The Hague, saw this as a good opportunity to 'make clear work in Africa'. However, a Dutch fleet under de Ruyter then captured the African settlements.[28] Such shifts in control greatly affected the local elites who were dependent on the slave trade. The Anglo-Dutch Wars, which were formally from 1652 to 1654, 1665 to 1667 and 1672 to 1674, left Britain with a stronger position in West Africa. Its new bases included Cape Coast Castle in 1652, Tasso Island in 1663, Fort James in 1664, and Accra, Apollonia, Elmina (the onetime Portuguese base of São Jorge da Mina), Winneba and Whydah in 1672.

The foundation of bases reflected changing opportunities on the African coast. In the late seventeenth century, there was a rise in the relative importance of slaves from sources from north of the Equator as opposed to Angola, in large part as a reflection of the greater *relative* significance of the West Indies as a market, as opposed to Brazil, although Angola and Brazil both remained crucial to the Atlantic slave trade. The Bight of Benin, off what is now Benin and western Nigeria, where Anecho became a Portuguese base in 1645 and Whydah an English one in 1672, was of particular importance for slaving. By the end of the century, this area had extended to the Gold Coast.

The prospects of profits from the slave trade encouraged many merchants and numerous rulers to enter into it. At the beginning of the seventeenth century, Spanish pressure had helped deter the Grand Duke of Tuscany from continuing with plans to create colonies in Sierra Leone and Brazil, and, in the second half of the century, the Duke of Courland in the eastern Baltic was unable to persist with his West African plans, but Denmark, Sweden and Brandenburg-Prussia all established bases in West Africa, although the Swedes had lost all of theirs by the end of the 1650s.

Greater European demand for plantation goods led to an increase in the number of slaves imported into the Americas in the seventeenth century. About half a million slaves were imported in the first half of the century, but a million in the second half, including over 600,000 in the last quarter.[29] The slave trade had initially been dominated by the need to supply the Portuguese and Spanish colonies with labour, but, as the Dutch, French and English expanded their colonial presence, so they played a more direct role in the trade, selling to their own colonies. The first slaving voyage from Bordeaux, which was to be a major base for the slaving trade, sailed in 1672, although the French slave trade only became important largely after 1713.

The English Company, which was re-formed as the Royal African Company in 1672, was granted, by its charter, monopoly rights over the English slave trade between Africa and the West Indies. However, the undermining of the Company's position after the overthrow of the Stuarts by William III in the Glorious Revolution of 1688–9 hit its finances and resulted in a decline in both government support and the assertiveness of the Company. Moreover, the Company's monopoly had become more unpopular due to its failure to meet rising demand for slaves in the New World. This led, in 1698, to the Company licensing private traders, in return for a 10 per cent tax, which freed up the African trade by legalizing the position of interlopers who became private traders. The role thereby granted to private enterprise helped propel England to the fore in slave shipments.[30] Much of the seventeenth-century French slave trade was by interlopers, and thus clandestine, but the wars with the Dutch in 1672–8 and with the English and Dutch in 1689–97 and 1702–13 hit French trade hard, not least because the French Navy was unable to provide much protection for trade after its severe defeat by the English at Barfleur in 1692.[31]

The ability to supply slaves to the colonies was important, because new slaves were continually needed to sustain the labour force. White labour was no substitute in the West Indies. Indeed, higher death rates in the West Indies than in North America, and higher death rates for white people than for slaves, ensured that the colonies there did not become settler societies with large, locally born white populations. Yellow fever, which first struck the West Indies in 1694, was to be a particular scourge; it was especially virulent in whites previously unexposed to the disease, while malaria was also a serious problem. In part, disease was due to the slave trade itself, as the ships that brought the slaves also carried mosquitoes from Africa that had the yellow fever virus, while the cutting down of forests for sugar affected the birds that were predators of mosquitoes. Moreover, clay pots used for sugar refining, once discarded and filled with rainwater, became breeding grounds for mosquitoes, and the latter also fed off sugar. In turn, the greater ability of black people to adapt to the American tropics, not least their stronger resistance to yellow fever,[32] was seen by Europeans as justifying their use for hard labour, not least because it was argued that this adaptation reflected the extent to which they were like animals.[33]

The slave trade in North America

Further north, in North America, the British established their first permanent colony at Jamestown on the Chesapeake in 1607. The colony expanded rapidly as a result of the continued arrival of new settlers, and tobacco became the major crop in both Virginia and Maryland. The long terms of service exacted in return for transportation to Virginia and 'the extreme demand for labor' encouraged a dealing in (white) servants, and the hiring of servants was harsher and more degrading than in England.[34] These indentured servants could be bought and sold between masters. Indentured labour was also sent to the French colonies, but most went back to France at the close of their service.[35] Moreover, those judged unwanted and/or deviant were sent to the colonies. Thus, in 1618, the street children of London were seized for work in Virginia, while in 1763–4 Parisian prostitutes were detained and dispatched to Cayenne (French Guiana).[36]

Tobacco's limited capital requirements and high profitability encouraged settlers and investment, while, because it was an export crop sold to England, the links with the mother country were strengthened. The needs and difficulties of tobacco cultivation and trade, however, created serious problems for farmers, and these problems ensured particular sensitivity to labour availability and cost. Prior to the 1680s, savings in the costs of production and marketing were important in expanding the market. Then there were about three decades of stagnation at a time of rising labour prices, followed, during the eighteenth century, by increased demand, but also rising production costs. Moreover, complicating the general pattern, booms and busts created serious problems for producers. Alongside this, there was a shifting regional pattern in production.[37]

As so often in the history of the slave trade, demographics proved a key element, in this case the fall in the birth rate in England in the 1640s. This fall hit Chesapeake planters in the early 1660s, with both fewer young men entering the Virginian labour market from England and a rise in real wages in Virginia. White indentured workers proved difficult to retain in the face of the opportunities offered by rapidly spreading English settlement.[38] These difficulties encouraged the move towards slaves in the Chesapeake labour system in the decades surrounding 1700.

An alternative labour source, Native Americans, was hit by European diseases. Furthermore, aside from an ambiguous attitude by government, including moves against the enslavement of native people in Virginia from 1659, the Native Americans fought against European control, for example on Grenada, St Vincent and across North America. Captured Native Americans were used as slaves, some being sent from Connecticut to Barbados after King Philip's War in 1675–6, while Tuscarora defeated in Carolina in 1715 were enslaved, but they were insufficient in number to meet labour requirements. Moreover, in both North and South America, Africans were also regarded as more effective and industrious workers than Native Americans and commanded higher prices. The profitability of the plantation economy made it possible to invest in these African workers, and desirable to do so, and even in Carolina, the British colony where there were most Native American slaves, they were outnumbered by Africans.

In contrast to the white people and Native Americans, slaves, thousands of miles from Africa in an unknown land, proved a more controllable labour force.[39] However, this was not always so for slave resistance developed, especially from Maroons, escaped slaves in the hills of Jamaica.[40] Across the Americas, large numbers of slaves fled, generally to the margins of white settlement, such as the Dismal Swamp in

North Carolina, where they played an important role in relations between black and Native Americans.[41]

The development of Atlantic slavery interacted with European ideas of race. In Virginia, economic advantage and coercive power were linked to a belief that Africans were inherently inferior, an attitude that drew on what were seen as 'their God-given characteristics and the circumstances of their arrival in America'.[42] Meanwhile, the establishment of Carolina as a separate colony in 1663 helped expand the English presence and also led to a rise in the slave economy of the English Atlantic. The new colony was closely linked to the English West Indies, providing opportunities for younger sons from the crowded islands, particularly Barbados. The settlers from these islands brought black slaves with them, ensuring that a sizeable black labour force soon developed in the new colony.[43] Carolina became a key exporter of colonial goods, including, from the 1690s, rice and rice cultivation, which required large numbers of slaves, as did that of indigo.[44] Nevertheless, by 1700, only 23,000 Africans had arrived in English North America, and most labour needs were still met by white servants. The crossing distance to North America, a key index of both slave fatalities and slave-trading profitability, was greater than that from Africa to Brazil and made the trade a risky business.

More generally, the price for male slaves was greater than that for females, both on the African coast and in the New World, and far more males than females were imported. This contrast reflected the role of demand factors in the slave trade, specifically the hard physical nature of the work that was expected. The profits and possibilities they provided readily explained the rise of both slavery and the slave trade, but it would be wrong to present the complex dynamics of enslavement simply in terms of rising demand for labour in the New World. It is also necessary to look in detail at the African dimension.

The slave trade within Africa and African Agency

Some accounts have focused on Western economic domination in Africa, and in particular on the way in which the Atlantic slave trade encouraged slavery within Africa. There has been an emphasis on the gun-slave cycle, by which slaves were obtained by the Europeans in return for the provision of European guns, shot and gunpowder to the Africans. Some accounts note the existence of goods that Africans could only buy from outsiders as well as the significance of the availability of European credit in encouraging trade with the Europeans, but this approach does not provide an adequate explanation.[45] This is not least because it was not until after the Industrial Revolution had transformed Western Europe's economy in the nineteenth century that traders could exert significant economic pressure on Africans, while European weapon sales, although important, do not provide the key to the trade. Similar points can be made about the sale of slaves to Arabs, as the economic pressure that could be exerted in this trade was also limited, and became more so in the nineteenth century due to Western industrialization.

Instead, it is necessary to focus on the supply of African labour, as well as the means for satisfying European demand, and also to offer a specific examination of the different slave-supplying regions in order to suggest the danger of broad generalizations. This process is made more complex by the widening impact of Europeans along the African Atlantic coast, although the coastlines of the Bight of Biafra to the east of the Niger delta, as well as the Sierra Leone coast, were not to become important sources of slaves until the mid-eighteenth century. What emerges clearly is a politics of frequent conflict within Africa that produced slaves, and of the rise and fall of empires such as the collapse of the Mali empire on the upper Niger in about 1660. Fighting was also often linked to serious droughts and famine, although the introduction of maize, manioc and peanuts from the Americas helped support population numbers in Africa just as the potato was to do in Europe. In Africa, the seizure of people for slavery was seen as a way to weaken rivals, while the availability of large numbers of slaves helped lower their price, which meant that their purchase by Europeans became more efficient as a way of addressing economic needs in the New World. This process was encouraged because the cost of slaves was further lowered by the relatively inefficient nature of African agriculture, with cultivation across Africa, except in Ethiopia, emphasizing the use of the hoe, an inefficient practice that acted to limit the value of labour ensuring that the benefit gained was not great.[46]

There have been serious difficulties in conceptualizing sub-Saharan statehood. The basic unit of African politics was a fairly small, discrete and well-bounded entity which John Thornton has termed the 'mini-state'. Larger units typically agglomerated mini-states, either by charging them tribute or by interfering in their institutional, judicial or leadership functions, creating an instability that may well have been reflected in violence. The point at which such a mini-state lost sovereignty and became a part of a larger unit is problematic: was it when one recognized the supremacy of another with nominal presents, or when significant tribute was assessed, or when judicial functions or leadership positions were taken over and appointed from outside, or when boundaries were completely redrawn? The complexity of the relations between states may help explain the frequency of conflict between them, as campaigning was a key aspect of the way in which states pursued their interests and redefined relations.[47]

Warfare between African powers certainly provided far larger numbers of slaves than European attempts to seize people. By far the most expansionist European power in Africa was Portugal, but its experience revealed the major limitations of European land warfare in Africa, and contrasted markedly with the situation in Brazil. In South-East Africa, Portuguese adventurers raised private armies from among their slaves to operate from their bases in Mozambique up the River Zambezi and to exploit the civil wars in Mutapa (modern Zimbabwe). However, they were thwarted in the 1690s with Changamire, the head of the Rozwi empire, driving the Portuguese from the plateau in 1693. Meanwhile, in Angola, the Portuguese were effective only in combination with African soldiers. Unlike the nineteenth-century pattern of European-organized units filled with African recruits, the Portuguese in seventeenth-century Angola were all organized together into a single unit with its own command structure, while the Africans, either mercenaries, subject rulers or allies, were separately organized in their own units with their own command structure. It was only at the level of the army as a whole that Portuguese officers had command, providing control for entire operations. The Portuguese also used slave soldiers, as did some of the African rulers.[48]

The Portuguese found the Africans well-armed with well-worked iron weapons, as good in some ways as Portuguese steel weaponry, and certainly better than the native wood and obsidian weapons of the New World. The slow rate of fire of Portuguese muskets and the openness of African fighting formations reduced the effectiveness of the Portuguese muskets, while their inability to deploy anything larger than a small force of cavalry ensured that they could not counter this open order, and their cannon had little impact on African earthwork fortifications. As in North America, the availability of firearms spread rapidly to the native people and Africans possibly even had them in equal numbers by the 1620s, when quantities of them were reported in 1626–8 in the first war against the formidable Queen Njinga of the Ndongo who challenged the Portuguese position in Angola. The Portuguese victory over the shield-bearing heavy infantry of the kingdom of Kongo at the battle of Mbumbi (1622) was the result of overwhelming numerical superiority, notably from an alliance with the Imbangala cannibal mercenaries, and not of weapons superiority, and the Portuguese army withdrew very quickly and even returned captured slaves when the main Kongolese army reached the region.

The Portuguese needed the support of local troops, otherwise, when they were left without African light infantry, their forces could well be destroyed, for example by the forces of Queen Njinga at the battle of Ngolomene (1644). In contrast, the combination of Africans and European infantry, with its body armour and swordsmanship as well as firepower, was effective, as in the Portuguese victories over Njinga at Cavanga (1646), and over Antonio I of Kongo at Ambuila (1665). In the latter, the Portuguese deployed 400 Europeans and 4,000 African slave soldiers, and captured thousands of Kongo slave soldiers. As a reminder that Europeans enjoyed no monopoly of firearms, Antonio's army included a small force of musketeers, as well as two cannon.

The Portuguese victory at Ambuila has attracted attention, but Kongo did not collapse rapidly and the Portuguese attempt to intervene in the Kongolese civil war led to a disastrous defeat at Kitombo (1670), which caused all hope of intervening in Kongo, even when it was severely divided in civil war, to be put aside. Since the civil war had only begun in 1665, after what many considered one of Portugal's greatest victories (Ambuila), it was unclear after Kitombo what openings were now available in a country that had previously been essentially invulnerable: Kitombo showed that there was little to be gained even against a weaker Kongo. In addition, a long series of wars against the kingdom of Ndongo that had begun in 1579 ended in stalemate for the Portuguese in the 1680s. Portuguese policy in the African interior shifted away from large-scale wars aimed at conquest after, at considerable cost, they took Pungo Andongo in a difficult siege in 1672, and central Angola was not to be conquered by Portugal until the late nineteenth century.[49] Portugal would have found it difficult to carry war much further east against any sort of organized and determined resistance because of the need for extended supply lines. The same was true of the north (into

Kongo), and the period of quiescence from the 1680s in part reflected acceptance of the fact.

Portuguese weakness in Africa and in contrast the strength of rival non-Western slave traders, was shown in East Africa. Fort Jesus, the powerful Portuguese position in Mombasa, the impressive remains of which survive to this day, fell in 1631 to a surprise storming by Sultan Muhammad Yusuf of Mombasa, and a Portuguese expedition from their major India base of Goa failed to regain it in 1632. The Portuguese were able to return when the Sultan abandoned the fortress under the pressure of Portuguese attack, but in 1698 it fell again, after a lengthy siege, to the Omani Arabs. The Portuguese presence north of Mozambique was thus lost, and a European territorial presence on the Swahili Coast did not resume until the 1880s when Germany and Britain established bases, the Germans at Pemba, Witu and Zanzibar in 1885, the British at Mombasa from 1887.

The development of new military forms and the spread of firearms in West Africa also affected Western options, influencing the pattern of slave availability. African warfare was transformed by the increasing preponderance of firepower over hand-to-hand combat, and by a growing use of larger armies. From the mid-seventeenth century on, the role of archers increased in Akwamu and Denkyira, inland states of the Gold Coast. In turn, the bow was supplanted by the musket. Firearms came into use in West Africa over a long timespan, in part because usage was restricted by the limited availability of shot and powder, both of which were obtained by trade from outside the region. The use of firearms in West Africa was first reported in the fifteenth century in Kano, one of the Islamic Hausa city states that traded slaves across the Sahara to North Africa, although a regular force of musketeers was not organized there until the 1770s. On the West African coast, the Asebu Army of the 1620s was the first to include a corps of musketeers, their guns being supplied by the Dutch, and muskets replaced bows in the 1650s to 1670s. Firepower increased in the 1680s and 1690s as flintlock muskets superseded matchlocks. In the forest interior of West Africa, muskets replaced bows in the 1690s and 1700s. The emphasis on missile weapons, bows and, later, muskets interacted with socio-economic changes, in particular with the transformation of peasants into militarily effective soldiers. This development led to the formation of mass armies and to wars which lasted longer. Larger armies increased the numbers who could be captured in conflict, which took place over much wider areas, producing large numbers of slaves. Warfare based on shock tactics had been selective in its manpower requirements, but in Akwamu and Denkyira all males fit to bear arms were eligible for conscription and therefore punishing a defeated power by large-scale enslavement hit its military potential.

These military changes were related to the rise of the states of Akwamu and Asante on the Gold Coast and Dahomey on the Slave Coast, and maybe to the late seventeenth-century expansion of Oyo further east, and these powerful states affected European options at a time of the major expansion of the slave trade. Yet, even without such states, it could be difficult to prevail over African resistance. Thus the Moroccan victory at Tondibi in 1591 was followed by persistent opposition to the Morrocans in southern Songhay which limited the expansion of the new Morrocan pashalik of Timbuktu and, notably, affected its slave raiding.

Unlike Portugal, other European powers did not try to make conquests in Africa, and the European presence in West Africa was anchored by coastal forts that served as protected bases for trade, although in some areas there were no settlements and the traders operated from their ships. Aside from rotting in the humid climate, these bases were vulnerable to attack: the Dutch position at Offra and the French one at Glehue were destroyed in 1692, the Danish base at Christiansborg fell in 1693, and the secondary British base at Sekondi fell in 1694. In contrast, the leading British base at Cape Coast Castle, the overseas headquarters of the Royal African

Company which was gained from the Dutch in 1652, was never taken by Africans and was successfully defended against African attack in 1688. Nevertheless, the British were well aware of the weakness of their position. The garrisons of European forts were indeed very small and, both for their own security and for the capacity for intervention in local conflicts, relied upon the forces of African allies.[50]

The emphasis was on cooperating with African rulers. British posts in West Africa were not held by sovereign right, but by agreement with local rulers – rent or tribute was paid for several posts, and the officials of the Royal African Company sought to maintain a beneficial relationship with numerous local *caboceers* (leaders) and *penyins* (elders) through an elaborate and costly system of presents and jobs. On the Gold Coast, the Swedish African Company was able to play a role in the 1650s because the Futu elite wanted to balance the influence of the Dutch West India Company. Their cooperation was crucial to the establishment of new trading posts, and cooperation was a matter not only of trade but also of military and political support.[51]

In so far as comparisons can be made, European slave traders did not enjoy coercive advantages in Africa greater than those of Arab counterparts on the Indian Ocean coast of Africa. Indeed, the Omani Arabs on that coast showed greater dynamism than the Portuguese. Moreover, the coercive advantages of Moroccan and other slave raiders operating across the Sahara, and from the *sahel* belt into the forested regions further south, were probably greater as they did not need to rely on ships and were not therefore dependent on the power relationships required to negotiate crossing to the shore and doing business there.

The major European advantage rested on purchasing power, not military strength, and this purchasing power derived from the prosperity of plantation economies in the Americas, and thus on the integrated nature of the Atlantic economy, but the Europeans did not have a monopoly of purchasing power. If the emphasis is on purchasing power, then a key element in the slave trade becomes not only the conflicts within Africa that produced slaves, but also the patterns of credit and debt between lenders and borrowers that transmitted this purchasing power, opening African society to demands for labour. In this approach, although there was no Western economic domination, the under-capitalized nature of the African economy emerges as import-ant in creating a reliance on European credit, with the same being true for other external sources of credit in the shape of Arab slave traders. The term 'undercapitalized', however, involves contentious value judgements for some commenta-tors. Local cooperation was crucial in the European slave trade with West Africa,[52] with financing a critical element and commercialization growing over time so that by 1750 loan sharks were setting borrowers, and their entire families, up for seizure and sale. Cooperation was also crucial in India where the collaboration of sections of the Hindu elite with Muslim rulers extended to taking part in the large-scale slave trade involving other Hindus.

In West Africa, where the Europeans did not wield control, and notably had no territorial presence comparable to those of the Muslim rulers to the north of the region, the slave trade entailed the interaction of the Western economic order and the dynamics of African warfare, at the cost of the victims of the latter.[53] The demands of the European-dominated Atlantic economy pressed on local African power systems and, in providing slaves, these systems served the Atlantic economy, although many slaves were kept for use in the local economy, which is an element that tends to be underplayed. The relationship between African states and the Europeans was similar to the cooperation of the kingdoms of Axum and Cush in the slave trade to Ancient Rome.

In the early-modern period as in the ancient world, African rulers proved more than willing to sell captives, deriving considerable profit from the trade. Indeed, the widespread belief among many Africans exported as slaves that they had been sold to cannibals to be cooked and eaten, possibly expressed a wider opposition to the cannibalistic social politics of selling slaves to foreigners as well as an association of cannibalism with evil witchcraft.[54] Similarly, in African attitudes, there was a linkage of the trade to disease and to death, and reasonably so. Indeed, if the Western and Islamic 'demand' side of the slave trade is morally reprehensible, so too was the African 'supply' side. African agency in the slave trade extended to the use of 'guardians' on the slave ships, a practice that exemplified the stratification that could exist within the slave population.[55]

The compromises entailed in sharing interests in the slave trade, a prime instance of the relations summarized as globalization, were thus made at the expense of others, the slaves, and it is important to see both elements. To treat the subject in terms only of compromise, or simply of coercion, is naïve and limited. Yet, alongside the acceptability of the trade to powerful African interests, there was opposition. In particular, reflecting longstanding Muslim views about the boundaries of appropriate behaviour, two popular religious movements in West Africa, led by Nasr al-Din in 1673–7 and Abd al-Kadir from 1776, included hostility to the sale of slaves to Christians among their Islamic reform policies.[56] The movements failed, but are a reminder of the contentious nature of the slave trade in Africa at that time, as well as of the extent of violence in West Africa.

The transportation and treatment of slaves
At the individual level, the reality of slavery was of the trauma of capture by African chieftains, sale to European merchants, often after passing through African networks, and transportation: violence, shock, hardship and disruption. These factors need emphasizing in each of the chapters of this book as they are a continual reality alongside the changes that are charted. Individuals were taken from their families and communities.

Many died in the process of capture, although this is very obscure. Others died in the drive to the coast, in which they were force-marched in coffles joined by shackles which secured them by the neck while leaving their legs free for walking. Again death rates in this stage are very obscure. Yet more died in the port towns where they were crowded together in hazardous circumstances while awaiting shipment. At Cape Coast Castle, the slaves were confined in the vaulted brick slave hole, a crowded, infected, twilight existence where they were chained round the clock, apart from when they were driven to the Atlantic coast twice daily in order to be washed. Others died on the ships that transported them across the Atlantic, the stage for which death rates have been calculated, and, also, soon after arrival, as the entire process exposed slaves to unaccustomed levels and types of disease. In the process of capture, transportation and sale, the slaves were also intimidated, humiliated and exposed to terrifyingly unfamiliar circumstances.

There are no precise figures for overall deaths, but many slaves died on the Atlantic crossing, where they were crowded together and held in poor, especially insanitary, conditions, with holds proving both foetid and crowded. Furthermore, the slaves had already been weakened by their generally long journey to the Atlantic coast, while there was also an unwillingness on the part of their captors to spend much on provisions. This situation exacerbated the serious health problems already caused by the severe impact of malnutrition, disease and conflict among those who became enslaved. As a result, the slaves were more vulnerable in their journeys. Most died from gastro-intestinal illnesses, such as dysentery, which were a reflection of the very crowded nature of the ships and the dirty conditions in the holds. Slaves were generally shackled, usually at wrist and ankle, and lay in their excrement, which contributed greatly to the pungent atmosphere in the holds. Ventilation panels were closed in bad weather and high seas.

The percentage of deaths on a crossing clearly varied, not least because, if the crossing was delayed, casualty rates rose; but the average percentage was grim. An average loss of 17.9 per cent on Dutch ships between 1637 and 1645 has been calculated, and the losses for the British Royal African Company between 1680 and 1688 were about 23.5 per cent.[57] Statistics record these experiences of brutal custody, for most involved are now nameless. The Atlantic crossing was but a part of a wider process of loss to which the organization of the slave trade contributed, and the terrible nature of the Middle Passage across the Atlantic should be added to the cruelties of the opening phases of the trade in Africa. Each of the stages brought suffering, not least because the sequential ownership of the slaves ensured that none of the owners was responsible for their long-term welfare. Instead, quick resale was the key, and only minimal care was taken to that end.[58]

Once arrived in the Americas, the slaves were exposed to fresh difficulties and renewed humiliation and intimidation. Becoming habituated to new living and working environments in the so-called seasoning period was difficult and led to a continuation of high death rates. These rates were accentuated by the harsh conditions of work and life. Rates of seventy deaths per thousand were the case on Barbados and Jamaica.[59] Furthermore, many slaves were moved considerable distances once in the Americas. Large numbers were transported from entrepôts such as Curaçao and Jamaica to eventual mainland destinations. This process involved fresh voyages, as on the route from Cartagena to Lima via Panama, and also frequently long marches overland, as on the route from Buenos Aires to Chile and Peru. Fresh voyages exposed the slaves to renewed crowding, and the hazards these entailed, while the marches led to major problems as new ecosystems were confronted. Furthermore, it was frequently necessary to wade rivers or to climb to considerable altitudes, each of which could be dangerous as well as difficult.

Such treatment can be related to the powerful racism of the

period, with its notion of a clear racial hierarchy, which was linked to false explanations, such as that of Marcello Malpighi (1628–94), Professor of Medicine in Bologna and the founder of microscopic anatomy, who believed that all men were originally white, but that the sinners had become black. The religious perspective was also instructive. In 1686, Pope Innocent XI condemned the slave trade, which was seen as harming missionary activity, but, whereas there was widespread disquiet about enslaving Christians, the plight of enslaved pagans received less attention. There was more attention about bringing Christianity to slaves and about treating them as fully human than about ending the slave trade, let alone slavery.[60] African slaves, many of whom were Muslims from West Africa, could find Christian proselytism disorienting, although some types of Christianity, for example that of the Baptists, could prove accessible.[61]

Transported, the Africans, however, used their culture to adapt to the Americas, developing social and cultural practices that variously reflected African and hybrid forms.[62] Although individual slave voices themselves are rare, and the authenticity of some accounts is controversial, the condition of slaves and former slaves was not simply that of oppression and labour. Urban slaves in Spanish America had, for example, reasonable opportunities to improve their position and freedom was granted there with some readiness, far more so than in British or French America.[63] Slaves and former slaves also had a varied associational and cultural life with black and mulatto brotherhoods, for example in Brazil, providing a range of social benefits for members. These brotherhoods, which were seen as important in encouraging Christian observance, responded in their composition to the very varied nature of Brazilian black and mulatto society, and also the capacity of this society to create its own hierarchies. Procedures included the election of governing bodies.[64]

This was part of the process by which migration, however coerced, was a dynamic in which the whites who wielded political and economic power did not, or were unable to, prevent the development of independent associational patterns, a key stage in the creation of Black America. The reality of slavery was as much this diversity as it was the harsh and exploitative working and living conditions that most slaves experienced with scant hope of improvement.

4

SLAVERY BEFORE ABOLITIONISM, 1700–1780

By any standards it was a bleak crossing. The *Rodeur* took on 160 slaves at Bonny to the east of the Niger delta, but, in the confined hold, infectious disease hit hard, first eye problems and then 'a violent dysentery'. Crowded in the noxious hold among their urine and excrement, the slaves found their water ration cut from eight ounces a day to half a wine glass. Allowed on deck for exercise, some threw themselves into the sea, which led to the others being continually confined. Contagion spread to the crew and, by the time the boat had reached Guadeloupe, thirty-nine slaves and twelve of the crew had lost their sight completely. Many others had lost their sight in one eye. Of the thirty-nine, thirty-one were thrown into the Atlantic.[1] The case of the *Zong* was more famous. Carrying 470 Africans for Jamaica, this Liverpool ship ran short of water and, concerned to ensure some of his cargo, the captain, Luke Collingwood, had 131 of the weaker slaves thrown into the Atlantic to drown. Their value was then claimed on the ship's insurance, which led to a legal case, while the public furore focused anger and provided a longstanding image of callousness and cruelty, not least thanks to a dramatic painting by Turner.

The eighteenth century proved the highpoint of the Atlantic slave economy, with more slaves shipped across than ever before. Yet, as a reminder of its diverse forms, the Atlantic world included not only those slaves consigned to gruelling and unhealthy labour in the sugar and rice plantations of the Americas, but also the corps of black slave soldiers created by Sultan Mawlay Isma'il of Morocco (r.1672–1727). Under his successor, Ahmad Adh-Dhahabi (r.1727–9), the slave corps became a force for chaos, trying, like the Praetorian Guard of Imperial Rome, to sell their political support. The varied nature of slavery was in part captured by Morocco, for European powers made efforts to win protection for their merchant trade from the attacks of Moroccan privateers, attacks that led to enslavement, although they were also an opportunity to raise money by selling captives back. Thus, in 1700, Captain George Delaval negotiated a treaty for the redemption of British captives, and further agreements between the two powers followed in 1713 and 1751.[2] Other European powers were forced to similar expedients, not least as attacks on the major Barbary bases were unsuccessful, most spectacularly with Spanish failures at Algiers in 1775 and 1784. The presence of the Royal Navy at Gibraltar from 1704 helped protect British trade but the limited technology of the period ensured that there was no capacity for long-range surveillance.

The century saw a continuation of large-scale Islamic slaving, with slaves obtained from sub-Saharan Africa, including northern Madagascar, moved to North Africa, the Middle East, the Arabian peninsula, the Persian Gulf and the west coast of India, notably to Calicut. There was also the movement of slaves into the Islamic world from the north, particularly from the Ukraine and Caucasus, although the scale of this movement was affected by the southward move of Russian power, especially the conquest of the Crimea in 1783. Earlier, Russian defensive lines had limited the potential for Islamic slave raiding, although it continued both west and east of the Caspian Sea. Moreover, into the nineteenth century there were regular cases of Russians being kidnapped in the Caucasus and ransomed; if they were not bought back, they in effect became slaves.

In turn, there was certainly Russian selling of Muslims, both captives gained through war and others, in the early eighteenth century, which probably meant slavery, but it was not stated nor legally acknowledged as such. Slave raiding also played a role in the frequent conflicts in Central Asia, notably between Kazaks, Uzbeks and Dzhungars. In India, however, the collapse of Mughal power in the early eighteenth century lessened the potential for raising slaves through warfare, although this collapse also led to a degree of instability and conflict that provided opportunities for enslavement.

The European slave trade to the New World
In aggregate terms, the resulting movements of slaves were considerable, while in detail they were hugely disruptive as well as the cause of much misery. Yet, it is the Atlantic slave trade and slavery in the New World, especially in the British empire, that commands attention, in large part due to the direction of scholarship but also because the voluminous reaction to the British slave trade proved the crucial background for the growth of Abolitionism.

In his futuristic novel *L'An 2440* (1770), the radical French writer Louis Sébastien Mercier described a monument in Paris in 2440 depicting a black man, his arms extended, rather than in chains, and a proud look in his eye, surrounded by the pieces of twenty broken sceptres and atop a pedestal with the inscription, '*Au vengeur du nouveau monde*' [To the avenger of the New World]. To his readers, this would have seemed a utopian prospect and also a proof of Mercier's radicalism. In the absence of photography, books, however, certainly brought home at least part of the nature of slavery to European readers. In his far more successful novel *Candide* (1759), the leading Enlightenment French writer Voltaire had his protagonist visit Surinam (on the Atlantic coast of South America), which had been colonized by the Dutch in the seventeenth century as a plantation economy. A black man told Candide,

> Those of us who work in the factories and happen to catch a finger in the grindstone have a hand chopped off; if we try to escape, they cut off one leg. Both accidents happened to me. That's the price of your eating sugar in Europe ... Dogs, monkeys, and parrots are much less miserable than we are. The Dutch ... who converted me, tell me every Sunday, that we are all children of Adam.[3]

This last comment was a reference to Christian hypocrisy directed at the Calvinist Dutch whose plantation economy yielding sugar, cocoa, coffee and cotton was both harsh and faced by slave risings as well as by flight. Similarly, 'SPG' was branded on the many Barbadian slaves owned by the Society for the Propagation of the Gospel. Voltaire's point about hypocrisy was to be echoed in 2003 when, on a visit to Africa, the American President, George W. Bush, travelled to the West African slave-trading post at Gorée, Senegal, which had been used by the Dutch, France and Britain. Now a major site in heritage tourism, this was a choice of destination designed to send a message about his concern for African Americans, as well as his awareness of their distinctive history, and his grasp of the role of suffering in it. Bush declared that 'Christian men and women became blind to the clearest commands of their faith ... Enslaved Africans discovered a suffering Saviour and found him as more like themselves than their masters.'[4] A similar point had been made by the Abolitionist Stephen Cave, who wrote that 'the African owes his degradation to his intercourse with the inhabitants of enlightened Christian Europe'.[5]

Gorée and other ports were indeed very busy in the eighteenth-century. It was the peak period of the slave trade, with about 52 per cent of those shipped from Africa to the Americas in the period 1450–1900 moved in this century alone,[6] and there was a clear sense of the trade as becoming larger in scale and more sophisticated. The Atlantic trade meant selling slaves to the colonies of other powers, as well as one's own colonies. Most obviously, both France and Britain sought to profit from demand in Latin America and the wealth of its economies. In doing so, they overcame Spanish and Portuguese attempts to retain commercial monopolies and thus contributed greatly to the illicit slave flows[7] that were to become even more important when steps were taken to stop the slave trade in the nineteenth century. Illicit slave flows made it difficult for contemporaries to know the size of the trade.

Nevertheless, in order to avoid the problems posed by the Spanish regulatory regime, which covered so much of the Americas from the Spanish colony of Florida southwards, it was far more desirable to gain permission to trade. Indeed, in 1701, as a sign of closer Franco-Spanish relations following the accession of the Bourbon Philip V, grandson of Louis XIV of France, to the Spanish throne the previous year, the French Guinea Company was granted the *asiento* contract to transport slaves to Spanish America for ten years, a lucrative opening into the protected trade of the Spanish empire.[8] In turn, the victorious British gained the *asiento* contract and the right to trade with Spanish America as part of the Peace of Utrecht at the close of the War of the Spanish Succession (1702–13), a conflict over the future of the Spanish empire in which they had defeated the French.[9] This right was exercised by the South Sea Company, and the extravagant hopes it gave rise to helped launched the vast speculative bubble in the Company's shares, which crashed in 1720, creating a major political scandal about governmental connivance in fraudulent practices. The role of the South Sea Company also created tensions in the British slave trade, with, for example, the Royal

African Company pressing the ministry for assistance against the Company. Such tensions were common throughout the history of the slave trade, as the quest for profit created rivalries and brought them to the fore.

Unlike Britain and France, powers that lacked important colonies were dependent on selling to others. The Dutch had bases on the Gold Coast of West Africa, including Axim, Hollandia, Accadia, Butri and Shama, but in the Americas lacked a market comparable to Portuguese Brazil, French Saint-Domingue (modern Haiti), or British Jamaica. Instead, they sold to all they could reach through entrepôts on their West Indies' islands of Curaçao and Saint Eustatius, and carried about 310,000 slaves during the century.[10] Based in Cape Town, which had been founded in 1652 as a base on the way to the Indian Ocean, Cape Colony was another Dutch slave society, with the slaves brought across the Indian Ocean, mostly from Africa, although some came from India.[11] However, Cape Colony was far less developed than the plantation economies of the New World.

In a weaker position than the Dutch, the Brandenburg (Prussian), and Danish companies were unable to make money from their West African bases. Indeed, in 1717, the two forts that the Brandenburg Company had on the Gold Coast, Fort Dorothea (Accadia) and Fort Friedrichsburg (Hollandia), were sold to the Dutch as there were no Brandenburg bases, let alone colonial territories, in the West Indies to help support the trade.

In succession, three Danish West Indian companies failed to make the necessary profits; the Danes owned several small islands in the West Indies, St Croix, St John and St Thomas (sold in 1917 to the USA, and now the American Virgin Islands), but lacked a large market. The Danes transported just over 50,000 slaves from Africa between 1733 and 1802.[12] The Danish colonial presence on the African Gold Coast had begun in the 1650s, with Christiansborg acquired from Sweden in 1653, and Fort Augustenborg in 1700. The motives of the government, which supported the companies involved with cash, monopoly rights and other privileges, were to help Danish commercial groups and to gain larger revenues for the Treasury. Thus, entry into the slave trade was an aspect of a more general policy intended to further trade and industry and to strengthen the state.

The Danish role in the slave trade really started in the eighteenth century, as – apart from the shortlived attempt in the mid-seventeenth century – did that of Sweden which gained the island of St Barthélemy from France in 1784; it was returned in 1877. In return for being ceded the island, Gustavus III of Sweden had granted his ally France a depot for naval stores at Gothenburg. Gustavus also had ideas about Swedish colonies in Africa, but the person he sent out to gather information, Carl Bernhard Wadström, became a rather prominent Abolitionist.

More generally, the slave trade was not a constant. Flows varied, as the sources and destinations of slaves changed, with smuggling and piracy adding further complications. The majority of Africans transported in the eighteenth century went to the West Indies and Brazil, and fewer than a fifth to Spanish and North America.[13] The biggest shippers, in order, were Britain, Portugal, France and the Dutch. Anglophone scholarship concentrates heavily on Britain, but France also was a key supplier to the West Indies and it is pertinent to note its role, not least because French competition helped shape the British trade. During the century, the French colonies, Saint-Domingue, Martinique, Guadeloupe, Cayenne (French Guiana) and Louisiana, obtained 1,015,000 slaves from French sources, although an illegal British trade to them was significant, which makes it difficult to assess the numbers imported into these colonies.[14]

The French West Indian islands were particularly important for the production of sugar, and this helped drive forward French trade, interacting with opportunities in domestic and foreign markets. At the beginning of the century, Bordeaux's sugar refiners enjoyed the right of transporting their product to much of France without paying many of the internal tolls of which their rivals in La Rochelle, Marseilles and Nantes complained. Bordeaux's imports of sugar, indigo and cocoa from the French West Indies tripled in 1717–20, the beginning of a massive increase in re-exports to northern Europe, which competed directly with those of Britain in key markets such as Hamburg. In 1778, Saint-Domingue exported 1,634,032 quintaux of sugar (100 kilograms to a quintal).

A decade later, the French West Indies contained 594,000 slaves, a phenomenal expansion. Whereas in 1687 Saint-Domingue, the largest French colony in the West Indies, contained 4,500 white people and 3,500 slaves, by 1789 the numbers were 28,000 white people, 30,000 free black people and 406,000 slaves. The free blacks owned about 100,000 of the slaves, which was an aspect of the effectiveness of hierarchy in controlling slave resistance, hierarchy in this cast including highly privileged slaves, slave drivers, slave over-seers, and the free black planters and slave-owners. Saint-Domingue benefited from the use of fresher, less exhausted soils than those of the rival British sugar colonies such as Barbados, and this was a factor noted by contemporaries. In the 1780s, thanks to strong re-exports from France to other European markets, notably Germany and the Baltic via Hamburg, and Italy via Livorno, sugar prices rose despite a general recession in France.[15] This rise ensured a profitability in sugar production that encouraged the importing of more slaves, and the 1780s was the peak decade for the receipt of slaves by the French West Indian colonies: nearly 30,000 annually. The numbers sent to Saint-Domingue alone rose from 14,000 annually in 1766–71 to 28,000 annually in 1785–9, and the strength of its economy ensured that it was able to get a better choice of slaves. Large numbers of slaves were also sent to the French West Indian island of Martinique, although Guadeloupe received far fewer. The French, having estab-lished their first base in Louisiana in 1699, imported the first slaves to the colony in 1719, although it never became a major slave society.[16] Differences in the number of slaves had consequences for the social and racial structure of colonies that explain the contrasts between them.

The major French source of slaves was the basin of the River Senegal, via the slaving ports of Gorée and St Louis. In contrast, Assinie on the Ivory Coast was only held by the French from 1687 to 1705, while Forcados on the Benin coast was only held from 1786 to 1792. The French could be forceful in West Africa, as in 1724 when a naval force seized the Dutch base of Arguin in an area where the French claimed exclusive commercial privileges. In a separate trade, slaves from East Africa and Madagascar supplied the French colonies in the Indian Ocean, Réunion (Ile de Bourbon) and Mauritius (Ile de France).[17] Réunion, which they had claimed in 1642, was a source of coffee, and Mauritius, seized in 1715, of sugar. In 1769–72 French expeditions acquired clove plants on Ambon in the East Indies and introduced them to Mauritius.

Commerce and slave-produced goods

As a result of the efforts of the slaves, exports from the Americas boomed, helping to lead to a major rise in European consumption: of coffee in Europe across the eighteenth century from two million to 120 million pounds, of chocolate from two million to 13 million pounds, and of tobacco, especially from Virginia, from fifty million to 125 million pounds; in each case it was a rise far above that of the European population.[18] Between 1663 and 1775, the consumption of muscovado sugar in England and Wales increased twenty-fold, while British rum consumption rose from the 207 gallons imported in 1698 to an annual average of two million gallons in 1771–5. In 1702, visiting the port of Falmouth, John Evelyn had 'a small bowl of punch made with Brazil sugar', while, in September 1764, the merchant fleet from Pernambuco in north-east Brazil was reported as arriving in Lisbon with 5,000 chests of sugar.[19] Thanks to its plantation economy, Jamaica in the early 1770s was the wealthiest British colony in the New World, and the average white man there was 36.6 times as wealthy as the average white man in the Thirteen Colonies.[20]

The role of the New World in the global economy continued to be strong because of the failure to produce significant quantities of its plantation goods elsewhere. Thus, while New England and North Carolina iron and timber goods competed in the British market with Scandinavian production, there was no equivalent competition for sugar. In 1792, the West Indies interest lobbied hard and successfully against the attempt by the British East India Company to export sugar from India, which might have led to a cut in the price of sugar.[21] This interest was a powerful one and it helped affirm the importance of the West Indies to British political economy. The merchants trading with the West Indies lacked a company structure comparable to the East India Company, but their pressure-group tactics and their ability to mount well-organized petitioning and propaganda campaigns were very important in persuading the Westminster Parliament, in which they were well-represented, to pass a series of measures in their favour, such as the Molasses Act of 1733, and also to influence other legislation, such as the Sugar Act of 1764. The press argued against additional duties on sugar, which the government supported, preferring to call for duties on foreign imports such as linens instead.[22] This lobby became even more organized and active as a result of the problems posed by the American Revolution, which broke out in 1775.[23]

It was not only sugar. Coffee was another major product from the New World and, thanks to slavery, the Europeans took over the bulk of the world trade in coffee. In 1660 Marseilles, France's leading Mediterranean port, imported only 19,000 quintaux of coffee, traded from Yemeni origin, via Egypt, providing an important aspect of France's relationship with the Ottoman empire; in 1785 it imported 143,310, of which 142,500 came from the West Indies. Introduced to

Martinique and Guadeloupe in 1725, and to Saint-Domingue in 1730, French West Indian coffee was more popular than that produced by the Dutch in the East Indies, and it swiftly became the principal global source. From 1722, the French also produced coffee in Cayenne on the north coast of South America. In 1770, 350,000 quintaux of coffee were produced by the French in the Americas, and in 1790 over 950,000. Most went to France and was then re-exported; from Marseilles principally to the Ottoman empire, reversing the earlier trade flow. By 1789, Saint-Domingue was probably supplying more than half the Western world's coffee. The Dutch began coffee production in Surinam in 1712, and by 1772 were producing over twelve million pounds per annum there,[24] which was part of the commercial rationale for the harsh situation depicted in *Candide*.

These developments showed how slavery provided major opportunities for new commercial initiatives that were wide-ranging enough to create new global links and to change existing trade patterns. To regard such slave-linked developments as progress is to misuse the language, but they indicated the competitive advantages brought by large-scale slavery and the economic transformations it could lead to as new opportunities were tested and exploited.

Cacao and tobacco were other important products from the New World produced by slaves. Aside from the prominent goods, the provision of other New World products also depended on slaves. Thus, the dye indigo was widely produced, including in both Jamaica and Venezuela. More-over, British logwood cutters who settled in Belize in Central America brought in African slaves from 1720, and, from the 1760s, brought in more to help with mahogany cutting, which required more slaves. When looking at fine mahogany pieces from the period it is easy to forget the slave labour involved in their production.

The European presence in the East Indies was far more limited, and also more dependent on local cooperation than that in the West Indies. The Dutch East India Company introduced coffee into Java, and also imported pepper, sugar and indigo from there. Coffee production on Java quickly became considerable, while cloves, tea and coffee came from Ambon (Amboina). However, due to political problems and distance, these trades could not match those from the West Indies, and the heavily regulated nature of the Dutch East India Company did not help. The Company wanted limited supplies at high prices, as opposed to massive quantities able to compete on world markets at low prices. Limits in the availability of investment capital and servile labour were also significant, although the Dutch East India Company had slaves in Java, Sri Lanka and Cape Town able to perform menial work as well as to fulfil private household roles. Most of these slaves came from the coastlines of India and Arakan, and there was much ethnic mixing. In Java, sugar production depended on servile labour from China provided by the Chinese to whom the Company franchised the production. The Dutch Indian Ocean slave world reached for sources of supply as far as New Guinea and the southern Philippines, benefiting from the weakness of governmental organization in such areas.[25] Slavery also played a role in British India, not least in the provision of concubines.[26]

Trade with the New World affected much of the European economy. For example, although at Bordeaux the colonial trade with the Caribbean was conducted by French merchants, re-exports were largely controlled by foreign firms established in the town. At the beginning of the century, most were Dutch, but by 1730 there was a significant German presence. Towards the end of the century, Milanese merchants brought coffee, chocolate, sugar and spices to Switzerland, purchasing the muslins of St Gall and Zurich in return.

European conflicts in the Americas and Africa
France's production of colonial goods and its slave trade were affected by war with Britain and eventually, in the 1790s, by

a major and, in the end, successful slave rebellion on Saint-Domingue. The war with Britain which broke out in 1793 was the last of a sequence of eighteenth-century wars that involved conflict in West Africa and the Americas. These conflicts, in 1702–13, 1744–8, 1756–63, 1778–83 and 1793–1802, affected the slave trade and the exports from the New World which it fed, although it was generally the case that disputes over competing interests in the West Indies and West Africa did not lead to sustained hostilities, let alone war. In 1739 Anglo-Spanish differences over trade in the Caribbean led to the War of Jenkins' Ear between the two powers, but, in the eighteenth century, disputes in West Africa did not have such dire consequences. Indeed, disputes were often with allies, as in the 1720s. The British Royal African Company frequently complained of attacks. In October 1723 the Portuguese destroyed its trading settlement at Cabinda, an example of the Portuguese determination to control the trade from the north of the River Congo; in 1725 the Company complained about French action on the Guinea coast; and in 1728 Dutch attacks upon its ships led to demands for naval protection and the dispatch of a British warship. The issue, however, did not arouse interest in Britain, and the same was true of Dutch–Portuguese rivalry over the slave trade from West Africa in the mid-1720s.

In the 1730s, tension in West Africa centred on Anglo-French competition, although this focused on the gum arabic trade from the River Senegal, rather than on the slave trade. Gum arabic was a product used in textile manufacture that was the other major European-controlled export from this region. The French sought to limit the establishment of a British position on the River Gambia, while the British argued that French settlements on one part of the coast did not give the French a right to the trade of the whole coast.[27] Conflict was avoided, because neither state sought to fight, and neither was under significant domestic pressure on the issue: the Royal African Company was unpopular in Britain as it suffered from the widespread dislike of the monopolistic position of chartered companies.

Later in the century, there was also reluctance in Britain to push disagreements in West Africa, whether with allies or with rivals. For example, in 1784, a memorandum about the French establishing a post on the River Gambia at once led to government enquiries in Britain, but the response was subdued.[28] In 1791, there was concern over the position at Ambriz to the north of the Portuguese settlements on the Angolan coast but to the south of the River Congo. British trade was seen as threatened by Portuguese claims, but the issue was not pushed forcefully by Britain.[29] Ambriz became part of Angola. Further north, clashes between France and Portugal over trading rights at Cabinda, to the north of the Congo, had led to the French demolishing a Portuguese fort in 1784.

Disputes over control of the sugar islands in the West Indies were more sensitive, although they did not lead to large-scale hostilities. British settlers were expelled by the French from St Lucia in 1723, but, although the issue created political difficulties for the British government, it did not become a major issue. Similarly, Anglo-Danish differences in 1733 over claims to the island of St Croix did not become important.

Once war had begun between Britain and France, the sugar islands became a major site of conflict. This was less the case in the War of the Austrian Succession, when Britain and France were at war from 1744 to 1748 and in which the British captured Port Louis on Saint-Domingue in 1748. The war ended with the two powers returning their conquests.

The prosperity of what had become the slave economy, however, was very much linked to imperial control. Thus, in 1754, when the British government was having to consider how best to respond to French expansion in the North American interior, one minister argued that this expansion might lead to France becoming the masters of the tobacco trade.[30]

In the Seven Years War (1756–63), the British were more successful than in the previous war, capturing Guadeloupe in 1759, and Grenada, Martinique, St Lucia and St Vincent in 1762. The French slave stations in West Africa, St Louis and Gorée were taken in 1758, the government being encouraged to this end by City merchants.[31] In addition, Havana was captured from Spain in 1762. Under the peace settlement, the Peace of Paris, of 1763, Martinique, Guadeloupe, Gorée, St Lucia and Cuba were returned, but Grenada, St Vincent, and St Louis in Senegal were retained. The importance of the slave trade was clear. John, Third Earl of Bute, George III's key adviser, had noted, 'When Choiseul [the French foreign minister] gives Senegal up and seems facile on Gorée, it is with an express proviso that the French be put in possession of a sea port on the Slave Coast.'[32]

After the war, the French mapped Martinique and Guadeloupe in order to provide information in the event of future hostilities with Britain. Mapping was carried out by engineers and was part of a policy of fortification. The maps recorded the plantation system, and the names of the owners were marked on the plantations.[33] In the War of American Independence, which France entered on the American side in 1778, Gorée changed hands in 1779, while, in the West Indies, the French also took Dominica (1778), Grenada (1779), St Vincent (1779), Tobago (1781), Nevis (1782), St Christopher (1782) and Montserrat (1782), although the British captured St Lucia (1778). The British slave trade was hit by the war, as was the profitability of the sugar plantations.[34] In the eventual peace settlement, the Treaty of Versailles of 1783, France gained Tobago and Senegal. In turn, in the French Revolutionary War, which broke out in 1793, the slave trade and the plantation economies of the West Indies were disrupted anew. The British captured Gorée in 1800, and, in the West Indies, Tobago in 1793, St Lucia in 1794 and (after it had been retaken in 1795) in 1796, Trinidad in 1797, Surinam in 1799, Curaçao in 1800 and the Danish and Swedish West Indian islands in 1801.

In contrast to the conflict between Britain and France, the Portuguese slave trade in the South Atlantic did not face a challenge comparable to that mounted by the Dutch the previous century in both Angola and Brazil. Angola, where the major bases were Luanda and Beneguela, supplied about two million slaves during the eighteenth century, mostly to Brazil, and the Portuguese had more bases further north, especially in Portuguese Guinea at Cacheu, and also traded along coasts where they did not have any bases. Off the Atlantic coast, the Portuguese also had the islands of Annobon, Fernando Po, Principe and São Tomé, although Annobon and Fernando Po were gained by Spain in 1776; otherwise, Spain had no direct presence in the African slaving world.

Slave production in South America

Growing demand in Brazil reflected its major economic expansion, but also economic change. The sugar plantations of the north-east declined in importance from the 1710s, as sugar production from the West Indies, especially the French West Indies, became more important in supplying European markets. This was an important aspect of the competition, and thus search for comparative advantage, that the slave trade reflected. However, there was major economic growth in the south of Brazil, where captaincies (provinces) were founded for São Paulo (1709), Minas Gerais (1720), Goiás (1744) and Mato Grosso (1748). Furthermore, gold and diamond extraction from the Brazilian province of Minas Gerais, where gold had been discovered in 1695, grew substantially in significance.[35] For instance, in 1723 the fleet from Rio de Janeiro arrived in Lisbon with a 'considerable quantity of unregistered gold'.[36] This activity produced, at once, a key demand for slaves in a different area and a major new stimulus for the slave trade that, at the same time, helped to fund it. Slaves worked both in mines and in tasks such as washing diamond-bearing rocks. Aside from in Minas Gerais, where the towns of Minas

Novas and Diamantina were founded in 1727 and 1730 respectively, there were also gold deposits in Goiás and Mato Grosso. From the late century, in another important geographical shift, sugar and coffee plantations near Rio de Janeiro became prominent; Rio had replaced Salvador (Bahia), further north, as capital of Brazil in 1763, and by 1775 a third of the population in the province were slaves.[37]

There was considerable differentiation in the slave trade. The Portuguese bases in Angola supplied Minas Gerais and Rio de Janeiro with slaves, while West Africa supplied the sugar plantations of north-east Brazil,[38] and this differentiation was an aspect of the wider specialization of the Atlantic slave trade. It took about forty to forty-five days to sail from Elmina in West Africa to Salvador (Bahia), and about fifty days to sail from Luanda in Angola to Rio.[39] The partnership between Europeans and elite Africans was crucial to this trade, with Luso-African families, who spanned the Portuguese world of the Angolan coast and the African world of the interior, also having links into the plantation-owning families of north-east Brazil. Plantation goods exported from Brazil included sugar, tobacco, coffee and, from the 1760s, cotton,[40] producing the profits that helped ensure there were over one million slaves there by 1800. The Portuguese slave-owners in Brazil preferred to import adult male slaves rather than to encourage slave families, and, combined with the physical strain of the work and a high mortality rate, this practice ensured a continual need for more slaves.

Although the Brazilian plantations relied on African slave labour, and most slaves came from Angola, slave raiding was still practised in Brazil at the expense of the native people. Slave traders from São Paulo, known as Paulistas or *mamelucos*, did much to lower native population numbers, although they were resisted by the *reducciones*, frontier settlements in Spanish America (notably in modern Bolivia and Paraguay) under Jesuit supervision where native people grew crops. Native slaves and forced labour in Amazonia were important for the collection of cacao, sarsaparilla and other forest products, but in 1743–9 possibly half the native population of the Amazon valley fell victim to measles and smallpox.[41]

Export growth from Spanish America was also linked to the intensification of slavery, which encouraged the import of slaves there. This was true of the export of sugar and tobacco from Cuba, cacao and sugar from Mexico, and cacao, tobacco, cotton, coffee, sugar and indigo from Venezuela. After the Caracas Company was founded in 1728 and given monopoly rights by the Spanish government to transport cacao from Venezuela, cacao exports increased and the already-established growth in production there continued. This growth encouraged the rise in slave imports: twice as many were imported into the region in the eighteenth century as in the previous century,[42] and, by 1800, about 15 per cent of the 800,000-strong population of Venezuela were slaves working in the plantations.

The economic importance of slave production in South America is generally underrated due to a concentration on the West Indies and on what became the USA, because the anglophone literature focuses on both. Alongside imports of slaves to Spanish America, there were movements within the Spanish world, with Florida, for example, receiving slaves from Havana as well as from the mainland colony of New Spain. At the same time, part of the black population of Latin America (as elsewhere) were not slaves. Moreover, there was a willingness to arm the free black people, who were increasingly recruited into the militia in Spanish America from 1764. Furthermore, defence of the interior of the French colony of Cayenne was entrusted to Native Americans and free black people, who were organized into a company of soldiers, while, in the 1760s and 1770s, black and mulatto Brazilians were recruited into companies of irregular infantry.[43] This practice was far less common in British America.

The British slave trade

Brazil was a market for British slave traders, while there were British and French sales to Spanish America, both legal and illegal, but for British, as for French, merchants, the core trade was that of selling slaves to their own colonies. The British were the most prominent in the slave trade. Between 1691 and 1779, British ships transported 2,141,900 slaves from African ports, and British colonial ships took another 124,000.[44] London dominated the trade until the 1710s, when it was replaced by Bristol. As an indication, however, of the range of difficulties faced by slave traders, Bristol merchants in the early 1730s were hit by shortages of slaves, falling profits on colonial re-exports as prices dropped, and deteriorating relations with Spain which created doubt about security and markets; war finally broke out in 1739 and with France in 1744. The number of slave voyages sailing from Bristol fell from fifty-three in 1738 to eight in 1744; war with France and Spain only ended in 1748 and British merchants were heavily exposed to privateering during it. The regulatory framework that had maintained London's control had been dismantled in 1698 when the African trade was freed from the control of the Royal African Company. This legalized the position of private traders, and made shifts in the relative position of ports far easier.[45]

The values of liberalization for increased trade were to be seen, at a different scale, with the removal of restrictions on the Portuguese slave trade from South-East Africa in the second half of the century. The monopoly role of companies was ended when the colony of Mozambique was removed from the jurisdiction of Portuguese India, and in 1786 the monopoly of the port of Mozambique over the slave trade was ended, so that other ports in the colony gained their own customs houses and began trading. This led to an expansion in the Portuguese slave trade from South-East Africa that was also related to the ability to expand the area in the interior from which slaves were obtained. This expansion rested on the purchase of slaves, not on the territorial expansion attempted earlier in the colony's history, and that was not resumed until the late nineteenth century, more particularly the 1890s.

The developing port of Liverpool took the leading position in the British slave trade from the 1740s and maintained it thereafter. In 1725, Bristol ships carried about 17,000 slaves and, between 1727 and 1769, thirty-nine slavers were built there, while, by 1752, Liverpool had eighty-eight slavers with a combined capacity of over 25,000 slaves. In 1750–79 there were about 1,909 slave trade sailings from Liverpool, 869 from London, and 624 from Bristol.[46] Liverpool had better port facilities than Bristol, not least the sole wet dock outside London. A wet dock was one with gates that were opened only at high tide, which kept the level of water within the dock at high-tide level so that ships could unload directly onto the dockside while still afloat. As a result, ships could be loaded and unloaded much more rapidly, which increased the efficiency of trade. The construction of the wet dock, built entirely by hand between 1710 and 1715, was followed by a major expansion of dock facilities, with the opening of the Salthouse Dock (1753), George Dock (1771) and Duke's Dock (1773), and the wet dock became the Old Dock, which was backfilled in 1826 and became the site of a splendid new customs house. The harbourside was a bustling centre of economic activity linked to trade and to satisfying sailors' needs.

By 1801, Liverpool, with a population of 83,250, dominated Britain's Atlantic trade, but was also a city faced with overcrowding, poor sanitation and disease. Dr Duncan of Liverpool, the country's first medical officer of health, calculated in the mid-nineteenth century that certain streets and alleys in the city had a density equivalent to 657,963 people per square mile. In 1840, the annual death rate in Liverpool was 34.4 per 1,000 and the average age of death 17 years, compared to 27 and 26.5 respectively in London. The nineteenth century was an age of statistics that threw light on earlier conditions. In 1846, Liverpool contained 538 brothels and in 1857 there were at least 200 regular prostitutes under the age of twelve in the city. Such was the varied infrastructure and human suffering supporting the slave trade and other commerce.

Most slaves were transported by the British to the West Indies, which were the centre of the British slave economy; but many also went to British North America. The number of African slaves there rose from about 20,000 in 1700 to over 300,000 by 1763, particularly as first South Carolina and then the newly established colony of Georgia were developed as plantation economies, supplementing those on the Chesapeake. In South Carolina and, eventually, Georgia rice became an additional plantation crop, reflecting the particular opportunities of the tidewater environment.

The slave trade was integral to the commercial economy and shipping world of the British Atlantic, crucial to important entrepreneurial circles in Britain, and to part of the financial world there, and had a range of influences elsewhere in Britain, particularly in, but not limited to, in the ports. Not only were the large ports of Liverpool, Bristol, Glasgow and London involved in a trade that affected more than the merchants and shippers directly engaged,[47] but there were also smaller ports, such as Barnstaple, Bideford, Dartmouth, Exeter, Lancaster, Plymouth, Poole, Portsmouth, Topsham and Whitehaven. The last sent about sixty-nine slaving voyages to Africa between 1710 and 1769, most after 1750, and its merchants were probably the fifth most important group of slave traders in Britain in the latter period, but they largely abandoned the trade after 1769.[48]

The role of the smaller ports helped spread the impact of the slave trade on the British economy, although many, including Devon's ports, only played a minor role, a process that owed much to the extent to which many merchants and ships were involved in the trade on a temporary basis. Because the majority of British ships involved made only one voyage in the trade, there was no substantial separate slave fleet. Partly as a result, many slave ships were not the large ships that tend to attract attention, but smaller vessels carrying a limited number of slaves. Most fell within the 50–150 tonnage range.[49] The use of ships not designed as slavers, but instead poorly adapted, often contributed further to the miseries of the journey for the slaves. Similarly, for the Portuguese trade, the large *galeras* were less important than the more modestly sized *bergantim*.

The triangular pattern of Atlantic trade – goods, both British manufactures and imports, such as East India Company textiles, from Britain to Africa; slaves thence to the New World; and colonial products, such as sugar and tobacco, back to Britain[50] – was practicable for small-scale operators, as the outlay of funds required was less than for the trade to the more distant East Indies. The triangular trade depended on credit and the ability to wait for payment, and Britain's financial strength provided both. The role of finance, particularly of the sugar commission business, ensured that London, where the business centred, was as heavily involved in the trade as Liverpool.[51] Financial buoyancy was particularly important in long-distance trade in which new ships often lasted only two or three voyages, financial returns were delayed, and merchants needed to obtain long-term credit on favourable terms.

The trade brought prosperity to British manufacturers, and the export of goods to Africa as part of the triangular trade helped broaden the range of groups in British society who were interested in the slave trade and who benefited from its expansion. Africa was seen as a sphere of opportunity, not least because trade to much of the rest of the world appeared blocked or limited by the role of other European states, for example Spain's determination to limit outsiders' trade with its colonies, as well as by the attitude of non-European powers, by the entrenched position of British chartered companies, such as the East India Company, or by the lack of any product worth obtaining in return for exports. The last, for example, limited Portuguese and Dutch interest in Australia.

In his 'Thoughts on the African Trade', published in 1730 in number 76 of the *Universal Spectator*, 'J. L.' attacked the position of the British East India Company in trade to the Indian Ocean, and urged the establishment of a trade to the south-east coast of Africa, with textiles and pewter exported, which, he argued, would help British industry, whereas, he claimed, the trade to India did not bring such advantages. The suggestion did not bear fruit, but was indicative of the sense of Africa as a land of opportunity for British trade, with the value of the exports redeemed in large part in slaves. The argument about the potential of Africa for exports was later to be taken up by Abolitionists who claimed that the abolition of the slave trade would create major new opportunities for British exporters by facilitating the development of stable and prosperous markets.

The triangular trade also offered considerable flexibility, so that, for example, when sugar became harder to obtain from the West Indies, Lancaster's traders found other imports in which to invest their proceeds from slave sales, particularly mahogany, rum and dyewoods, each of which was in demand in Britain. This enabled them to maximize their profits on each leg of their enterprise, a maximization which was particularly important for marginal operators trading in a competitive field, while, when competition did eventually make the slave trade less viable at Lancaster, the contracts and experiences forged by the African trade ensured that other opportunities were on offer to merchants.[52] It would not have benefited the slaves to know that they were part of a more dynamic economic system in which consumerism, capital accumulation and investment in industrialization were all linked.[53] For example, profits accumulated in Glasgow from sugar and tobacco trading helped fund the development of the chemical industry in west-central Scotland, and also increased the liquidity of Scottish banks. This rate and range of activity was an aspect of the extent to which the British Atlantic stood out from the Atlantics of the other European states in terms of the combined degree and intensity of the processes of exchange and linkage.[54]

As far as the profitability of French trade was concerned, La Rochelle's colonial trade was affected by the wild fluctuations in slave trade profits, as well as by wars and attendant colonial losses. As a result, merchant families limited their business endeavours neither to maritime trade, nor to any one branch of it.[55] Nevertheless, long-distance trade was more profitable than private notarized credit, while being as profitable and also safer than government bonds.[56] Risk and solvency were also serious problems in the slave trade from Angola to Brazil, while difficulties in attracting investment affected the Coriso Company established by Portugal in 1723 to export slaves to north-east Brazil, and it collapsed in 1725.

The triangular trade was not the sole commercial system that was developed to help finance and exploit slavery. Supplying food and other products to the slave plantations was also important. Kendal was an English inland town that did not have close links to a major port, yet, in his *Tour of Scotland 1769* (1771), Thomas Pennant recorded how trade had encouraged industry there, 'chiefly engaged in manufactures of ... a coarse sort of woolen cloth called cottons sent to Glasgow, and from thence to Virginia for the use of the Negroes ... the manufactures employ great quantities of wool from Scotland and Durham'.

Similarly, some of the expansion in French exports to the West Indies was for the growing population of the French Indies, although many of the goods were re-exported to the Spanish empire. In 1741–2, Bordeaux exported over eight million livres worth of produce to the French West Indian colonies annually, principally wine and textiles. The comparable figure for 1753–5 was over ten million.

There was also, as part of the British commercial world, the development of a trade in salt cod from Newfoundland, both to the West Indies and to Charleston, the port for South Carolina. Moreover, food was shipped from the Thirteen

Colonies to the British West Indies. The colonial contribution to the economy of the Atlantic slave world included slaving from the Rhode Island ports of Newport, Bristol and Providence. Rhode Island lacked the agricultural opportunities offered elsewhere in the bigger colonies, and produced rum that could be exported in return for slaves.[57] There were similar developments in other colonial systems.

Accumulated experience in the slave trade helped improve the ability of merchants and shippers to respond to opportunities, lessen risk and increase the efficiency of the trade. This efficiency encompassed the dealings with the Africans, contributing to an African supply system that was also responsive to opportunities.[58] It was possible to expand supply to meet changes in demand, and there was also a successful search for new sources of supply. The slave trade, nevertheless, involved serious commercial risks, created for example by a lack of sufficient slaves or, alternatively, by the glutting of markets, issues greatly affecting profitability. The trade could be expensive to enter, and the scale of the profits are unclear. Alongside evidence of considerable profits, and a major contribution as a result to investment and economic growth in Britain, there are more modest estimates, and suggestions that, at the level of the individual voyage, the slave trade did not, on the whole, bring great profits, or sometimes even any. Concern about the profitability of the trade was a major factor in the pronounced variation in the number of voyages per year from individual ports. Returns from slave-trading ventures were risky, but also sufficiently attractive to keep some existing investors in the trade and to entice new investors to join up; the returns could enable men of marginal status to prosper sufficiently to enter the merchant class. Yet, larger firms had a considerable advantage.[59]

The accumulated actions of individual merchants and voyages were the key context for the profitability of the trade.[60] This was particularly the case for the British trade after the collapse of the role of the Royal African Company. The

Company's bases meant that it exercised a function of sovereignty in a sphere where the state did not wish to do so, but this entailed a considerable financial and organizational burden and, in 1730, the near-bankrupt Company petitioned for a subsidy for the maintenance of its forts and settlements. Indeed, from 1730 to 1747, it received an annual subsidy from the government, but the financial arrangement agreed in 1698 could not save the Company's poor finances, and in 1750 it was abolished by the African Trade Act, which opened the trade to all subjects willing to pay a fee.[61] With the help of a block grant from Parliament, the Company's bases were to be maintained by a successor company, the Company of Merchants Trading to Africa, which was controlled by the leading slave traders. Elsewhere, the poor financial state of the Dutch West India Company and the heavy cost of its West African operations also led it to depend on government subsidies.

Aside from the uncertainty of the slave trade, profitability was also hit by the human cost of slavery, in the shape of the frequently (although not invariably) high death rate on the Atlantic crossing among both slaves and crew. If, with time, the percentage of slaves who died fell appreciably, this was largely owing to shorter journey times, rather than to improved conditions, although a reduction in the crowding on ships was also important.[62] Slaver captains were less committed than the slave-owners to the survival of the slaves. In particular, there was little interest in costly medical care when the sick could be thrown overboard alongside the dead, a practice that led to outrage on the part of Abolitionists.

Many of the officers and crew involved in the trade also died, in part as a consequence of their exposure to tropical disease. In 1785–1807, 10–15 per cent of the British captains died each year. Of the 940 men who made up the crews of twenty-four Bristol ships in 1787, twenty-six died during the voyage, and 239 deserted or were discharged in the colonies. With such casualties, it was scarcely surprising that the slave trade was very unpopular among the sailors, which may well have encouraged a harsh, not to say sadistic, treatment of the slaves, notably frequent beatings.[63]

The situation in Africa

Warfare in Africa among African powers continued to provide large numbers of slaves, which contributed greatly to the high proportion of slaves in the population of sub-Saharan Africa.[64] The intensive nature of warfare in much of the Atlantic hinterland, for example the long civil war in Kongo,[65] and the westward advance of the Lunda empire, fed the slave trade, as did droughts and famines. In Kongo, civil war led to the enslavement of the partisans of rivals, ending the distinction in the supply of slaves between foreign-born slaves and freeborn Kongos who should not be enslaved.[66] The *sahel* belt also saw widespread conflict. For example, the pashalik of Timbuktu declined under pressure from the Tuareg and was destroyed by them in 1787. In its place, the Bambara people, whose principal town was Segu, extended their power down the River Niger. In the forest zone of West Africa, Asante on the Gold Coast and Dahomey on the Slave Coast were expansionist powers whose conflicts produced slaves.[67]

Alongside this supply-side account, it is also pertinent to note the degree to which the slave trade helped transform African society, hitting earlier patterns of hierarchy and identity, and savaging agrarian communities. Trends in slave prices suggest that the external (European) demand factor became more important from mid-century and, as a result, that domestic (African) forces became less important in the history of the regions affected.[68] For most of the century, however, variations in the productivity of the trade, not least the time spent by ships off Africa, reflected African forces, namely shifts in slave supplies within Africa. Indeed, British terms of trade with West Africa had fallen heavily in the 1720s and then again in the 1750s to 1770s, before rising in the 1780s and 1790s, although to a figure that was only about a third of that of the 1700s. From the last quarter of the century, European advances in shipping and organization became important and helped lead to major gains in the productivity of the slave trade.[69]

In West Africa, there was diffusion of European arms without European political control, although the traffic in firearms developed more slowly at a distance from the coast. Muskets, powder and shot were imported in increasing quantities, and were particularly important in the trade for slaves. For example, in the Senegal valley, gifts of guns were used to expand French influence. There is little evidence that Europeans provided real training in the use of firearms, although rulers showed a keen interest in seeing European troops and their local auxiliaries exercise in formation. The auxiliaries were crucial to the security of the European positions and to the offensive capability of European forces, and were probably the key figures in the transfer of expertise. Since they often worked seasonally for the Europeans and were trained to use firearms, for example in the riverboat convoys on the River Senegal, they had ample opportunity to sell their expertise to local rulers.

There is evidence that the troops of some African kingdoms trained in formation. Further, there are a few cases of Africans capturing European cannon and putting them to use, but field pieces were normally not sold to them, although some were given as gifts. West African blacksmiths could make copies of flintlock muskets, which replaced the matchlock as the principal firearm export to the Gold and Slave Coasts from about 1690; but casting cannon was probably beyond their expertise.[70]

African firearms can be criticized by European standards, but they served their purpose and became the general missile weapon over much of Africa, for example in Angola and on the Gold and Slave Coasts. Musketeers largely replaced archers on the Gold Coast in the seventeenth century, and did so on the Slave Coast in the eighteenth. The kingdom of

Dahomey under King Agaja (c.1716–40) in part owed its rise to an effective use of European firearms combined with standards of training and discipline that impressed European observers; weaponry alone was not enough. Two French officers provided the Dahomians with military guidance in the 1720s, including instruction on how to dig trenches.[71] Europeans on the Slave Coast had to take careful note of Dahomey views, not least in ensuring that their quarrels did not disrupt relations with that kingdom: Dahomey supplied the slaves exported from the Bight of Benin. Moreover, the widespread availability of firearms in Dahomey facilitated the slave trade by contributing to its aggression.

An emphasis on firearms puts the Europeans centre-stage in the power relationships of the slave trade, but the role of firearms should not be exaggerated. The Mahi, whose warfare was based on bows and arrows, successfully resisted Dahomian attack in the 1750s. Cavalry was more important to the north of the forest belt in West Africa, and it was largely thanks to cavalry that the kingdom of Oyo (in modern north-east Nigeria) was able to defeat Dahomey and force it to pay tribute from the 1740s. The Lunda of eastern Angola, who expanded their power in mid-century, relied on hand-to-hand fighting, particularly with swords. The successful forces in the *jihad* launched by Usuman dan Fodio and the Fulani against the Hausa states in modern northern Nigeria in 1804 initially had no firearms and were essentially mobile infantry forces, principally archers, able to use their firepower to defeat the cavalry of the established powers. Their subsequent acquisition of cavalry, not firearms, was crucial in enabling them to develop tactics based on mobility, manoeuvre and shock attack. By 1808, all the major Hausa states had fallen to the *jihadis*, indicating that firearms were not crucial for warwinning in Africa.[72] This *jihad* proved the basis of the Sokoto Fulani kingdom.

In West Africa, furthermore, the Europeans remained confined to coastal enclaves, and not always in a satisfactory fashion. British cannon drove off Dahomey forces that attacked their fort at Glehue in 1728, but these forces had already captured the Portuguese fort there in 1727, while the French fort was partially destroyed by a gunpowder explosion in 1728. In 1729 and 1743, the Dahomians succeeded in capturing the Portuguese fort at Whydah, where Brazilian tobacco was exchanged for slaves. In 1761, the British governor of the slave trade port of Fort Louis, which had been captured from the French in 1758, reported, 'the troops here are exceedingly sickly, and we have lost many officers and men, the whole garrison has suffered prodigiously . . . it is not in my power to mount an officers' guard'.

The difficulties the Portuguese encountered in East Africa are also instructive. They regained Mombasa in 1728, after a mutiny by African soldiers against Omani control, but lost it again to the Omanis in 1729, with the Portuguese garrison capitulating as a result of low morale and problems with food supplies. Further south, the Dutch, expanding east from Cape Colony, overran the San and Khoekhoe peoples with few difficulties, but then encountered the Xhosa, leading to a war between 1779 and 1781. The Xhosa mounted serious resistance, but were defeated on the Fish river.

The dependence of the Europeans on local support was illustrated by the problems facing Europeans due to their lack of knowledge about the African interior, which increased their reliance on the intermediaries in the coastal zone. This was only lessened from the close of the eighteenth century with the Association for Promoting the Discovery of the Interior Parts of Africa, or African Association, being founded in London in 1788. The Association sought to explore the interior of Africa from the River Gambia. Daniel Houghton, an ex-army officer who had served at Gorée, went further beyond the River Senegal into the interior than previous European travellers, but his efforts to open a trade route were unsuccessful, and he was robbed and died in 1791, well short of his goal, Timbuktu.

From 1802, the British government took over the sponsorship of the major expeditions from the Association. It supported Mungo Park who died in 1806 negotiating rapids on the River Niger. His *Travels in the Interior Districts of Africa* (1799) provided new information for mapmakers, as did William Browne's *Travels in Africa, Egypt, and Syria* (1800). In 1798, Francisco Lacerda e Almeida, the Portuguese governor of Sena on the River Zambezi, who was concerned about the recent British conquest of Cape Colony from the Dutch, decided that the Portuguese needed to link their colonies of Mozambique and Angola. He reached Lake Mweru in central Africa, but died of disease there. This was the end of the attempt, although, in 1806–11, two Portuguese mixed-race slave traders, Pedro Baptista and Antonio Nogueira da Rocha, crossed Africa from Cassange in Angola to Sena.

The problems faced by explorers were one element of the difficulties confronted by Europeans. As another aspect, the British Royal African Company had sought the support of warships, which was a product of the vulnerability frequently felt on the peripheries of the European world. A sense of precariousness about the European presence was conveyed by Captain William Cornwallis in a report to the British Admiralty about a voyage to the River Gambia in February 1775,

> I thought the appearance of a man of war might be of service. I therefore went up the river in the *Pallas* to James's Fort, which I found in great distress for want of stores, and particularly gun-carriages, not having above three or four serviceable ones in the Fort, and most of their guns rendered totally useless for want of them . . . I stayed in the River eight days, during which time we got the king of the country on board, and showed him all the civility we could; he seemed very well pleased, so I hope all will go on well again.[73]

Trade with Africa was only possible thanks to the active cooperation of African rulers, which extended, on the part of

King Agaja of Dahomey in the 1720s to an interest in permitting the establishment of European plantations in Dahomey, although these were intended as a supplement to, rather than a substitute for, the slave trade.[74]

In Madagascar, plentiful firearms were obtained from European traders in return for slaves and use of these firearms played a major role in the powerful kingdoms of Menabe and Boina. In 1719, the crew of a Dutch ship recorded their surprise at the skilful use of muskets by the 4,000–5,000-strong army of the King of Menabe, and, three years later, another Dutch commentator was impressed by that of Boina. Indeed, by mid-century, the King of Boina had at least thirty large cannon, while his army was estimated as 15,000 strong in 1741. The availability of these arms probably played a role in the consolidation of powerful kingdoms in Madagascar, but there were also political and economic dimensions to this process.

France's coastal base at Fort Dauphin was shortlived (1746–68), but Madagascar's proximity to the Portuguese bases on the Mozambique coast and the French possessions of Réunion and Mauritius in the Indian Ocean were such that the island remained essentially in the European slave-trading system rather than the Arab one further north. Yet, there was an Arab slave-trading presence in Madagascar, which serves as a reminder of the overlap between slave systems. Cooperation with Africans was also the pattern for the Arab slavers, based on ports such as Zanzibar, Kilwa and Mombasa, who played the key role in the Indian Ocean slave economy.

The relationship between foreign slavers and Africans was often a complex one. Within the wider context set by the European inability to coerce the Africans, there was an emphasis not simply on trade, but also on credit. This was more generally true of the European-dominated Atlantic trading system. Credit was given to encourage coastal Africans, such as the Fante of the Gold Coast, to purchase slaves from the interior. Mutual trust was important, but there was also a reliance on the security provided by connections of the

African traders who were left with the European merchants, and themselves shipped as slaves if they did not deliver.

This practice led to complaints when African merchants felt that these pawns were wrongly shipped and there were demands for redress. Evidence for this situation, which has been described as a moral community linking African and European slave trades, survives in letters from African traders at Old Calabar in the Cross river region, one of the major slave-trading centres on the Bight of Biafra in modern south-east Nigeria, the leading region of supply for British slavers later in the century.[75] A comparable situation probably prevailed in the Arab-dominated trading systems but there is not similar surviving material, in part because of the efforts made by Abolitionists, notably Thomas Clarkson, to accumulate information about the Atlantic trade. Thus, there is evidence for a role by British traders in a massacre of African traders at Old Calabar by their rivals in 1767.

African traders and rulers served the needs of a European-dominated Atlantic economy. The Atlantic economy pressed on the local, and the local served the global, and vice versa, with Anglo-African and Franco-African slave traders matching, and indeed supplanting their Luso-African equivalents.[76] In the valley of the River Senegal, patterns of trade between the Sahara desert and the *sahel* were annexed to the Atlantic world, as the export of slaves and gum arabic reconfigured local economies and interregional trade. The cloth and metallurgical industries in West Africa were hit by European imports,[77] which anticipated problems that were to be more widespread in the nineteenth century.

The resistance, treatment and conditions of slaves
There was a degree of African resistance to slavery, entailing both action against African slave hunters and against Westerners, the latter extending to 493 known risings on slave ships especially in the late eighteenth century,[78] but it was far less significant than the active cooperation that fed the trade, while

hatred among the chained slaves for each other was also noted by commentators opposed to the slave trade.[79] Nevertheless, the prospect of risings on the ships ensured that the crew was considerably larger – usually twice – than on merchant ships of a similar size, and this requirement affected the profitability of the trade.[80] From this perspective, African resistance, or its threat, actively moulded the trade and limited the numbers transported.

Suicide was another form of opposition, with some slaves jumping overboard, while the melancholia noted by ship surgeons was also conducive to high rates of illness. The conditions of shipboard life also affected the sailors, who suffered from depression, illness, and the strain of guarding and restraining the captives.[81] These conditions became an issue during the Abolitionist campaign when, in reply to the claim that the trade was important for the training and support of British sailors and the merchant marine, it was claimed that it was a toxic task characterized by brutality and disease. These claims were pushed hard in the *Observations of a Guinea Voyage* (1788) by James Field Stanfield who had worked as a sailor on a slaver.

The European position was far more powerful as far as the slaves in the Americas were concerned than it had been in Africa, although there were both slave risings and the problems created by escaping slaves. In 1739, in the Stono rising in South Carolina, 100 slaves rose and killed twenty colonists, before being defeated by the militia and their Native American allies, notably the Chickasaw. The determination of some of the slaves to escape to Spanish Florida helped prompt the rising. Although their scale varied, there were slave risings in the British West Indies: on Jamaica in 1746, 1760, 1765 and 1776, Montserrat in 1768, and Tobago in 1770, 1771 and 1775, and this is not an exhaustive list. There were also conspiracies discovered by the authorities before they could be launched, including on Nevis in 1725 and Antigua in 1736. There was a major rising in the Dutch colony of Berbice (now part of

Guyana) in 1763–4, but Native American support helped the Dutch suppress it. The slaves had cited cruel treatment, poor rations and a denial of customary rights as reasons for rebellion. In Mexico, there were slave risings in the Córdoba and Orizaba region in 1725, 1735, 1741, 1749 and 1768 that involved attacks on the sugar industry, notably with the burning of cane fields and sugar houses.

As with serf risings in Europe, slave risings in the colonies were usually brutally suppressed, and followed by savage punishments and harsh retribution, notably executions, in order to deter fresh upheavals. This situation was a variant on the view of Emmerich de Vattel, the leading European writer on international relations, that the laws of war need not apply when fighting 'savage' peoples.[82]

Circumstances, however, did not favour slave risings, as the white people limited the availability of firearms to slaves and made efforts to prevent them plotting.[83] Frequent declarations of martial law served as a means of control in the British West Indies.[84] Indeed, slaves were unable to coordinate action, except in very small areas. In Pensacola in West Florida, which was under British rule from 1763 until regained by Spain in 1781, no slave was allowed out without his owner's written permission, and meetings of more than six slaves were forbidden after 9 p.m.[85] Those plotting what was to be known as Gabriel's Conspiracy in Richmond, Virginia in 1800 had first to consider how to acquire guns, horses and swords. In the event, the plan was betrayed by other slaves before the rising could take place.[86]

Flight was a more common form of resistance. It led, in Jamaica, to unsuccessful expeditions by British forces against the Maroons – runaway slaves who controlled much of the mountainous interior. Edward Trelawny, the governor, reported in 1738, 'The service here is not like that in Flanders or any part of Europe. Here the great difficulty is not to beat, but to see the enemy . . . in short, nothing can be done in strict conformity to usual military preparations, and according to a regular manner; bush-fighting as they call it being a thing peculiar by itself.' The failure of these expeditions were followed in 1738 and 1739 by treaties that granted them land and autonomy.

Particularly in Brazil, but also elsewhere, there were organized communities of fugitive slaves, for example those in the mountains of Oaxaca in Mexico or the numerous 'Bush Negroes' in Surinam. The *Briton*, a London newspaper, in its issue of 11 December 1762, argued that gaining St Augustine in northern Florida from Spain would prevent 'the desertion of our Negro slaves' from Georgia across the border. Further north, slaves fled to the Dismal Swamp on the Virginia-North Carolina border. In Europe, there was similar flight by serfs to forested and mountain areas at the margins of authority.

Alongside slave risings and flight, there were also murders of individual overseers, as well as many suicides, the latter owing something to a slave belief that it would take them back to their homeland. Similar anger and reckless despair could be seen with European serfs. As with the slaves, most peasant violence was local, the response to specific grievances directed against particular landlords and overseers. In 1764–9, at least thirty landowners were slain by their serfs in the province of Moscow alone. Risings frequently revealed desperation, as in Bohemia in 1775, where some peasants asked the soldiers to kill them, and others burned grain that they were obliged to cut. Ethnic tensions were also important, as in western Ukraine where Ukrainian peasants following the Uniate rite reacted violently to attempts by Polish landlords to extend labour services and impose Catholicism, or in Transylvania, where Greek Orthodox Romanian peasants felt oppressed by Hungarian Calvinist landlords.

Slaves who did not flee could, if circumstances were propitious, also engage in social protest and labour bargaining, matching points made about the degree of peasant autonomy in Europe.[87] In Barbados during the eighteenth century, the insurrectionist attitudes that had led to plans for revolts in

1649, 1675 and 1692 were replaced by an emphasis on limited protest that was designed to secure the amelioration of circumstances. This possibility contrasted with the other British islands, such as Jamaica, where circumstances were harsher, and, in general, the situation was less favourable than on Barbados. White concern about slaves reflected multiple anxieties, and it was easy to misinterpret poor slave health or understandable black complaints about conditions as active defiance and to react harshly accordingly. This reaction contributed to the coercive nature of the slave economy and the reliance on force.

Equally, force was part of an economy of control in which slaves understandably sought to pursue their own interests. In January 1825, the fiscal in the British colony of Berbice on the Guiana coast recorded a dispute between a slave and a manager on a coffee plantation. The slave, Woensdag, stated:

> On Christmas Friday we worked till four, we went home. I was sweating and went to wash in the back dam trench and I drank in some water. Driver asked me where do you come from, I said I have been nowhere, I went only to wash. He said when you at work you must not turn about. I said when I feel hot and thirsty I must wash and drink, I then feel strong [enough] to finish my work. The driver said, Oh, I know you, you are a lazy bugger.[88]

The circumstances of slave life varied greatly.[89] For example, some slaves became skilled men in the plantations, and hence acquired a self-respect which owners could recognize as a mutual advantage. Moreover, conditions in individual colonies were far from uniform. For example, alongside the situation in Surinam described by Candide, came the *Rule on the Treatment of Servants and Slaves* introduced there by the Dutch in 1772 in order to counter slave unrest. This *Rule* was to be enforced by the fiscal, an official to whom slaves had the right of appeal, although this right was of course not intended to challenge slavery. Moreover, the racial dimension was clear as the testimony of white people was preferred to that of slaves.

There were also significant differences between colonies, and regional variations in plantation economies had important consequences for the slave trade. As far as British America was concerned, owing to the varied demands of tobacco and rice cultivation, and to related economic and social characteristics, slaves in the Chesapeake were more affected by white life, living in close proximity to owners in relatively small farms, and benefited from the less arduous work regime focused on tobacco. In contrast, in the rice lands of South Carolina, there were fewer, but larger, plantations, the percentage of slaves was greater, and the higher death rate ensured that, although by the 1750s the slave work force could reproduce itself, there were more imported African slaves than American-born slaves. As a consequence, slaves were more autonomous and more influenced by African culture and material life, and relations between slaves and owners remained more antipa-thetical than where they lived in closer proximity,[90] although it is not easy to assess slave attitudes. Indeed, the 'first strictly autobiographical account by an enslaved African' was published only in 1772.[91] The growing need for slaves in South Carolina and Georgia helped ensure that the balance of the British slave world shifted, so that, by 1775, alongside the continuing large number of slaves in the British West Indies, there was also an increasing percentage of the slaves in the British world living in British North America. In part, this also reflected the amelioration of the slave position in the Chesapeake, which led to a growing rate of natural increase, which was to become more apparent in the nine-teenth century.

The slave situation in Jamaica, where slaves were also treated harshly, was more similar to South Carolina than the Chesapeake; the majority of both slaves and white people in Jamaica were immigrants. The diaries of Thomas

Thistlewood, who was a slave-owner and agricultural manager in west Jamaica from 1750 to 1786, indicate clearly that he treated his slaves cruelly, not least abusing his female slaves sexually. Similarly, on Sir William Stapleton's profitable sugar estate on Nevis there were very exploitative working arrangements, and in the 1730s the black population fell by nearly 25 per cent. In the British Windward Islands – Dominica, Grenada, St Vincent and Tobago – in the 1760s and early 1770s, there was harsh treatment that did not encourage family life and reproduction, in large part because it was easier to buy new slaves than to raise children to working age. The resulting regime led to high mortality and low fertility, with far too little food provided to slaves. Sir William Young, whose father owned land there, wrote of Tobago in the early 1770s that slaves newly arrived from Africa,

> had the laborious task of cutting down woods hanging on steep declivities, and of smoothing paths for intercourse and conveyance over or through hard and pointed rocks: scanty food, a food they were unaccustomed to, accompanied with the severities attending first coercion aggravated the grievances of their toil. Hence a sullen and refractory spirit had shown itself in the deportment of the Negroes.

The severity of treatment contributed to flight and suicides.[92] The slave situation in Brazil was also more similar to that in South Carolina and the West Indies than that in the Chesapeake.

Sexual exploitation was part of the lot of female slaves. It could bring them a privileged situation, as with the 'Surinam marriage',[93] but there was also exploitation, as when Princess, a newly bought slave, noted her treatment by her twenty-seven-year-old master, Dr Hugh McGee, who pressed her to 'come and sleep with him'. Princess replied that she was 'just come out of lying in, and that it was too soon to take a husband'. Princess's mother told her to go or 'the Doctor would lick me', and indeed McGee threatened her with '39 lashes', which led Princess to go to bed with him. She was subsequently whipped for grumbling about the work she was made to do.[94]

Rising prices for slaves in British North America from mid-century indicate that demand was outstripping supply, but differing needs for slaves were a key aspect of variety. For example, the Ibo shipped from the Bight of Biafra were favoured by Virginia planters, but seen as insufficiently strong by Carolina and Georgia planters, who preferred Bambara and Malinke from Senegambia as well as Angolans. In South Carolina, Georgia and East Florida, opinion among planters about slavery was divided. The better established commercial agriculture was, the more its participants wanted to reform or diversify it, especially to prevent greater dependence on slavery. Conversely, newer settlers welcomed such dependence.[95] Indeed the relationship between slavery and economic development could be very varied. Thus, in the lower Mississippi in the 1760s, Spain and Britain, the new rulers in Louisiana and West Florida respectively, took measures to increase the number of colonial inhabitants, both white settlers and black slaves, and an export economy based on indigo, tobacco and timber developed.[96]

The treatment of slaves was related to the racism of the period, which was far from restricted only to the unlearned. Religious and biological explanations of apparent differences between races, whose genesis was traced back to the sons of Abraham, with black people as the children of the cursed Ham, were important. Influential writers argued in favour of polygenism – the different creation of types of humans. This led to suggestions that black people were not only a different species, but also related to great apes, such as orangutans, suggestions that were linked to the argument that, although black people were inherently inferior, they were particularly adapted to living in the tropics. Black people's ability to cope better than whites with diseases in the tropics was believed to exemplify an inherent difference that was linked to a closeness to animals that lived there. This thesis was held to justify slavery, and the same argument was used about the alleged nature of African society. For example, in his *A New Account of Some Parts of Guinea and the Slave Trade* (1734), William Snelgrave defended the trade on the grounds that being sacrificed was the alternative for prisoners, an argument that was to be taken on by opponents of Abolition later in the century.

Physical attributes, particularly skin colour, attracted much attention, and Montesquieu explained colour as due to exposure to the tropical sun. The argument that bile was responsible for the colour of human skin, advanced as a scientific fact by writers in antiquity, was repeated without experimental support by eminent eighteenth-century scientists, including Feijoo, Holbach and La Mettrie. An Italian scientist, Bernardo Albinus, proved to his own satisfaction in 1737 that Negro bile was black, and in 1741 a French doctor, Pierre Barrère, published, in his *Dissertation sur la cause physique de la couleur des Nègres*, experiments demonstrating both this and that the bile alone caused the black pigment in skin, a thesis which was discussed in *The Gentleman's Magazine* (of London) the following year. This inaccurate theory won widespread acclaim, in part thanks to an extensive review in the *Journal des Savants* in 1742, and played a major role in the prevalent mid-century belief that black people were another species of man without the ordinary organs, tissues, heart and soul. In 1765, the chief doctor in the leading hospital in Rouen, Claude Nicolas Le Cat, demonstrated that Barrère's theory was wrong, but he was generally ignored and Barrère's arguments continued to be cited favourably.[97] They accorded with a hierarchical classification of humanity that served the interests of the slave trade.

It is instructive that the most successful sentimental critique of slavery published in early eighteenth century Britain related not to a black slave but to a Native American. The tale of

'Inkle and Yarico' published in the leading periodical the *Spectator* on 13 March 1711 was one of humanity affronted, and morality breached, by slavery,

> Mr. Thomas Inkle, an ambitious young English trader cast ashore in the Americas, is saved from violent death at the hands of savages by the endearments of Yarico, a beautiful Indian maiden. Their romantic intimacy in the forest moves Inkle to pledge that, were his life to be preserved, he would return with her to England, supposedly as his wife. The lovers' tender liaison progresses over several months until she succeeded in signaling a passing English ship. They were rescued by the crew, and with vows to each other intact, they embark for Barbados. Yet when they reach the island Inkle's former mercantile instincts are callously revived, for he sells her into slavery, at once raising the price he demands when he learns that Yarico is carrying his child.

This was but a stage in a tale that had surfaced in Richard Ligon's *History of the Island of Barbados* (1657), and whose iterations were to include George Colman the Younger's much-performed play *Inkle and Yarico* (1787),[98] which, in the fashion of the time, was provided with a happy ending.

The popularity of the story reflected the way in which the transoceanic world could provide a setting for moral challenges, a setting that in practice was largely safe for Europeans. Slavery became a key instance of such a moral challenge, although, prior to the late eighteenth century, there was an ambivalence about the treatment of black people. The portrayal of them could be sentimental, and the harsh world of their work and lifestyle was generally ignored, although this criticism could also be advanced of the extensive artistic treatment of the European peasantry. Joseph Wright's intimate and gentle portrayal of *Two Girls with their Black Servant*, which may have been his *A Conversation of Girls* exhibited in 1770, probably depicts the daughters of a merchant in Liverpool where Wright worked in 1769–71. The service depicted here seems agreeable, and bore little reference to the grimmer nature of slavery. The same was even more true of the double portrait, attributed to William, Lord Zoffany, of Mansfield's great-niece, Lady Elizabeth Murray and her black companion, Dido Elizabeth Belle who was left a substantial bequest by Mansfield.

Sentimentalism was not the relevant factor when slavery was banned by the Trustees of the new colony of Georgia in 1735. This decision was not so much because of hostility to slavery as due to the wish to base the colony on small-scale agrarian activity rather than aristocratic plantations. Defensive considerations also played a role and the law was entitled 'An Act for Rendering the Colony of Georgia More Defencible by Prohibiting the Importation and Use of Black Slaves or Negroes into the Same'. The colonists, however, opposed the measure from the outset, not least because they had to watch their South Carolinian neighbours getting rich using cheap labour while they could barely eke out a living. The Malcontents, the leading political faction in Georgia that opposed the Trustees, published several pamphlets calling for legalization of the slave trade, but they were unsuccessful. The Stono Rebellion in South Carolina was cited by the Trustees, but they finally caved in in 1750, arguing that, since Spain had been unsuccessful in 1742 when it invaded Georgia from Florida during the War of Jenkins' Ear (1739–48), it was safe to import slaves.

This compromise followed those on other restrictions regarding issues such as land tenure and alcohol consumption. It was an aspect of the collapse of the Trustees' position, and they surrendered their charter in 1752.[99] Their objective of a colony of virtuous small farmers had not been realized, but it prefigured the goal of slave-owning Thomas Jefferson, the American president from 1801 to 1809 and a keen proponent of agrarianism. The Trustees had wanted silk or wine as their monoculture, but neither worked out very well. The economy of Georgia only came close to being a success after the Trustee era, and real wealth there had to wait for King Cotton.

By the end of the eighteenth century, most advanced opinion no longer regarded black people as a different species of man, but as a distinct variety. This interpretation, monogenesis – the descent of all races from a single original group – was advanced by Johann Friedrich Blumenbach, a teacher of medicine at the University of Göttingen, who in 1776 published *De Generis Humani Varietate*, an influential work of racial classification that went through several editions. However, the misleading assessment of the inherent characteristics of non-Europeans, combined with the association of reason with European culture, encouraged a hierarchy dominated by the Europeans, and therefore a treatment of others as inferior. Thus, although monogenesis can be seen as a benign theory that could contribute to a concept of the inherent brotherhood of man that was voiced during the Enlightenment, and especially in the period of the American and French Revolutions, it was also inherently discriminatory. Blumenbach assumed the original ancestral group to be white and that climate, diet, disease and mode of life were responsible for the developments that led to the creation of different races. Sir Jeremiah Fitzpatrick, Director-General of Health for the British Army, pressed for better care of slave women in order to ensure fewer deaths in childbirth and of babies, and proposed an inspection system for the slave trade, but also used supposed inherent characteristics to justify slave labour: 'The African is not less dear to me than the European, and the sole reason I have for cultivating the plantations by him, rather than by the latter, is that the climate is in every sense to him more congenial.'[100]

Racial characteristics and developments were understood in terms of the suppositions of European culture, and this approach led to, and supported, the hierarchization already referred to. Irrespective of the nobility of non-Westerners, their societies appeared deficient and defective, and thus inferior. This was seen in writing on history and sociology, for example William Robertson's influential *History of America*

(1777). This approach also tended to be true of the developing idea of cultural relativism, although subversive themes could be offered, as by the British painter William Hogarth, in his perceptive *Analysis of Beauty*. He pointed out that 'the Negro who finds great beauty in the black females of his own country, may find as much deformity in the European beauty as we see in theirs'.[101]

At the same time, black subjects of European powers who were not slaves were increasingly granted civil rights. The French made efforts to incorporate free blacks as subjects, following Louis XIV's *Code Noir* of 1685. Furthermore, in 1761, Asian and East African Christian subjects of the Portuguese crown were given the same legal and social status as Portuguese whites, on the grounds that subjects should not be distinguished by colour. Pombal, the leading Portuguese minister, explicitly cited the Classical Roman model of colonization in which citizenship had eventually been granted irrespective of origins. However, extending rights for non-whites in Goa, a long-established Portuguese colony, where syncretism and mutual interest were both important, provided no guidance to the more coercive treatment of slaves and Native Americans in Brazil.

As a reminder of the very different contexts provided by the politics and policies of European states, slaves as a legal social group in Russia had largely ended when Peter the Great introduced the poll tax in 1719–23 as all the subjects of landowners were listed together, be they serfs or various categories of slaves. So, in this instance, it was tax which largely ended slavery – Peter being the most pragmatic of rulers – for serfs paid tax, whereas slaves did not. In practice, however, Russians could still fall into slavery by debt servitude, being sold in contracts known as *kabala* for a fixed period, their status lasting as long as the debt. It could pass from one generation to the next if the debt was not paid off.[102] There were also slaves in areas annexed by Russia, such as Bessarabia (which had been part of the Ottoman empire) in

1812, and this slavery continued until the emancipation of the serfs in 1861.

There was increased criticism of slavery among progressive intellectuals. The *Encyclopédie* (1751–65) had been character-ized by contradictory or tentative views, alongside criticism, for example by the Chevalier de Jaucourt in his entry on slavery, an entry devoted to slavery as a whole and not specifically to colonial slavery. Jaucourt claimed that 'all men are born free' and that slavery is 'a right based on force', so that slaves were entitled to flee. He also argued that it lacked utility, as free men, encouraged by rewards and helped by machines, could do everything that was done by slaves.[103] In contrast to the variety of views in the *Encyclopédie*, Abbé Raynal's influential *Histoire philosophique et politique des établissements et du commerce des Européens dans les deux Indes* (1770) became, especially in its 1774 and 1780 editions to which the prominent *philosophe* Denis Diderot made important contributions, a channel for the expression of progressive ideas, such as anti-slavery.[104] The *Histoire* was condemned by the Inquisition in Spain, but was widely read by European reformers, for example in Italy, and it was translated into English.

Such views on colonial slavery were matched by longstand-ing opposition in particular European countries to slavery at home. Thus, the Dutch had no African or Arab slaves at home and, unlike the British, did not even tolerate temporary slavery to exist in the United Provinces, so planters from the West Indies were not allowed to come home accompanied by their personal slaves.

American liberty is generally seen as a progressive cause, but, in the case of the War of American Independence (1775–83), the cause of freedom in the case of American liberty did not extend to the slaves.[105] Dedicated to the most prominent French radical, Jean-Jacques Rousseau, the third edition of Thomas Day's *The Dying Negro* criticized the American Patriots for supporting slavery, a theme he returned to in his *Reflections on the Present State of England and the Independence of America* (1782). The Hessian soldiers sent to fight the Americans felt that the American treatment of their slaves formed a hypocritical contrast with their claims of the equality of man, and this argument was also made by black Africans after independence.

Black soldiers

The war led to a focus on the sensitive issue of the use of black soldiers in conflict against white people. This use was not new. In 1688, William of Orange's army that invaded England included Native Americans from Surinam. In 1741, Etienne de Silhouette, a French agent in Britain, in a letter intercepted by the British, reacted with alarm to the news that the British were arming black people in order to use them against Spanish-ruled Cuba. He felt this might be very dangerous for all American Europeans, but argued that the British were too obsessed by their goals to consider the wider implications.[106] In practice, the issue did not become important until the War of American Independence, when the British were very short of manpower, which led them to turn to Native Americans, Loyalists, and German-subsidy troops in order to make up for the shortage in regular troops. In November 1774, James Madison, a prominent Virginian, warned,

> If America and Britain should come to a hostile rupture I am afraid an insurrection among the slaves may and will be promoted. In one of our counties lately a few of those unhappy wretches met together and chose a leader who was to conduct them when the English troops should arrive – which they foolishly thought would be very soon and by revolting to them they should be rewarded with their freedom. Their intentions were soon discovered and proper precautions taken to prevent the infection. It is prudent such attempts should be concealed as well as suppressed.

Madison returned to the theme the following June,

It is imagined our Governor [John, Fourth Earl of Dunmore] has been tampering with the slaves and that he has it in contemplation to make great use of them in case of a civil war in this province. To say the truth, that is the only part in which this colony is vulnerable; and if we should be subdued, we shall fall like Achilles by the hand of one that knows that secret.

That summer, Jeremiah Thomas, a black pilot who himself owned slaves, was sentenced to death in South Carolina for supplying arms to the slaves and encouraging them to flee to the British.[107] Later that year, Dunmore added Loyalists and black men to his forces, seizing the towns of Gosport and Norfolk. He issued a proclamation emancipating slaves who joined his army, creating an 'Ethiopian Regiment' of several hundred escaped slaves, but was defeated at Great Bridge on 9 December 1775. Moreover, General Prevost armed 200 black men at the time of the American-French siege of Savannah in 1779, a step that was criticized by the Americans.[108] When the British threatened Charleston in May 1779, a large number of slaves fled to their camp in search of promised freedom, and, during the city's siege by the British in 1780, they encouraged slaves belonging to Revolutionaries to run away, although those of Loyalists were returned to their masters on condition they were not penalized. Slaves of Revolutionaries fleeing to the British were to work on sequestered estates or perform other designated tasks in return for which they would receive their freedom at the end of the war. In contrast, the Revolutionaries punished fleeing slaves. The first three captured attempting to flee to Dunmore in 1776 were publicly hanged, decapitated and quartered. In turn, the Revolutionaries were reluctant to arm slaves.

Towards the end of the war, there was increased British interest in the idea of black troops. In January 1782, Dunmore backed John Cruden's proposal for arming 10,000 blacks, who would receive their freedom under white officers. Two months later, the British commanders at Charleston proposed the raising of a black regiment; but the British were hesitant to take full strategic advantage of slavery.[109] The British failure to employ black men for military purposes on any scale can be regarded as a missed opportunity, but it would have greatly complicated the British position in the South where the British were dependent on the winning of Loyalist support. It was also necessary to consider the impact on the West Indies. In November 1779, William, Second Earl of Shelburne, a leading member of the opposition, warned the House of Lords about the danger of arming black Jamaicans.[110] As yet, there was not the large-scale use of black troops that was to be seen in the French Revolutionary and Napoleonic Wars,[111] but both American independence and interest in the use of black troops underlined the dynamic nature of circumstances and the extent to which the slave trade was affected by external factors.

Although inexperienced in the use of firearms, black soldiers, during the War of American Independence, acted with success as irregulars, fighting on the eastern shore of the Chesapeake alongside Loyalist partisans. Others, calling themselves the King of England's soldiers, fought on from the swamps by the River Savannah after the British had evacuated Charleston and Savannah preparatory to the peace settlement. In May 1786, a combined force of militia and Catawba Native Americans defeated them, but, a year later, a governor's message mentioned serious depredations by armed black forces 'too numerous to be quelled by patrols' in southern South Carolina.[112]

The American Constitution did not end slavery and prohibited the government from interfering with the slave trade for twenty years. In 1791, the Tenth Amendment, the reserved powers clause, left the issue of slavery to the individual states. Slavery was slowly abolished in the states of the North, although, with the exception of Massachusetts, this did not involve the emancipation of slaves, but, rather, as in New York under legislation of 1799,[113] the freeing of slave children born thereafter once they reached maturity. The majority of the black population (which was 19.3 per cent of the national population in 1790), nevertheless, was in the South where slavery continued. That this situation was to be transformed by the abolition of slavery within seventy years was totally unexpected.

5

REVOLUTION, ABOLITIONISM AND THE CONTRASTING FORTUNES OF THE SLAVE TRADE AND SLAVERY, 1780–1850

Rear-Admiral George Cockburn had no doubt of what British power and law meant for escaped slaves when he replied in 1815 to a request from Governor Kindelen of the Spanish base of San Augustin, Florida, for their return: 'As this island now appertains to His Britannic Majesty by right of conquest, and for the moment must of course be governed by the laws of Great Britain (which know not of slavery) I do not conceive it to be within my power *forcibly* to send back any individuals of the description mentioned by your Excellency'.[1]

The Royal Navy was to play a key role in ending the slave trade, both directly and indirectly. Thus, in Navarino Bay on 20 October 1827, thanks largely to overwhelming British firepower from 32-pounders at almost point-blank range, an Anglo-French-Russian fleet under Sir Edward Codrington destroyed the Ottoman-Egyptian fleet. There was concern about the responsibility for starting the battle and the result exacerbated governmental anxiety about Russian expansionism, but the public responded with pleasure while Codrington received chivalric orders in France, Greece and Russia. The last great battle of the age of fighting sail, this key event in the struggle for Greek independence from Ottoman rule led toward success in 1830. The battle therefore stopped the Ottoman campaigning in Greece that had produced scenes such as those depicted by William Allan, whose painting *The Slave Market, Constantinople* was supposedly based on what he saw, in 1829–30, when he accompanied the British diplomats to Constantinople who negotiated the independence treaty. The painting, which caused a great impression when it was exhibited in London in 1838, depicted a black Egyptian slave merchant selling a Greek slave girl to an Ottoman pasha, and was a scene of distress and pathos.[2] The Royal Navy did not act at Cape Navarino to end the slave trade, but the effect of its actions was to help stop it, and part of the reason for philhellenism in Britain was the depiction of the Ottomans as slavers.

It is possible to cite sources questioning the value of naval action against the slave trade, or at least of the enthusiasm for the mission. Thus, in 1862, John, First Earl Russell (until 1861 Lord John Russell), the Foreign Secretary, noted that the Admiralty did not like having to tackle the slave trade, adding of an earlier Foreign Secretary, 'Palmerston says that in his time the Admiralty always sent their slowest and worst craft to catch the swift vessels used by the slave traders.'[3] Yet, whatever the drawbacks, this effort was very different to that by the Royal Navy a century earlier, and British naval action was crucial to the suppression of the trade.

Change and force, indeed, were key themes in what was seen with reason as an Age of Revolutions, most dramatically with the overthrow of both slavery and French imperial control in Saint-Domingue in the 1790s. The account of these years understandably focuses on the Atlantic world, but there were also changes elsewhere, although not to the same extent.

The last stages of the Atlantic slave trade

The last stages of the slave trade and slavery, as widely understood, invite two separate narratives. On the one hand, there is the Abolitionist narrative, the how and why of the ending of both. On the other, there is room for an emphasis on the continuation of both the slave trade and slavery prior to, or even after, Abolition; indeed, the slave trade and slavery each remained important in the nineteenth century. In part, this situation was a reflection of the limited purchase of liberalism in the Western world (let alone elsewhere), and the strength, instead, of anti-radical sentiment and counter-revolutionary policy in the first half of the nineteenth century,[4] but in truth, both continuation and Abolition need to be included in the same narrative, because they cannot be understood apart, as this and the following chapter indicates.

In Europe, the slave trade was abolished first by Denmark in 1792, an abolition that reflected the variety of factors at play in the general process. The key Abolitionist currents were provided by religious pressure and secular idealism, but governmental concern and political calculation were important to timing. Religious pressure was particularly influential in the Protestant world, although there had always also been a significant current of Catholic uneasiness about, and sometimes hostility to, slavery, which can be seen in particular among Spanish religious thinkers in the sixteenth century. Despite some ambiguity about the status of enslaved persons entering Europe, slave trading and slavery were illegal in much of Europe, and had been for some time, which was significant in shaping the norms of public opinion, providing a different dynamic to those of government and business interests. The absence of slavery in Europe was striking in comparison with many other parts of the known world, and contributed to a situation in which slavery lacked normative value for public opinion. In British polite society, by the early 1770s, both slavery and the slave trade were increasingly seen as morally unacceptable.[5] An extraordinary number of international relationships and contingent factors came into play, however, to take this situation to the point of ending the slave trade.

In Denmark, the role of government was central in ending the slave trade, and, unlike in Britain, there was no Abolitionist campaign, although the law banning the trade did not come into force until 1803. Also, in the meantime, the slave population in the Danish West Indies (from 1917 the American Virgin Islands) was built up from about 25,000 slaves to about 35,000, which was a comment on the abortive plan to transfer the slaves to the West African base of Fort Christiansberg. In part, Danish Abolition prefigured the situation with most powers over the following century in that it reflected an awareness of the international context. Such concerns were particularly the issue for lesser powers, such as Denmark. It was believed in Denmark that Britain and France would soon abolish the trade and would then seek to prevent other powers from participating, which proved to be an erroneous expectation in the short term. The Slave Trade Commission in Denmark also argued that slave conditions on the islands would improve if imports were banned, as it would be necessary to look after the slaves in order to encourage them to reproduce. In short, slavery would become less reprehensible; a view also taken by British Abolitionists.[6]

Changes in Britain were more important, because of its position as the leading European imperial and naval power. Furthermore, its key role in the slave trade and in the Caribbean slave economy ensured the importance of British attitudes, as did its potential influence on other states. This influence rose greatly due to Britain's major, and eventually totally successful, role in resistance from 1793 to 1815 to Revolutionary and Napoleonic France, a resistance that ensured that Britain was increasingly the pre-eminent global power.

Abolitionism was to be an aspect of the ideology of this power. Reflecting the range of British concerns, Abolitionism was part of the same current that saw growing missionary activity in the West Indies and, increasingly, Africa, while Christian assumptions about the inherent unity of mankind and the need to gather Africans to Christ played a major role in influencing British opinion. The influential Methodist leader John Wesley strongly attacked both slavery and the slave trade in his highly influential *Thoughts upon Slavery* (1774) and, in 1791, he was to send William Wilberforce a dying message urging him to maintain the Abolitionist cause. Visions of Christian liberation from sin could be linked to the slaves breaking free from chains. Methodists also fused evangelical moral universalism with the more secular universalism of natural rights and Enlightenment thought. Elsewhere in the Protestant world criticism of the slave trade and slavery developed in the Netherlands, although less actively than in Britain.[7]

Commercial benefits from the abolition of the slave trade were also predicted by some commentators, the influential writer Malachy Postlethwayt arguing, in his *The Universal Dictionary of Trade and Commerce*, that the trade stirred up conflict among African rulers and thus obstructed both British trade and 'the civilising of these people'.[8] Belief in such benefits became far stronger in the early nineteenth century, not least as British merchants looked for new export markets, particularly in the face, first, of the Continental System – the Napoleonic attempt to weaken Britain by banning her trade with Europe – and, subsequently, after the defeat of Napoleon in 1815, of Continental protectionism, for example the German Zollverein (Customs Union) established in 1834. Competition from American producers was an additional problem. Furthermore, the massive expansion of British industry during the Industrial Revolution meant that there were more goods for sale, as well as a desire for raw materials. Thus, a very different basis for trade with Africa was proposed to that in the eighteenth century.

The ruling of William, Lord Mansfield, in the case of James Somerset in 1772, that slave-owners, in this case James Steuart, could not forcibly take their slaves from England made slavery unenforceable there, and was matched by a reluctance among Londoners to help return runaway slaves. Somerset's American master had tried to send him out of England to be sold, but Abolitionists had pleaded habeas corpus on his behalf so that he could be brought before the court. Mansfield ruled that 'the state of slavery is of such a nature that it is incapable of being introduced on any reasons, moral or political, but only by positive law, which preserves its force long after the reasons, occasions and time itself from whence it was created, is erased from memory. It is so odious that nothing can be suffered to support it, but positive law.'

Abolitionist sentiment directed against the slave trade became more overt from the 1780s, and was an aspect of the powerful reform pressure and religious revivalism of the period, as well as a reaction to the loss of the American colonies as a result of the War of American Independence in 1775–83. Quakers played a prominent role in Abolitionism, but they and others were effective in part because of a more widespread shift in opinion, a situation more generally true of campaigning movements in Britain and elsewhere.[9]

The ready possibilities for organization presented by the strength of associational practices was also significant. In 1787, the Society for Effecting the Abolition of the Slave Trade, a national lobbying group with a guiding London Committee, was established. Most of the committee's members were Quakers. Provincial liaison committees were established that year, and they mobilized extensive support. Exeter's list of supporters the following year contained over 250 names, and if many came from outside the city, they nevertheless showed the range of support, including sixty women among the subscribers. The last was indicative of the prominent role of women in British Abolitionism.[10]

Pressure from the Society helped lead to debate in

Parliament and to the Dolben Act of 1788, by which conditions on British slave ships were regulated, the number of slaves limited according to the tonnage, and each voyage required the presence of a doctor. The ready responsiveness of the slave trade to the change in circumstances was speedily demonstrated, however, as its profitability had to be brought into line with legislation that increased the costs to the slave trader: the legislation thus encouraged the use of larger ships. In 1789, a less rigorous, but similar, Act was passed by the Dutch, and in 1799 British restrictions were strengthened.

Abolitionist sentiment also affected the arts, leading to the production of visual and literary images of the horrors of slavery, such as the medallion of the Society for the Abolition of the Slave Trade designed by William Hackwood and manufactured at Josiah Wedgwood's factory. Women wore anti-slavery emblems and jewellery. Anti-slavery became a fashionable cause, joining the powerful sentimental, Romantic and evangelical currents in the British culture of the period. Furthermore, there was a mass of pamphlet literature and discussion of the issue in humanitarian novels, and also extensive comments on the Abolitionist fight. Moreover, the information on the slave trade and the colonies that was sought by Abolitionists was publicized, in particular with Thomas Clarkson's *The Substance of Evidence of Sundry Persons in the Slave Trade* (1788) which was based on interviews he had conducted, largely with the captains and crew of slavers.

Popular action included the boycott of West Indian sugar and rum in 1791–2. This boycott indicated the synergy between different Abolitionist forces, notably public pressure, organizational capability and the culture of print, especially William Fox's *An Address to the People of Great Britain, on the Utility of Refraining from the Use of West Indian Sugar and Rum* (1791). Similar action had played an important part in the growing crisis of imperial rule in the North American colonies prior to the outbreak of revolution in 1775.

Pressure to abolish the trade, however, was hindered by the importance of the West Indies to the British economy, as well as by the opposition of the King, George III, and much of the House of Lords. Dolben's Act, for example, was bitterly opposed in the Lords by the Lord Chancellor, Lord Thurlow, a favourite of the King, while other ministers such as Lord Hawkesbury, the President of the Board of Trade, another royal favourite who was greatly concerned about the prosperity of the West Indies, and Viscount Sydney, the Home Secretary, offered more muted opposition.

The votes also indicated the strength of opposition. On 19 April 1791, although supported by William Pitt, Charles Fox and Edmund Burke, William Wilberforce's motion to bring in a bill for the abolition of the trade was defeated in the House of Commons by 163 to 88. The following year, his motion for abolition of the slave trade in 1796 was passed by 151 to 132, but the Lords postponed the matter by resolving to hear evidence. Every county was represented in the petitioning movement that year, unlike in 1787, and this increase in petitioning was an aspect of the mutually reinforcing relationship between popular pressure and parliamentary discussion.[11]

In 1793, Wilberforce's motion to hasten the actions of the Lords was rejected, as was that to abolish the supply of slaves to foreign powers, while in 1794 the latter motion passed the Commons, but was rejected in the Lords. In 1795, the Commons refused leave to bring in a bill for abolition, and in 1796 the bill was rejected on a third reading. In 1799, the Slave Trade Limiting Bill designed to prohibit the slave trade with Sierra Leone was quashed in the Lords. In 1804, a bill to abolish the slave trade passed the Commons, but was defeated in the Lords, and in 1805 it failed the second reading in the Commons. Wilberforce's efforts, however, were successful in helping to shift the parameters of parliamentary debate and in keeping the issue before Parliament.

Yet, aside from technical arguments, for example claims that restrictions would affect other aspects of Britain's trade with

West Africa,[12] there was also a populist tone to opposition to Abolition, one that is too often overlooked in the stress on a benign shift toward a more evangelical Zeitgeist in Britain. In William Dent's caricature 'Abolition of the Slave Trade, or the Man the Master', published in London on 26 May 1789, colonial produce is shown waiting for a purchaser because its price has gone up.[13] Part of the opposition to Abolitionism derived from the continued conviction that slavery was compatible with Christianity, and also that it was sanctioned by its existence in the Bible, notably the Old Testament, an argument that indicates the range of views that could be squeezed from Christian teaching and the Christian heritage.

Although the argument was not widespread in Britain, the Dutch Reformed Church, the established church in Cape Colony, claimed that slaves were not entitled to enter the Church, and that conversion to Christianity would not make slaves akin to Europeans because they had been born to slavery as part of a divine plan. Thus, the Dutch settlers opposed missionary activity among their slaves; as did many plantation owners in the West Indies.[14] By 1800, there were nearly 17,000 slaves in Cape Colony who were brought by sea from the Indian Ocean. Convicted criminals from Batavia were also part of the slave population in the colony.

The authority of the Classical world also contributed to the acceptability of slavery. To supporters of slavery, an acceptance of black people as fully human did not preclude slavery. Instead, black people were presented as degraded by their social and environmental backgrounds and, partly as a result, it was claimed that they would not greatly benefit from the end of the trade.

Abolitionism in France and the French territories

In part, opposition to Abolition reflected the conservative response in Britain to reform in general as a result of the French Revolution. The Revolution, which began in 1789, indeed had been linked to a secular idealism in France that had embraced Abolitionism as one of its themes and, in February 1788, *La Société des Amis des Noirs* had been founded in Paris, with help from British Abolitionists. Although, as was seen by the limited mention of the issue in the *cahiers de doléances*, the reform demands prepared for the meeting of the Estates General in 1789,[15] the French were far less active in Abolitionism than their British counterparts, the Société pressed for the abolition, first, of the slave trade and, eventually and without compensation, of slavery. One of its founders, Jacques-Pierre Brissot, argued that, with education, black people had the same capacities as whites.[16] In the utopian idealism of the French Revolution, the liberties affirmed by the Revolutionaries were believed to be inherent in humanity, and thus of global applicability. In January 1792 the Colonial Committee of the National Assembly pressed for an alliance with the people of Madagascar, not conquest and enslavement.[17]

Revolutions rarely, however, conform to utopian hopes. Indeed, initially, far from the slave trade being banned by France, it reached its peak in the French Atlantic during the years 1789–91. This maintenance of the trade reflected the value of the West Indies to the French economy, especially during the boom that followed the War of American Independence. Moreover, it was argued that slaves were not French and, therefore, that slavery and the freedoms of revolution were compatible.

The large-scale slave rising in France's leading Caribbean colony, Saint-Domingue, in August 1791 altered the situation. This rising overthrew both slavery and imperial control and led to a complex conflict in Saint-Domingue. The slave rebels liberated themselves from slavery and, to win their support for the French cause, in August 1793, the Civil Commissioner, Léger Sonthonax, freed the slaves in the Northern Province. The following February, the National Convention abolished slavery in all French colonies, a step that was unwelcome to most of the white settlers.[18] This idealism, however, did not protect the French position in Saint-Domingue, which after a complex and bitter war, became, in 1804, the independent black state of Haiti. There were important African echoes in the rising and the subsequent warfare with French forces, but the rising also drew on European military practices and on the ideology of Revolutionary France.[19] Fighting in Haiti demonstrated what was also seen with the British West Indies regiments, that black people were far better than Europeans as warriors in the West Indies, especially because their resistance to malarial diseases was higher.[20] The conflict displayed brutal racist anti-societal violence on both sides, notably the slaughter of civilians.[21]

French Revolutionary idealism also fell victim to the reaction and consolidation associated with Napoleon, who seized power in France in 1799. Slavery was restored in Guadeloupe (after the bloody repression of opposition by former slaves) and Cayenne (French Guiana) in 1802, and the entry to France of West Indian black and mixed-race people was prohibited while the slave trade was also restored.[22] In 1802, Napoleon sent 22,000 troops to Saint-Domingue under the command of his brother-in-law, General Charles Leclerc. Successful amphibious landings followed by rapid advances led to the overthrow of the defenders under Toussaint L'Ouverture, who was deported to France. Most of his generals defected to Leclerc. However, resistance continued in parts of Saint-Domingue and, in the autumn of 1802, it was joined by many of the officers who had fought under Toussaint. These took the initiative and the French forces, hit very hard by yellow fever which killed maybe 35,000–45,000 troops,[23] were reduced to isolated ports. Prefiguring their very different later role in subsequently ending the slave trade, the British played an important part in ensuring the success of the Haitian revolution with a crucial blockade of Saint-Domingue's ports in 1803 when war between France and Britain resumed after the peace negotiated in 1802. Alongside the strength of the resistance within Haiti – a resistance that

owed much to opposition to re-enslavement – thi
wrecked the costly French attempt to recapture the
and thus Napoleon's western strategy. The remaining F ich
forces abandoned Saint-Domingue in November 1803, becoming British prisoners of war, and its independence, as the
new state of Haiti, was proclaimed in 1804.

The sale of Louisiana to the USA in 1803 was linked to
French failure, as Louisiana was regarded as a crucial source
of food for the French West Indies. In turn, the Louisiana
Purchase permitted the spread of American slavery and
created the possibility for further American expansion into the
Spanish empire, which exacerbated New England concerns
about the Southern domination of the federal government.
Slavery was a challenge politically to the Northern states as
the apportionment of representation in the House of Repre-
sentatives and the Electoral College by the Constitution
counted each slave as three-fifths of a freeman. New England
concerns were taken further in the War of 1812–15 with
Britain, a conflict that was economically disruptive and
unpopular in New England and blamed on the Southern
states, which helped mobilize anti-slavery sentiment in New
England.[24]

There were also slave revolts elsewhere in the Caribbean
world in the 1790s, including, in the British colonies, Fedon's
rebellion on Grenada in 1795–6, and risings or conspiracies in
Dominica and St Vincent, followed by a conspiracy on Tobago
in 1802.[25] All were unsuccessful, as was the Pointée Coupée
slave rebellion in Louisiana in 1795, and smaller-scale slave
violence. Nevertheless, the Maroons of Dominica, who were
already a serious problem in 1785, were only suppressed in
1814, in part as a result of defections and in part due to the
burning of their cultivated patches.

Moreover, slave rebels were less successful in Latin America
than in Saint-Domingue. The small-scale 'Revolt of the
Tailors' in Salvador in Brazil in 1798, which included slaves as
well as mulattos and whites, called for the abolition of slavery,

but was suppressed in the context of white fear.[26] However, the success of the Haitian revolution, a key development, led to a marked increase in the always-present climate of fear in white society. This fear was accentuated by the killing of settlers by rebels on Grenada in 1795. The extent and impact of slave revolts, both on the slave ships and in the colonies, are important issues as they relate to the question of black agency in reducing the profitability and appeal of the slave trade and slavery, and thus of encouraging Abolitionism on economic grounds. The evidence for this thesis, however, is limited. Moreover, far from leading to a determination to end slavery as dangerous and costly, revolts and the pervasive fear of revolt encouraged a determination to maintain slavery as a form of control.

The end of the slave trade in Britain, and British pressure on its allies

The British situation differed from that in France as Abolitionism in Britain declined in the 1790s for both economic and ideological reasons. The boom in sugar exports from the British West Indies caused by the chaos in rival Saint-Domingue was important, as was the widespread opposition to populist reform that stemmed from hostility to the French Revolution. Thereafter, however, there was, in contrast in France, an upsurge in Abolitionism in the 1800s, which led to the formal end of the British slave trade.[27]

In 1805, the ministry of William Pitt the Younger, a statesman who saw himself as progressive and who profited from his appeal to this reforming middle-class constituency, issued Orders in Council that banned the import of slaves into newly captured territories after 1807 and, in the meantime, limited the introduction of slaves to 30 per cent of the number already there. This proclamation was taken much further by the next government, the more reformist Ministry of All the Talents, under the strongly Abolitionist William, Lord Grenville, which took power after Pitt's death in early 1806. As an aspect of its reform drive, this ministry was also to try (and fail) to secure Catholic Emancipation, a failure that led to its own fall.

In May 1806, the new ministry supported the Foreign Slave Trade Act, ending the supply of slaves to conquered territories and foreign colonies. This measure was presented on prudential grounds, as a way to limit the economic strength of these territories when some were returned as part of the peace settlement at the end of the war as they would be: Cuba, Guadeloupe and Martinique had been returned by Britain in 1763, and the last two were to be returned anew after the Napoleonic Wars. This Act hit the slave trade hard as much of it by then was focused on supplying the conquered colonies. In June, Parliament, declaring the trade 'contrary to the principles of justice, humanity and sound policy', agreed to consider abolishing the slave trade to the West Indies in the following session. The public mood also came into play, with the general election in 1806 leading to the election of many Abolitionist MPs. The election affected the subsequent debates, with Walter Fawkes, MP for Yorkshire, speaking in the key debate of 23 February 1807 to fulfil 'a solemn but voluntary pledge made to my constituents'.

The highpoint of the Abolitionist process occurred when the Abolition Act of 1807 banned slave trading by British subjects and the import of slaves into the British colonies. Introduced and pushed hard by Grenville, the Prime Minister, in the House of Lords on 2 January, the bill passed the Lords on 5 February by 100 votes to 34, followed by the Commons. By passing the legislation first in the Lords, where it was unsuccessfully opposed by William, Duke of Clarence (William IV from 1830 to 1837), Grenville ensured that the backstop behind opposition in the Commons had been removed. The Leader of the Commons, Charles, Lord Howick, was, as Earl Grey, to be Prime Minister at the time of the Slave Emancipation Act of 1833. At about four o'clock on the morning of 24 February, after a ten-hour debate, the motion to commit the bill passed the Commons by 283 votes to 16, a far larger majority than had been anticipated, albeit scarcely voted by all of the 658 MPs, many of whom had been listed as 'Doubtful' by the Abolitionist lobbyists. Liverpool's representation was divided, with Isaac Gascoyne pressing the commercial and maritime value of the trade, only to be opposed by William Roscoe. The bill received the royal assent on 25 March. The Act came into force on 1 May 1807, and on 1 March 1808 for those slave ships already at sea. Subsequently, in 1811, participation in the slave trade was made a felony.

The end of both the British slave trade, and, later, of slavery itself, has been ascribed by some commentators to a lack of profitability caused by economic development, rather than to the humanitarianism usually stressed in the nineteenth century,[28] but this view underplays the multiplicity of factors that contributed to the decisions. Some studies attribute much to economic problems in the plantation economy of the West Indies, problems stemming from the impact of the American Revolution, and, crucially, of subsequent British protectionism, on the trade between North America and the West Indies, trade that was very important to the supplies for, and markets of, the latter.[29] Moreover, problems were created for the sugar producers during the French Revolutionary and Napoleonic Wars by over-production following the seizure of French colonies, and by the exclusion of British exports from European markets stemming, in part, from the extent of French conquests but also due to low-cost Spanish sugar growers in Cuba who took over the competitive role formerly provided by Saint-Domingue.[30] There are, on the contrary, also indications that slave plantations in the West Indies remained profitable,[31] which, in part, reflected the ability of plantation owners to innovate. An aspect of this innovation included better care for the slaves and therefore improved survival rates, although Jamaica, Trinidad and British Guiana were still not approaching demographic self-sufficiency by the 1820s. As a result, unlike Barbados and the USA (where self-sufficiency had been early achieved in the Chesapeake region), they would have greatly profited from continuing slave imports, which would have helped with labour costs.

Instead of problems within the slave economy of the British West Indies, it is more appropriate to look at the outside pressures towards Abolition, which led swiftly to a situation in which it became the general assumption of the 'official mind' that action against the trade was a proper aspect of British policy.[32] These pressures included, and contributed to, a marginalization of groups, especially West Indian planters, that had encouraged and profited from British, and indeed European, demand for tropical goods. Instead, the reforming, liberal, middle-class culture that was becoming of growing importance in Britain, one that was helping to define both civility and Britishness, not least against aristocratic values and cosmopolitanism, regarded the slave trade and slavery as abhorrent, anachronistic and associated with everything it deplored. Abolitionists indeed were encouraged and assisted by a confidence in public support. Moreover, this confidence helped greatly influence the debate amongst the elite, forcing the defenders of slavery onto the defensive, and thus further ensuring that slavery seemed out of date. In addition, all sorts of reform impulses in Britain converged on and supported Abolitionism, including concern over the treatment of animals.[33]

Abolitionism offered Britain, tired by the travails of seemingly intractable war with Napoleon, the opportunity to see itself as playing a key moral role in the advance of true liberty, and Abolitionist medals show how self-conscious this was.[34] This factor was particularly valuable in 1806–7, as Britain's leading allies, Austria and Prussia, succumbed after sweeping French victories at Austerlitz (1805) and Jena (1806) respectively. Abolitionism enabled Britain to present itself as civilized and progressive in a way that Napoleon could not match. Indeed, on 23 February 1807, Sir Samuel Romilly, the Solicitor-General and a prominent Whig, told the Commons that Wilberforce, who had 'preserved so many millions of his fellow creatures', was far better than Napoleon, who 'had waded through slaughter and oppression', a speech which was followed by a standing ovation for Wilberforce.

Britain also used its international strength and influence to put pressure on other states to abolish or limit the slave trade, for not only did the trade now seem morally wrong, but, once abolished for British colonies, it was also correctly seen as giving an advantage to rival plantation economies and thus to their general economies. George Canning, the Foreign Secretary from 1807 to 1809, ordered British diplomats to begin negotiations aimed at securing treaties that would end the trade. Naval power, amphibious capability and transoceanic power projection ensured that the British were in a dominant position and well placed to advance their views. Indeed, once war resumed with Napoleon in 1803, a war that lasted until 1814 and was briefly and successfully resumed in 1815, the British seized St Lucia, Tobago, Demarara, Essequibo (now both in Guyana), and Surinam in 1803–4, following with the Danish West Indies – St Croix, St Thomas and St John in 1807, Martinique and Cayenne in 1809, and Guadeloupe, St Eustatius and St Martin in 1810. Fort Louis, the last French base in West Africa, fell in 1809.

Abolitionist voices applauded this expansion of the British empire and called for more British conquests in order to help the Abolitionist cause. Robert, Viscount Castlereagh, the Foreign Secretary, was pressed in 1812 to support the capture of Dutch and Danish settlements on the West African coast as this would lead to: 'the more effectual abolishing the Slave Trade, which, during my residence on the coast, was carried on to a great extent with the said Dutch and Danish settlements by Spanish and Portuguese vessels and Americans under Spanish colours'.[35]

Although their pressure against the slave trade was widely resented by others, both during the Napoleonic Wars and thereafter, as self-interested interference and undesirable moralizing, the British were in a position to make demands. In 1810, pressure was exerted on Portugal, then very much a dependent ally, protected from Napoleon by British troops, to restrict the slave trade to its territories as a preparation for Abolition; because Brazil, the leading slave economy, and Angola, its prime source of slaves and the largest colony in Africa, were Portuguese territories, the Portuguese position was important. The export of sugar from Brazil had particularly benefited from the rising on Saint-Domingue.

In 1815, Napoleon, on his return from exile in Elba, abolished the French slave trade, possibly as a way to appeal to progressive British opinion and encourage acceptance of his position. Subsequently, after Napoleon was defeated at Waterloo, the returned Bourbon regime of Louis XVIII in France was persuaded to maintain the ban on the slave trade. This was of great concern to British Abolitionists, as the French slave trade, if it continued, was seen as an opportunity for British investment. Like Portugal, Louis XVIII was very much a dependent ally of Britain. Under British pressure, which owed much to public opinion and the advice of Abolitionists,[36] the international peace Congress of Vienna (1814–15) issued a declaration against the trade. Signed on 8 February 1815 and eventually attached to the Congress treaty as an annex, the declaration called for the 'prompt suppression' of the trade, but accepted that individual states would have to consider how best to achieve this goal. Indeed, the Congress led, albeit only temporarily, to the institutionalization of suppression in the form of the short-lived, but multilateral, diplomatic committee established in London to monitor the trade.

This was not the end of the process of incessant British pressure. In January 1815, an Anglo-Portuguese treaty limited the slave trade in Brazil to south of the Equator, ending the supply of slaves from the Guinea coast in West Africa,[37] and, again in return for money, in September 1817, an Anglo-Spanish treaty contained similar provisions. Spain, in contrast, had rejected such pressure in 1814, but it did little to enforce the 1817 treaty, which itself was ambiguous in that it was possible to take on slaves after ships had left Spanish ports. In

1814, with effect from 1818, the Dutch slave trade was abolished. Again, this reflected British influence, as the Netherlands was also a dependent ally and wished to regain control of its conquered possessions in the East Indies.

The continuation of the slave trade to the Americas

In 1807, with effect from 1 January 1808, the slave trade was also abolished by the United States, but there was scant attempt to enforce the ban. Orders in Council, however, issued on 11 November 1807 were used by the British to justify seizing American slavers and in 1810 the Court of Appeals accepted the argument of the barrister James Stephen, Wilberforce's brother-in-law and a member of the Clapham Sect who had become convinced of the horrors of slavery by his time in the West Indies, that slave trading was a violation of the law of nations, the laws of humanity and Anglo-American law, and that therefore neutral slave ships could be legitimately seized.[38]

During the War of 1812–15, the British willingness to receive and arm escaped slaves aroused American anger, while British commentators suggested encouraging slave resistance as a way to weaken the USA. In 1814, Henry, Viscount Sidmouth, the Home Secretary, received a proposal suggesting that the British change the politics of America by turning to the slaves: they were to be emancipated in Virginia and Maryland, which was to be supported as a separate country.[39] In the closing stages of the war, the British military devoted particular attention to supporting slave resistance, but the Peace of Ghent that ended the war brought this option to a close and the British-armed Negro Fort on the Appalachicola river in Spanish West Florida was destroyed in 1816 by an American amphibious force; those black defenders who were not killed were enslaved.

Despite the efforts of the British government, the Atlantic slave trade continued because slavery had not been abolished and therefore provided an opportunity for slave traders.

Slavers used the flags of France and the USA, states that did not permit search by British warships. The British attempt, at the international conference at Aix-la-Chapelle in 1818, to establish an agreement of all maritime states that was to be supported by an international police force on the coast of Africa was rejected, with the French playing the key role.[40] Moreover, even British participation in the trade persisted, both legally and illegally, directly and indirectly. This participation included the purchase of slaves, both for British colonies and for British-owned operations elsewhere, such as mining for gold in Brazil and for copper in Cuba, as well as the provision of goods, credit, insurance and ships to foreign slave traders. Delays in emancipation enabled British and other investors to continue to invest in other slave systems, and helped maintain the profitability of the slave trade. They also encouraged purchases of slaves to pre-empt the end of legal imports, while the slave trade between British colonies remained legal for a time.

The provision of capital by British lenders was particularly valuable to slave societies which otherwise found it difficult to obtain sufficient capital to pursue economic activity, and this lending was an aspect of Britain's dominance of, and role in, what was otherwise an undercapitalized Atlantic world. The range of this role was extensive. For example, as also with free societies, British finance helped support rail construction, and this was important to plantation economies, in Brazil, Cuba and the USA. The British were not alone in this process. American manufactured goods supplied to Africa came to play a significant part in the slave trade from the 1840s.[41]

Although demand for new labour in the plantation economies was in large part met by the children of existing slaves, the continuation of slavery ensured that, even where the slave trade had been abolished, smuggling persisted, although it was not very extensive to the British West Indies. An illicit slave trade continued in the French Atlantic world, especially to Cayenne (French Guiana), but also to the French Caribbean.

The French had at least 193 slaving voyages between 1814 and 1820, although few after 1831 when the government in Paris pressed the colonial officials in Senegal to end the trade. Deception extended to the shipping of slaves termed *libertos* by the Portuguese and *engagés à temps* by the French. The French financed their trade with the export of goods to Africa, but this was a small flow compared to that from Britain. The French and Dutch also sold slaves to Puerto Rico, a Spanish colony until 1898, circumventing treaties banning their import direct from Africa by moving them via their Caribbean ports and reclassifying them.[42]

In response to action against the trade, there was a need, however, to search for new sources of slaves, and this need led to the development of slaving from South-East Africa. This was a distant source, where the slaves were in part purchased in return for textiles shipped from Bombay. However, distance hit profitability, and, as a result, most slaves shipped from Africa via the Portuguese bases in Mozambique, such as the ports of Mozambique and Quelimane, went to nearby Mauritius and Réunion in the Indian Ocean, and not to Brazil: proximity took precedence over the political link. The impact of European slaving activity in Mozambique on African society has been a source of controversy. It, rather than Zulu expansion, has been held in part responsible for the serious conflict in the interior of southern Africa known as the *Mfecane*,[43] although this revision has been rejected by other scholars.[44] A more appropriate approach is one that rejects mono-causal interpretations, and, instead, emphasizes the role of dynamic internal forces in generating change in African societies, which provides a context within which to consider European pressures and opportunities.[45]

Demand reflecting labour needs kept the slave trade alive. In particular, the trade to the leading, and increasingly important, market, Brazil (independent from Portugal from 1822), was not effectively ended until 1850, and that to the second market, Cuba, until 1867; the relevant Spanish legislation was passed the previous year. Brazil imported 60,000 slaves in 1829 and again in 1830. Cuba, which, until conquered by the USA in 1898 was a Spanish possession, imported an annual average of 10,700 slaves in 1836–60. The profitable nature of the sugar economies of Brazil and Cuba, as coffee and sugar exports rose helped by free trade moves in Britain,[46] kept the trade successful, as did the commitment to the lifestyle and ethos of slaveholding, and a lack of relevant European immigrant labour. The decline of the slave economies of nearby Haiti and Jamaica encouraged an increase of slavery in Cuba, which led to interest in American pro-slavery circles in annexing Cuba, and thus strengthening the slavery lobby in American politics. Despite the abolition of the slave trade by the United States, American slavers greatly profited from demand in Brazil and Cuba.

Demand for slaves encouraged supply and shifts in the supply system. For example, the number of slaves shipped through Portuguese-controlled ports in the Cabinda region to the north of the River Congo rose in the 1820s. In part, this was due to the decline of the French and Dutch trade from this region, but the expansion of the Atlantic slave trade further east into the African interior was also significant.[47] Until the late 1830s, the Bight of Benin and, until the 1850s, the Angolan coast north to Cabinda remained important sources of slaves. The export of slaves to Brazil helped keep the trade buoyant, and the British role in the Bight of Benin had been replaced by Brazilian, Dutch, Portuguese and Spanish traders.

Furthermore, the raiding warfare that provided large numbers of slaves remained important across Africa, and responded to shifts in the Atlantic transit system. For example, Opubu the Great, ruler of the important port of Bonny on the Bight of Biafra (1792–1830), responded to British moves against the slave trade by selling palm oil to Britain while, at the same time, developing his slave interests with Portugal.[48] Moreover, the slave trade helped Asante expansion, although this expansion was also financed from other sources.[49] Dahomey too played a prominent role in the slave trade,[50] as did Madagascar.[51] In the interior of sub-Saharan Africa, Islamic *jihads*, such as that of al-Hajj Umar Tal in the 1850s, were linked to slaving.[52] At the same time, the remarkably rapid African shift to palm oil and other 'legitimate' exports also had a huge impact on Africans.

The flow of slaves to Brazil was principally financed by the shipping to Angola, in return, of textiles, cheap brandy and firearms. Britain and Brazil were the leading sources of the textiles, and Britain's role was important to Anglo-Brazilian trade. This helped complicate the attitudes of the British government to the continuation of the slave trade, for there was pressure over the issue on behalf of British manufacturing interests. The textile trade to Africa also helped spur Brazilian production. As a result of the continued flow of new slaves, Brazil and Cuba remained more African in the nineteenth century than the British West Indies or the southern USA, which had important long-term consequences in terms of their societies and cultures, consequences that continue to this day.

Changes in the United States

In the USA, the initial acceptance of slavery was a product of the federal character of the new state, and of the fundamental role of slaveholding, not only in the economies of the Southern states, but also to their sense of identity and distinctiveness. It is a common mistake to say that the framers of the American Constitution agreed that the American slave trade would be abolished in twenty years. In fact, the Constitution prohibited the government from interfering with the slave trade for twenty years, and this was one of the Constitution's provisions that was unamendable. South Carolina and Georgia both expected a future need for slave imports.

From 1808, however, the slave trade to the USA was no longer legal. Nevertheless, indicating the extent to which the international slave trade was not the sole element to consider, there was still an important slave trade within the USA, and, indeed, it became more important in the nineteenth century. The extent of the slave states, combined with the contrasts among them, ensured that there was still a very extensive slave trade, particularly from the Old to the New South, which was a situation similar to that in Brazil, where the sugar planters of the north-east sold slaves to the coffee planters further south, who were expanding west into the province of São Paulo using the railway to create new links and opportunities.[53] Similarly, delays in emancipation provided a market for slave trade within the Caribbean, particularly once direct trade with Africa was limited. Caribbean slave supplies, for example, became more important to the Spanish colony of Puerto Rico from 1847.[54]

Aside from slave sales, the prevalence of slave hiring in the American South further ensured considerable geographical mobility among slaves, which helped keep slavery responsive to the market, and thus part of a dynamic economic system. Without a trade in slaves, there would have been less room for such entrepreneurship, or for the interaction with capital that purchase and hiring offered.[55] The slave economy in the USA was transformed and greatly expanded as a result of the major expansion of cotton production, which owed much to Eli Whitney's invention in 1793 of the cotton gin, a hand-operated machine which made it possible to separate the cotton seeds from the fibre. This process, which was subsequently improved, encouraged the cultivation of 'upland' cotton. It was hardy, and therefore widely cultivable across the South, but was very difficult to de-seed by hand, unlike the Sea Island cotton hitherto grown, which had been largely restricted to the Atlantic coastlands. Annual cotton output in the USA, as a result, rose from 3,000 bales in 1793 to over three million in the 1850s.[56] This raw cotton helped drive the Industrial Revolution by providing the raw material for the cotton industry, notably in Lancashire in Britain. Thus, slave labour played a significant role in economic change in the Western economy.[57]

The profitability of the cotton economy was important to the continued appeal of slavery in the South, and, as tobacco became less well-capitalized, so slaves from the tobacco country – where, anyway, in contrast to the situation further south, there had been a natural growth in the slave population from the 1720s – were sold for work on cotton plantations. This sale ensured that slaves became less important in the Chesapeake states. The success of the cotton economy and the ability to boost the birth rate of American slaves were such that Southern apologists did not regard the slave system as anachronistic. Their argument had considerable weight and cannot be disproved by reference to the later problems of the South, problems that led to a presentation of the slave economy as backward.

American Abolitionists had hoped that the end of the international slave trade, combined with the high death rate among American slaves, would lead to an extinction of slavery by natural causes, but, instead, this death rate declined and the slave population increasingly sustained its numbers. As a consequence, Abolitionists became more convinced that slavery had to be ended by state action, a belief encouraged by its abolition in the British empire in 1833. This belief affected the political atmosphere in the North, contributing to the conviction that beneficial change could, and should, be introduced.

Conversely, the greater centrality of slavery to the expanding cotton economy led its Southern advocates to become more vocal and to add a conviction of potent economic need to the arguments they offered for sustaining their socio-political world. Racial exclusion was presented as both form and focus of Southern cultural identity and this identity interacted with economic factors to ensure that slavery was not an issue of the fading past. The earlier support of Thomas Jefferson and others for ending what he saw as the slave problem by expatriation (sending slaves abroad) now seemed anachronistic. Indeed, the number of slaves rose considerably until the Civil War, providing an economic dimension to ideological debates about slavery.[58] That racism was an integral element was shown by the increasing marginalization of mulattoes, who were frequently treated as black.[59]

Furthermore, there was a strong interest in spreading slavery to nearby areas, an interest linked to the Southern commitment to expansionism and seen as likely to strengthen the position of the slave states politically. Fear of soil exhaustion played a part, as did a concern that slaves, as well as poor whites, would become too numerous for the stability of the South unless it could gain new territories. The spread of slavery was envisaged both within the USA where, for example, Indiana nearly became a slave state in 1824, and with the expansion of the USA.

With other topics, particularly relations with Britain, more prominent the issue of slavery was in abeyance as far as most politicians were concerned during the 1810s, but the consequences of expansionism threw the issue to the fore in 1819 when the Missouri Territory applied for statehood. The proposals from James Tallmadge, a New York congressman, for the gradual ending of slavery in Missouri, by prohibiting the entry of new slaves and freeing all existing slaves born after admission to statehood once they had turned twenty-five, won extensive support in the North, but was seen in the South as a threat to its identity and existence, and by April 1820 Thomas Jefferson was expressing his concern at the prospect of division.

In the event, the Missouri Compromise of 1820 allowed Missouri to enter the Union as a slave state in 1821, but banned slavery elsewhere above the 30°36' Parallel, which ran along Missouri's southern boundary. This measure, which left most of the Louisiana Purchase free from slavery, was scarcely an authentic compromise.[60] Instead, it was seen as a challenge by Southerners opposed to Northern interference, notably by means of federal power over the sovereign authority of the states. As a result, the Missouri Compromise led to an increase in support for slavery[61] as well as encouraging Southerners to press for expansion to the west to develop an interest in Mexico and the Caribbean. In 1822, the British envoy in Washington thought that interest in creating a new state out of West Florida was related to the wish to establish more Southern states, while, in 1823, he noted pressure for slavery in Illinois in order to cut labour costs and raise land values.[62] Keen on expansion, the mental space of the South expanded to include Texas, other parts of Mexico, Cuba and Haiti. While Texas was under Mexican rule (1821–35), the attempt by the Mexican government to prevent the import of slaves there aroused much anger among the American colonists. As a reminder of the prevalence of slavery, the south-eastern Native Americans, such as the Cherokee and Creek, owned thousands of African slaves by the 1830s.[63]

The British attack on the slave trade

Britain, meanwhile, expended much diplomatic capital on moves against the slave trade, which the Foreign Secretary, George, Fourth Earl of Aberdeen, described in 1842 as a 'new and vast branch of international relations'.[64] Henry, Third Viscount Palmerston, who had three spells as Foreign Secretary – in 1830–4, 1835–41 and 1846–51, and two as Prime Minister (1855–8 and 1859–65), and Edward, Fourteenth Earl of Derby, Secretary of State for the Colonies in 1833–4 and 1841–4, and Prime Minister in 1852, 1858–9 and 1866–8, were particularly committed opponents of the slave trade, as was Derby's son Edward, the Fifteenth Earl, who was Foreign Secretary in 1866–8 and 1874–8. In 1862, Palmerston responded to a deputation pressing for action to end the 'barbarous practices' of King Gelele of Dahomey, who had succeeded to the throne in 1858 and was not interested in ending the slave trade. Palmerston replied that he and the Foreign Secretary, John, First Earl Russell, were 'quite as desirous of putting the slave trade down as any of them can be',[65] while his language made clear his grasp of the cruelty involved and his emotional commitment: 'Half the evil has been done by the time the slaves are captured in the American waters. The razzia [devastating raid] has been made in Africa, the village has been burnt, the old people and infants have been murdered, the young and the middle aged have been torn from their homes and sent to sea.'[66] Russell, Colonial Secretary in 1839–41 and 1855, Foreign Secretary in 1852–3 and 1859–65, and Prime Minister in 1846–52 and 1865–6, noted in 1865, 'I hate slavery and the slave trade beyond measure.'[67]

The major effort of the British government against slavery led to a spread in diplomatic representation and negotiations, and to the development of a new and large bureaucratic department, the Slave Trade Department, within the Foreign Office in London.[68] This was not only one of the first functional departments of the Foreign Office, but was also, in its emergence and evolution, a measure of the bureaucratization of diplomacy, while it provided the Foreign Office with a degree of expertise, particularly on African matters, that it might otherwise not have had.

The granting of recognition to the states that arose from the collapse of Spain's empire in Latin America depended on their abolition of the slave trade. British support was important to Abolitionism in formerly Spanish America, but so also was the example and process of rebellion against Spain which had led to independence. These rebellions challenged existing patterns of authority, but also saw a breakdown of order far greater than that in the War of American Independence, and one that was exploited by many slaves in order to escape or rebel. The Latin America societies were also more ethnically complex than the USA, with a large mixed-race sector, and this had a major consequence in the Latin American Wars of Liberation. Simon Bolivar, the most prominent leader of the independence struggle, freed his own slaves and pressed for the abolition of slavery, but also supported continued control by a white elite. Slavery itself was abolished in Chile in 1823, in Mexico in 1829 (although with Texas exempted), in Bolivia in

1831, and in Paraguay and Uruguay in 1842. In Argentina (1853), Colombia (1851), Peru (1855) and Venezuela (1854) abolition took longer.[69]

Trade and Abolitionism were linked in British government policy, not least as slave economies seemed a threat to the economic viability of the British West Indies. Thus, Charles Elliot, the British envoy to Texas, which had won independence from Mexico, advanced the idea of an independent pro-British Texas partly reliant on free black labour, and therefore a suitable ally for Britain. In 1839, the British radical Daniel O'Connell floated the idea of no recognition of Texan independence from Mexico without its abolishing slavery and, in addition, of negotiations with Mexico for the creation of a British protectorate in its territory that would be a safe haven for free black people.[70] In the event, British recognition was granted in 1840 in return for agreeing to suppress the slave trade. Indeed, in 1844, the pro-slavery American Secretary of State, John C. Calhoun, told the British envoy that Britain had promoted the abolition of slavery in Texas in order to undermine it in the USA.

Pressure was also exerted by Britain on other states to implement their bans on the trade, although there was considerable anger on their part about British demands, not least over the issue of searching ships. Albeit with only limited energy, the American Navy also took part in the struggle with slavery, sometimes in cooperation with the British. This action overlapped with the protection of American and international trade against privateering and piracy, and looked towards modern concepts of a benign role for American power. The combined goals led to a major American naval commitment to the Caribbean from the 1820s, with operations offshore and ashore Cuba, Puerto Rico, Santo Domingo and the Yucatán. In 1822, Commodore James Biddle commanded a squadron of fourteen American ships in the Caribbean, and, in 1823, David Farragut won notice in command of a shore party in Cuba while on anti-slavery duties.

American naval activity also ranged further afield, with the Webster-Ashburton Treaty of 1842 with Britain leading to a more active stance in the shape of the creation of an Africa squadron to help in stamping out the slave trade in African waters.[71] In 1843, sailors and marines from four American warships landed on the Ivory Coast in West Africa in order to discourage the slave trade and to act against those who had attacked American shipping. American naval activity, however, was handicapped by limited resources,[72] and the British repeatedly saw the American government and public as unhelpful in measures to try to suppress the slave trade,[73] although other navies did not take a comparable role against the trade. British pressure against the slave trade was in part countered by the American refusal to accept the abolition of slavery in the USA, and American influence in particular helped in the continued slave trade to Cuba. So also did the lack of a Spanish Abolitionist movement.

The perception among Protestant nations by the 1830s that Catholic Europe was tepid in its determination to extirpate the slave trade was broadly correct. However, Pope Gregory XVI issued a Bull in 1839 condemning slavery as unworthy of Christians, and this acted as a catalyst, at least in France. The Bull, however, was not well received in Catholic America, with the bishops there remaining silent.[74] The British government meanwhile was active. In 1839, the Act for the Suppression of the Slave Trade authorized British warships to seize slave ships registered in Portugal and sailing under the Portuguese flag, a unilateral measure in part intended to hit the use of the flag by Brazilian slave dealers. It was vigorously implemented, but some traders then switched to the use of the French flag. New treaties to enforce the end of the trade were signed with Spain in 1835, Portugal in 1842 and France in 1845.[75] The treaty with Portugal crucially extended the mutual right to search.

This issue caused particular problems in Anglo-Brazilian relations. In 1826, newly independent Brazil, concerned about its international position in the face of Portuguese interest in reconquest, accepted a treaty with Britain, ratified in 1827, promising to make the trade illegal within three years of ratification. Furthermore, in 1831, the Brazilian General Assembly passed a law ordering the liberation of all slaves entering Brazil. In anticipation of the abolition of the slave trade, the treaty led to a marked rise in demand for slaves, and also in their price, in 1828–30. There was also renewed interest in the recruitment of native labour. Thereafter, demand for slaves and prices fell in 1830–3, but both, however, later rose anew. This rise reflected the weak nature of Brazilian enforcement, which arose from a strong feeling that slavery and the slave trade were essential, a feeling that drew on the continuing demand for slaves, as well as anger about British interference and about Brazilian measures to enforce the law.

Plantation agriculture did well in Brazil for other crops as well as coffee and, in the late 1830s, political pressure there for the end of restrictions on the slave trade grew, and the trade was openly conducted. The Brazilian Navy came to do very little against the trade, which increased British anger. The low price of slaves in Africa indeed encouraged the revival in the transatlantic trade to the New World, another instance of the adaptability of the slave trade. The inflow of slaves to Brazil greatly increased, to an annual flow of over 50,000 in the late 1840s (the annual average in 1826–50 was 38,000), so that by 1850 there were over two million slaves in Brazil.[76] As a reminder of the variety of slave societies, the situation therefore was very different to the USA, the leading slave society, as the latter was no longer linked to the international slave trade.

In 1842, however, an Anglo-Portuguese treaty abolishing the trade was signed, which extended the mutual right of search to south of the Equator, threatening the (illegal) trade from Angola to Brazil, which provided the prime source of Brazil's slaves. However, it proved difficult to stamp out the trade, not least because Portuguese officials in Angola colluded with it. In 1861, Palmerston passed on to the Foreign Secretary a letter from Charles Buxton, an MP concerned about the slave trade, who claimed that there was now 'scarcely any slave trade except from' Portugal's African colonies. Buxton suggested offering Portugal the assistance of two or three British consuls to watch the conduct of officials,[77] the sort of infringement of sovereignty that other powers found unacceptable.

In 1845, meanwhile, Parliament had passed a Slave Trade Act authorizing the Royal Navy to treat suspected slave ships as pirates. In doing so, Parliament was seeking to enforce unilaterally the provision of the Anglo-Brazilian treaty of 1826 which deemed the Brazilian slave trade to be piracy. The Act of 1845, known as the Aberdeen Act after the Foreign Secretary, was a piece of legislation that testified to a strong sense of national power as well as mission, but it also reflected longstanding tension with other powers over British rights over their nationals and property, a tension that proved damaging in relations with the USA, not least in the late 1850s. The Act led to the capture of nearly 400 ships within five years. In June 1850, moreover, British warships entered Brazilian ports to seize and destroy suspected slavers, much to the anger of Brazil. However, the Brazilians were not in a good position to resist Britain, either politically or economically. Coffee and sugar, which Brazil sold in great quantities, could have been obtained by Britain from elsewhere, and Brazil greatly needed British capital. Despite calls for war with Britain, the Brazilian government temporized and in 1850 passed the Eusébio de Queiroz law, which banned the import of slaves. This measure owed much to British action, and the British, indeed, subsidized Brazilian Abolitionism. The last cargo of slaves to Brazil was unloaded in 1856. More generally, by helping push up the price of slaves, which rose greatly in the 1850s, and yet more thereafter, British actions ensured that slave owning was too expensive for many Brazilians, and therefore reduced the role of slave owning.[78]

Coercion thus helped make it economically redundant and politically weaker.

Pressure was also exerted on Cuba, sufficiently so for David Turnbull, the British Consul in 1840-2, to be accused of incitement to slave risings,[79] but in 1863 Palmerston could suggest that 15-20,000 Africans, and possibly more, were imported into Cuba each year, and the British felt it necessary to press Spain to implement its treaty commitments.[80] The bribery of officials to ignore restrictions was widespread. Nevertheless, the situation in Brazil and Cuba underlined the extent to which the slave trade and slavery came to an end in slave societies as a result of external pressures. The varied role of such pressures was an instance of a more general characteristic of both the slave trade and slavery.

Public Abolitionist sentiment remained strong in Britain and encouraged government action. This sentiment was directed both against foreign activity and against British participation, for example in the Brazilian mining industry. The British role in the suppression of the slave trade affected British institutions, not least the Foreign Office and the Royal Navy, especially as a result of the scale and continuity of the task and the enthusiasm displayed by many younger naval officers of the West African Squadron. Indeed, the navy became a global force for change, challenging not only slavers but also established maritime law. The sense of moral purpose behind British policy rested on the state's unchallenged naval power,[81] and was given a powerful naval dimension by the anti-slavery patrols off Africa and Brazil and in the West Indies. In 1807, when Britain was at war with France, and naval resources were very stretched blockading its ports, two warships were sent to African waters to begin the campaign against the slave trade. Subsequently, Abolitionists pressed for the retention of bases in West Africa in order to increase the effectiveness of naval action against the trade.

The use of naval pressure against the Barbary states of North Africa which seized Europeans as slaves acted as a bridge that helped to make such pressure against slave traders elsewhere, both Western and non-Western, seem more acceptable. This pressure against the Barbary states was a longstanding theme, but it is indicative that the biggest deployment of this type occurred in 1816, when Admiral Lord Exmouth and a fleet of twenty-one British warships with the support of a Dutch frigate squadron demanded the end of Christian slavery in Algiers. When no answer was returned, he opened fire and 40,000 roundshot and shells destroyed the Algerine ships and much of the city. Umar, the Dey (ruler), yielded, and over 1,600 slaves, mostly from Spain and the Italian principalities, were freed, which was seen as a great triumph.[82] The British presented themselves as acting on behalf of the civilized world, and as assuming a responsibility formerly undertaken by the Bourbon powers. In 1819, a British squadron returned anew to Algiers, and, in 1824, the threat of bombardment led the Dey, now Husain III, to capitulate again to British demands. That year also, the Bey (ruler) of Tunis was made to stop the sale of Christian slaves.

Slavery in the Islamic world continued without pressure for its abolition, but, as a sign of state-directed reform that challenged traditional practices, the Ottoman Sultan Selim III tried to reform the janissaries as part of his shift toward a *nizam-i cedid* (new order army) organized and armed on European lines, only to be overthrown in 1807 and for his new army to be dissolved.[83] The failure of Selim's successor, Mahmud II, to re-establish control over the janissaries in the 1810s indicated the deep-rooted ideological, political and social obstacles to reform, but in 1826 he suppressed them. This step scarcely equated with the end of the slave trade, but it indicated the extent to which there was a widespread volatility in the period, one that was not limited to Western powers. Also in the 1820s, the Chinese government ceased to use large-scale banishment in order to provide labour for the posts established in Xinjiang, a process begun after its conquest from the Dzhungars in the 1750s.[84]

Non-Western societies might be able to follow their own course on land, but the seas of the world were increasingly under the control of the Western powers. The most important active British anti-slavery naval force in the first half of the century was that based in West Africa (until 1840 part of the Cape Command), which freed slaves and took them to Freetown in Sierra Leone, a British colony for free black people. The anti-slavery commitment led to a major expansion of this force from the 1820s to the 1840s, and, by the end of the decade, there were thirty-five anti-slaving patrol ships off West Africa. In the late 1830s, British naval action helped greatly to reduce the flow of slaves from the Bight of Biafra.[85] The Royal Navy was to lose 17,000 seamen to disease, battle or accident in this lengthy commitment off West Africa, a commitment that many naval officers disliked. Their reasons included a belief that freeing the slaves often exposed them to difficult circumstances. Lieutenant Gilbert Elliott, who served on HMS *Sampson*, was horrified by the conditions of liberated Africans, who were kept in barracoons (coastal forts) while awaiting movement: 'thousands of poor wretches huddled together where no sea breeze can blow on them'. He claimed that Abolition had been poorly conceived: 'I should very much like to freight a ship with philanthropists and send them to sea – to show them . . . what dreadful misery it has brought on those poor unfortunate savages whose condition they pretend to better.'[86]

Warships based in Cape Town, a British possession from 1806, also played an important role, as anti-slavery patrols were extended south of the Equator in 1839, enabling Britain to enforce the outlawing of the slave trade to Brazil. Anti-slaving activities were not restricted to the Atlantic, but were also important in the Indian Ocean and in East Asian waters, which contributed considerably to the great expense of the British naval deployments.[87] Activity in the Indian Ocean focused on preventing slave shipments from East Africa into the Islamic world, but also elsewhere. In 1863,

Palmerston complained about large-scale movements of slaves from East Africa to Réunion by Portuguese slavers.[88] There were also attempts to prevent the shipment of slaves from India: Hindu women were seized and shipped from Bombay to Zanzibar. From 1820, the British negotiated agreements with the rulers of the Persian Gulf in order to provide an agreed basis for naval action against the slave trade by sea to the Arabian peninsula. A 1822 treaty with the Imam of Muscat (Oman) had only limited success, but, in 1845, Sultan Said II of Muscat agreed to stop exports from his African dominions, which essentially meant Zanzibar. However, these and other treaties were widely ignored.

There were also operations against piracy, which was often focused on slave raiding, for example off Sarawak in northern Borneo, an aspect both of the relationship between criminality and enslavement still seen today, but also of the extent to which such criminality was the product of particular societies and geographical milieux. Such activity was limited in the nineteenth century as the state increasingly became *the* main form and expression of organized violence.[89] In 1843–9, HMS *Dido* and other warships joined James Brooke, the British 'White Raja' of Sarawak, in stamping out pirates who resisted his influence there. In return for helping suppress a rebellion in Sarawak, Brooke had been appointed raja by the Sultan of Brunei in 1841, and, thanks to British help and his own entrepreneurship, he was able to have Sarawak recognized as an independent state in 1863.

The advent of steam power added a new dimension to the naval struggle. Coal was costly, but it increased the manoeuvrability of ships, making it easier to sound inshore and hazardous waters and to attack ships in anchorages, which made a major difference in the struggle against the slave trade, as slavers were fast, manoeuvrable and difficult to capture, and could take shelter in inshore waters. It was also necessary for the Royal Navy, from the 1840s, to respond to the use of steamships by slavers keen to outpace the patrols.[90] In West

Africa, Lagos, a major slaving port that exported many slaves as a result of the bitter Yoruba civil wars and that served as an entrepôt for Hausa slave traders, was attacked in 1851, and the slaving facilities were destroyed. In 1851–2, the local rulers on the western Slave Coast, including of Porto-Novo, Badagry and Abeokuta, were obliged to sign treaties with Britain ending the slave trade. In 1861, concern about continued slaving from Lagos led to successful pressure for its cession to Britain.

The role of the Royal Navy ensured that opposition to the slave trade would not simply be a matter of diplomatic pressure. It also meant that there was a constant flow of news to help keep Abolitionism at the forefront of attention in Britain. The role of the navy also demonstrated the extent to which external pressures were crucial to the last stages as well as the end of the slave trade.

British power was also important on land in South Asia. Wholesale enslavement during political and dynastic upheavals ceased under the British hegemony established in the early nineteenth century, which was also the period when adopted slave heirs to Indian princes were disinherited by the British. The latter practice illustrates the variety in the status and condition of slaves.

Aside from action against the slave trade itself, British pressure was brought to bear on African rulers in order to agree to end the slave trade and, instead, to agree to legitimate trade,[91] which was an aspect of a more general interest in deriving benefit from inland Africa. For example, in 1812, Major-General Charles Stevenson sent Robert, Second Earl of Liverpool, Secretary for War and the Colonies, a memorandum urging the need to gain control of Timbuktu on the Niger river in order to dominate trade and recruit soldiers.[92] Alongside coercion, there was a more benign attempt to link steam power with Abolitionism. Macgregor Laird, who founded the African Steamship Company, sought in the 1830s, with the use of steamships, to make the River Niger in

West Africa a commercial thoroughfare for British trade, which he hoped would undermine the slave trade. This was also a theme of Sir Thomas Buxton's *The African Slave Trade and its Remedy* (1839), and of the Society for the Extinction of the Slave Trade and the Civilisation of Africa, which held its first public meeting on 1 June 1840 with Prince Albert in the chair. Buxton's campaign against slavery drew heavily on the work of his female relatives.[93]

In 1862, a deputation pressing Palmerston on the slave trade from Dahomey claimed, he thought accurately, 'that Africa would, if the slave trade were abolished, prove a better supply for cotton than India', as it was nearer to Britain's mills and produced better cotton, and because there were fewer alternatives for Africans to cultivate. Palmerston keenly supported the idea of persuading African rulers to switch from the slave trade to the production of export crops.[94]

As with the continuing slave trade, pressure to end the trade, however, was exerted in Africa within a context in which due allowance had to be made for the continued strength of its rulers, and their ability to chart their own path, which was brought home in 1821, when the 5,000-strong British Royal African Colonial Corps under Colonel Sir Charles McCarthy, Governor of Sierra Leone, was destroyed by a larger, more enthusiastic, and well-equipped Asante army. The Governor's head, which became a war trophy and was used as a ceremonial drinking cup, was a particularly lurid instance of Western failure. McCarthy's replacement, Major-General Charles Turner, recommended total withdrawal from the Gold Coast, but, instead, the British withdrew to hold only Cape Coast Castle (which had been their key position in the slave trade) and Accra.[95]

Indeed, in the 1810s and 1820s, Egyptian expansionism in North-East Africa was more successful than its European counterpart in West Africa. From 1821, captured Sudanese were vaccinated, instructed in Islam and trained as slave soldiers for Mehmed Ali's *nizam-i cedid*. Armed with effective modern guns, these soldiers helped support slave raiding, which was a state monopoly from the 1820s to 1853, when private merchants took over.[96] The slave market in Khartoum was closed the following year. This Egyptian expansionism continued to be important into the 1870s, with Darfur, Equatoria and Harrar all acquired that decade. In 1872, Egyptian forces under Samuel Baker moved south into modern Uganda, fighting the Bunyoro. Slave raiding and trading were important aspects of this spreading Islamic control.[97]

They were also seen in other areas where Muslim powers continued traditional patterns of activity. Robert Adams, a sailor from New York who was enslaved after his ship was wrecked near Cape Blanco, ended up in Timbuktu on the River Niger in 1811, and subsequently described how:

> a party of a hundred or more armed men marched out ... to procure slaves ... they were usually absent from one week to a month, and at times brought in considerable numbers. The slaves were generally a different race of people from those of Timbuktu ... The greatest number of slaves that he recollects to have seen brought in at one time, were about twenty ... The slaves thus brought in were chiefly women and children.

These slaves were principally used to tend animals.

Adams also noted the use of enslavement as a form of punishment: 'Twelve persons were condemned to slavery during the six months of Adams's resident at Timbuktu [for] poisoning, theft, and refusing to join a party sent out to procure slaves.'[98]

At the same time, enslavement continued in Western, Central and Southern Africa as an aspect of warfare there. For example, in what is now Botswana, the expanding Ngwato kingdom conquered and enslaved the Sarwa.[99] This relatively greater success for non-Western powers repeated a longstanding pattern in Africa, and one that is underplayed in some of the literature.

It was only, in fact, from the 1840s that European power really became more insistent on the West African coast. French imperialism was extended, with colonies established in Gabon (1842) and Ivory Coast (1843), while Spain established another, Rio Muni, the basis of the modern state of Equatorial Guinea, in 1843. The spread of this imperial power gathered pace in the second half of the century, creating the basis for a transformation of the situation within Africa.

6

THE END OF SLAVERY, 1830–1930?

When the sun is down, if our row is not finished we get flogged. I received thirty lashes, as did Joe. We are taken to the stocks at night, and flogged next morning. We told the manager the work was too much, that we had no time to get our victuals, and begged him to lessen the task: this was the reason we were flogged.

Complaint of a slave in British Guiana.[1]

Your slave trade suppression schemes are very good, and if they can be carried out, which seems quite feasible, they will go far to smash the slave traders. It would be a great glory to your administration of our foreign affairs, if you could exterminate that hydra'.

Viscount Palmerston, 1861.[2]

It is very easy to shift from the abolition of the Western slave trade to that of slavery, but they were not simultaneous, and there were cross-currents, which explains the overlap with the previous chapter. Clearly, the Southern states in the USA did not think that abolition of the trade made abolition of slavery inevitable. In pressing in 1792 and 1807 for the abolition of the slave trade, William Wilberforce, indeed, had denied that he supported immediate emancipation as he considered the slaves not yet ready. Abolitionists themselves had hoped that the end of the slave trade would lead to greater care of the remaining slaves by their owners so that healthier slaves lived longer and were able to reproduce, which would thus make pressure for more imports of slaves redundant. A kinder slavery would make it less reprehensible, but would also prepare for a gradual withering as slave labour became more like other labour. Yet, an ability to sustain slave numbers without the slave trade was also a way to maintain slavery.

Moreover, there is a sense that the slave world was being strengthened in some respects at the same time that the slave trade was being ended. This was true not only of Mauritius in the Indian Ocean, but also of the colonies of Demerara-Essequibo and Berbice on the Guyana coast of South America, seized by the British from the Dutch in 1803. Plantation agriculture, the large-scale importation of African slaves, and a switch from cotton and coffee to sugar, all followed British conquest there, as they did on Trinidad, seized from Spain by Britain in 1797 and retained at the end of the Napoleonic Wars. Thus, these colonies were more like those of the late seventeenth-century West Indies than the more mature slave societies of the West Indies of the period, where a lower percentage of the slaves were African-born and where the work regime was less cruel.[3] The expansion of plantation agriculture in these colonies reflected the credit and investment readily available as part of the British world and the opportunities presented by trade within it.

From the mid-1820s, the continued strength of slavery helped lead to fresh Abolitionist pressure in Britain, although it is necessary to note that this was less important politically than successful pressure for the end of civil disabilities on

Catholics and on Protestant Nonconformists. In 1823, the House of Commons passed a resolution for the gradual abolition of slavery, although it had been modified to take more note of the planters' interests. The Society for the Mitigation and Gradual Abolition of Slavery throughout the British Dominions was also founded that year, with Thomas Clarkson and William Wilberforce, the stalwarts of the earlier campaign against the slave trade, being made vice-presidents. This pressure was mirrored in the West Indies by slaves keen to gain their freedom: some believed that their owners were withholding concessions granted by the Crown.

Slave-owners, in turn, showed no desire to end slavery and, aside from its continued profitability, the West Indies' plantation economy remained an important asset base. Furthermore, the limited convertibility of plantation assets did not encourage the movement of investment into other activities: too much money was tied up in mortgages and annuities that were difficult to liquidate in a hurry. Yet, profitability was affected by the rise in the cost of acquiring and sustaining the workforce, a rise that in part was due to moves against the slave trade and in part to market forces. Indeed, as an aspect of costs, by the time of emancipation, the material consumption levels of the slaves were similar to those of manual workers in Britain,[4] although this point, which was made by supporters of slavery, does not extenuate it as the primary problem was not ill-treatment (treatment could, and did, vary) but, rather, the absence of freedom, civic status and rights to family and self. A similar point can be made about coerced labour throughout history.

The determination by slave-owners to control the situation led to criticism in Britain.[5] In 1830–1, in Jamaica there was talk by the slave-owners of secession from British rule in response to Abolitionist pressure in Britain and legislation aimed at the owners' powers of discipline over their slaves. Racism, indeed, remained strong in the Caribbean world. It was brutally displayed in the harsh suppression of slave rebellions, as on

Barbados in 1816 (Bussa's rebellion), in Demerara in 1823, and on Jamaica in 1831–2, the Baptist War, the last in part a rebellion in response to pro-slavery agitation among part of the white population and the largest slave rising in the British West Indies.[6] The rising led to reprisals by the militia including the burning down of mission buildings, notably the Baptist chapel at Salter's Hill. Such action was part of the attempt by both sides to weaken their opponents in practical terms and symbolically.[7] Justifying the rebellion led supporters of Abolition to press for emancipation at once, rather than for gradual improvement.

Opposition to the continuation of slavery

There was also opposition to slavery elsewhere. In the French colony of Martinique, there was a major rising in 1831. There were also slave risings in Virginia in 1800 and 1831, Louisiana in 1811 and Cuba in 1812.[8] Abolitionists argued that opposition to slavery by the slaves was undermining the system and that, to avoid bloodshed, it would be much better if it was abolished legally,[9] but, in practice, organized opposition by the slaves was limited, in large part due to the coercive context in which slaves were held and the difficulties of coordinating opposition. Thanks largely to the power of planters, but also to measures such as state-sponsored and large-scale slave patrols to recapture escaped slaves in the USA,[10] control over the slaves was maintained by coercion without the need for any full-scale suppression of slave activity. Nat Turner's rebellion in Virginia in 1831, in which Turner presented himself as deploying his men like soldiers, was the most prominent slave rising in the USA, and it was swiftly suppressed. Nine years earlier, Denmark Vesey's planned slave revolt in Charleston was betrayed and pre-empted, although evidence for the plans has been questioned on the grounds that they were devised to give credence to the idea of a slave revolt. From that point of view, it is instructive to note that such a rising did not occur, but other recent work has argued the case for a real conspiracy.[11] At any event, the lack of slave revolts thereafter in the South is striking.

Coercion took many forms. The American determination to end slave flight from Georgia to Florida lay behind the costly Seminole Wars (1817–18, 1835–42, 1855–8), as the Seminole Native Americans in Florida provided refuge for escaped slaves.[12] Indeed, in the second war, an armistice came to an end and Seminole resistance revived in 1837 when the Americans allowed slavers to enter Florida and seize Seminole and black people. In contrast, an important success for the Americans was obtained in 1838 when Major-General Thomas Jesup announced that black slaves who abandoned the Seminole and joined the Americans would become free, which cost the Seminole 400 black fighters. Religious zeal played an important role in slave risings in this period, for example on Jamaica and around Bahia in Brazil between 1808 and 1835: the 1835 Bahia revolt was of Muslim slaves and freedmen.[13]

Opposition to slavery was also expressed in murders, flight and suicide, each of which was frequent. In part, they reflected harsh conditions, such as in north-east Brazil, where conditions remained hard and often violent, particularly in the sugar and coffee plantations. Food and clothing for the slaves was inadequate, and the work was remorseless, hard and long. Death rates among slaves were high, in part due to epidemic diseases, but also partly due to the work regime which was not abated in harsh weather. There was also a gender dimension to the appalling conditions. The conditions of work for pregnant women led to many stillbirths (as also in the British West Indies[14]), while, through poor diet, mothers lacked sufficient milk. However, underlining the variety of slave life, the 1872 census showed that 30 per cent of Brazilian slaves worked in towns, and conditions were better there, as again was more generally true in the history of slavery. A more humane treatment of rural slaves in Brazil only began in about 1870 when their price rose.[15]

The end of slavery in the British Empire

In Britain, Abolitionist tactics reprised those earlier directed against the slave trade, with press agitation, public meetings, pressure on Parliament and a prominent role for women.[16] Thus, a large meeting in Exeter on 3 April 1833 supported Abolitionist petitions, pressing for nothing short of 'the immediate and entire extinction of slavery'; the proceedings were reported at length in the *Western Times* of 6 April. A week later, the paper noted that the Anti-Slavery Committee in London had told the Devon Society that pressure on the government had to be maintained in order to indicate public concern, and that there had been between 1,500 and 1,600 people present in a public meeting in Exeter, including a 'great number of elegantly dressed ladies who could not procure seats'. The 1831 census figure for the city was 28,242.[17]

Concern about the plight of Christian slaves, especially those who were fully converted by Methodist missionaries, who often established schools for slaves, made the issue more potent, as did increased scepticism that the end of the slave trade would lead to the end of slavery. Instead of confidence that the situation would gradually improve, pressure grew for immediate emancipation. Moreover, reports of the slave rising in Jamaica in 1831–2, and of the brutality of its suppression helped make slavery appear undesirable and redundant as the colonists clearly could not keep order.

The Whig ministry that pushed through the Great Reform Act of 1832 that revised the electoral franchise (right to vote) to the benefit of the middle class also passed the Emancipation Act of 1833, with slaves emancipated from 1 August 1834, Emancipation Day. Influenced by Whig evangelicals, many Whig candidates had included an anti-slavery platform in their electoral addresses and Whig victories in the general elections of the early 1830s were crucial. The bill received the royal assent on 28 August 1833. Charles, Second Earl Grey, the Prime Minister, had been Foreign Secretary and Leader of the House of Commons when the slave trade had been abolished in 1807 and he had opened the key debate in the House of Commons on 23 February 1807. Thus, emancipation was an aspect of the more general process by which the Whigs, returned to power, replayed their earlier aspirations.

The Reform Act of 1832 contributed directly to this legislation as many seats with small electorates traditionally occupied by members of the West Indies interest group were abolished and replaced by constituencies that favoured Abolition. These seats tended to be large or medium-sized industrial or shipping towns, especially those with many Nonconformists. The debate on Abolition itself did not follow party lines, however. Most of the (opposition) Tories did not play a role in the debate nor vote against the government. Instead, the West Indies interest played a crucial role and, accepting the weakness of the cause of slavery, much of the debate revolved around the financial issue of compensation. However reprehensible in modern terms, the slave-owners had a good pragmatic case for the generous compensation they pressed for and received, rather than the loan originally proposed. The compensation, distributed by the Commissioners of Slave Compensation, was raised to a grant of £20 million, which, in the short term, strengthened the plantation owners' position in the West Indies by freeing up capital, although at least half of the compensation was paid to beneficiaries in Britain.[18]

Furthermore, initially, as a transition, all slaves aged over six were to become apprenticed labourers, obliged to work for their former masters for forty-five hours a week: field workers for six years, and others for four, although a clause forbade the punishment of former slaves. This system reflected uncertainty about the practicality of emancipation, an uncertainty also seen in the preferential tariff granted to sugar imported from the British West Indies, a measure to support the economy against the competition from the colonies of other powers that maintained slavery. In the end, this interim labourer system, which led to protests from many former slaves, was ended in August 1838, so that about 800,000 slaves were now free.

Abolition elsewhere

This was far from the end of the story as far as Britain was concerned. The already-strong opposition to the slave trade elsewhere was joined by action directed against slavery in other countries. Moreover, anti-slavery agitation continued after the Emancipation Act, with the British and Foreign Anti-Slavery Society founded in 1839 being particularly influential. World Anti-Slavery Conventions were held in London in 1840 and 1843. The former, held at the Freemasons' Hall, was in part a celebration of the British role in the movement. Addressed by Henry Beckford, a freed slave from Jamaica, it was presided over by Thomas Clarkson, who had played such a major role in the anti-slavery struggle from 1787 on, and the scene, with Clarkson speaking, was commemorated in a major picture by Benjamin Haydon which hangs in the National Portrait Gallery. This painting was an aspect of the public affirmation and commemoration that were important to Abolitionism.

Whereas the slave trade was under great pressure by 1840, slavery was still well established, including around much of the Atlantic and in the Islamic world.[19] Serfdom continued in Russia, as did slavery in Bessarabia, the province annexed from the Ottoman empire in 1812; it was only abolished there in 1861. In 1840, Brazil, Cuba, the USA and the French colonies were all major slave economies, producing valuable goods for export, and were attractive to slave traders. Many slaves worked in Brazil in the booming coffee industry, which benefited greatly from increased demand from the growing population of Europe and the American North, as did the Cuban sugar industry and cotton production in the American South, which was particularly important for British manufacturers. The relationship between the dynamic industrial economies of Europe and the northern states of America, and plantation agriculture was an aspect of the linkage between globalization and involuntary labour movements, whether of slaves or of other forms of coerced labour.

Imports of sugar from Cuba, as of coffee from Brazil and cotton from America, ensured that British consumers were heavily dependent on slave production, which led to anger from Abolitionists in Britain. In Cuba, which, like Brazil, was a low-cost producer, slavery remained important to the sugar monoculture of much of the economy, especially in western Cuba. The sugar economy depended on American investment, markets and technology, while the British embrace of free trade greatly helped Cuban production by ending the preferential measures that had ensured markets for sugar from Britain's colonies. Some British plantation owners indeed emigrated to Cuba.

In contrast to the British in 1840, the French government banned a world anti-slavery conference planned for Paris in 1842. For France, as for other slave societies such as the American South, the economic problems that affected the British West Indies appeared to demonstrate the continued value of coerced labour. So also did the British acceptance of indentured Indians into the region, which was not a remedy open to the French, Spaniards or Americans. Indeed, emancipation seemed an uneconomic risk.[20] The case of the British West Indies thus fortified the lesson learned from Haiti in that, if the latter apparently demonstrated the serious, destructive and bloody risks posed by Abolitionism and independence, the former indicated the problems that would follow from Abolitionism and continued imperial control. A different, but supportive, lesson for continued slavery also apparently came from the gradual emancipation in the Northern states of the USA after independence from British rule, as this emancipation was followed both by a rise in white racism and by parlous circumstances for many of the freed black people, who tended to be at the bottom of the social pyramid and who were disproportionately present in prisons.

At the same time, the Abolitionist cause remained a potent one linking both sides of the Atlantic,[21] rather as Puritanism had done in the seventeenth century. Thus, *Clotel: Or The President's Daughter: A Narrative of Slave Life in the United States* (1853) by William Wells Brown, a former slave, the first novel published by an African American, was published in London and aimed at a British audience, and sought to deploy religious arguments of the universality of divine and Christian benevolence. Moreover, American Methodism had split in 1844, with Northern Methodists looking to Britain.

Anti-slavery, however, was less important or popular in most of Continental Europe, whether in Catholic France or the Protestant Netherlands,[22] than in Britain. In part, this was due to the lack of a public politics comparable in form or content to Britain. There was not much of an Abolitionist movement in Spain in the late eighteenth and early nineteenth century, and even the liberal Cortes (national assembly) twice rejected measures, in 1811 and 1813. A genuine Abolitionist movement did not spring up in Spain until the 1830s. Slavery in peninsular Spain was abolished in 1837, although not in the Spanish colonies until the 1870s and 1880s. A link between religious persecution and slavery was clear to British Abolitionists. Russell commented in 1862, 'Persecution for religion and the slave trade are both odious to Britons, and both dear to Spaniards. So much the worse for them.'[23]

In France, the Société de la Morale Chrétienne, founded in 1821, was small, and a disproportionately high percentage of its members were Protestants, a marginal group politically. However, in the more liberal July monarchy that followed the 1830 revolution, laws were passed in 1833 ending the branding and mutilation of slaves and giving free black people political and civil rights. Effective action against the French slave trade was also taken in part because the new government was readier to ignore popular complaints about British pressure but also due to Anglo-French diplomatic cooperation over other topics.

The end of slavery in the French colonies, including French Africa, principally Algeria and Senegal, followed in 1848. The British example was important in weakening French slavery, not least because it provided French slaves with new opportunities for escape to British colonies where there was no slavery, and the intermixing of French and British colonies in the West Indies was significant. The increased influence of reforming middle-class circles was significant in France, but the decisive pressure came from a small group of writers and politicians, especially Victor Schoelcher, who argued for immediate emancipation, rather than the slow processes that had long been favoured, such as helping slaves towards purchasing their freedom.

There have been efforts to ascribe abolition to slave unrest in the French colonies, but this argument is contentious and distracts attention from the crucial metropolitan context of decision-making, not least the establishment in 1848 of the Second Republic which passed the necessary legislation. However, major uprisings in Martinique and Guadeloupe in 1848 certainly speeded the application of emancipation, and the argument that revolt was a possibility had been pushed hard by French Abolitionists.[24] As in Britain and Denmark, there was compensation for the slave-owners.

In 1848, slavery in the Danish West Indian islands (now the American Virgin Islands) was abolished when the threat of rebellion among the slave population forced the Danish Governor-General to free the slaves. Sweden had done so the previous year for its tiny West Indian colony of St Barthélemy, while much of formerly Spanish America abolished slavery between 1842 and 1855. In Europe, slavery was abolished in Moldavia in 1855 and in Wallachia in 1856. An earlier attempt to do so in 1848, during the Year of Revolutions, had been reversed when the liberal regime was suppressed.

Emancipation in the United States

Yet, these were not key territories in the world of slavery, which, instead, saw significant expansion in extent and scale in mid-century, in the USA, Cuba and Brazil. Texas' independence from Mexico in 1836 was followed by the reversing of earlier Mexican attempts to limit the scope of slavery, and in 1840 the immigration of free black people to Texas was restricted. The spread of cotton cultivation led to a major increase in the number of slaves in Texas from 443 in 1825 and about 5,000 in 1836 to 58,161 in the 1850 census and 182,566 in the 1860 census. The annexation of Texas to the USA in 1845 was opposed by the American Whigs, who were suspicious of the likely consequences of increasing the number of slave states.[25] From that perspective, Texas' entry as a single state, rather than, as had been feared, a number of (slave) states, was very important. The annexation led to war with Mexico (1846–8), which resulted in America gaining vast territories between Texas and the Pacific. The status of slavery in the newly acquired territories became a key topic of controversy. Southern politicians saw off the argument that it should be illegal and, instead, a compromise in 1850 left California, a new state, free. However, slavery was to be legal in the New Mexico and Utah territories, subject to popular sovereignty in the shape of the settlers, as well as in the as-yet-unorganized territory that in 1907 became Oklahoma.

The fate of slavery in the West, however, remained highly contentious, with extensions to the lands opened to slavery provided by the Kansas-Nebraska Act of 1854 and the Dred Scott decision of the Supreme Court in 1857, which determined that slave-owners could take their slaves into any territory. George, Fourth Earl of Clarendon, the British Foreign Secretary, was in no doubt that these issues would push slavery to the fore, although he got the eventual outcome wrong:

The Yankees seem to have got a good large internal bone to pick. The Nebraska and Kansas affair will I suppose bring the

whole slavery question under discussion again, and in a manner
the least likely to lead to an amicable solution. It may *threaten*
the union, but I have no idea that anything in our time will
dissolve it ... much bluster and insult and menace will
stimulate the sense of danger, and then some compromise will
be patched up.[26]

Southern advocates of slavery, such as Jefferson Davis, later
the President of the Confederacy, saw it as a way to guarantee
a labour force in the West that would bring prosperity,
notably by making irrigated agriculture feasible, and thus
overcoming the constraints of geography, as well as providing
the security of continuous white-dominated settlement and
thus lessening the power of the Native Americans. These were
themes in his speech to the Senate on 14 February 1850 and
his annual report as Secretary of War in 1853.[27] The demands
of irrigation in the pre-mechanized age were a frequent reason
for controlled labour, including slavery. Slavery and race also
played a role in American foreign policy, with interest in
gaining Cuba from Spain linked to a determination to
strengthen Southern slavery, while there was also talk of the
need to 'put down completely the black population of Haiti'
by annexing, at least, much of the state,[28] and of reviving the
slave trade.[29] The American determination not to let British
ships search those carrying the American flag for slaves was
very important to the continuation of the (illegal) slave trade
to Cuba.

The admission of California as a free state in 1850 gave the
free states a majority in the Senate, and the minority status of
the South in the Union was a key feature of the sectional
controversy of the 1850s. A sense of being under challenge
ensured that Southern secession was frequently threatened in
the 1850s, before the 1860 election of Abraham Lincoln led to
secession becoming policy. Abraham Lincoln, the Republican
candidate, won none of the Southern states in an election in
which effective national parties no longer existed. Lincoln

intended to ban slavery in the federal territories, but secession-
ism pushed the agenda of national integrity immediately to the
fore and, with Lincoln determined to use force to resist the use
of force against federal positions, led to civil war.

The variation in the prevalence of slavery in the South was
linked to the degree of support for the war, although many
who fought for the South did not own slaves and were more
motivated by a sense of the need to defend communities,
culture and the states' rights that were believed to protect
both. These states' rights, however, were defined in part in
terms of the defence of slavery, a defence in which self-
interest, regional identity, a sense of imperilled masculinity
and religious conviction all played a role. Indeed, Richard,
Second Lord Lyons, the British envoy, noted that 'The
orthodox notion seems to be that slavery is a divine
institution.'[30]

Paranoia also played a role. Many Southerners were
convinced that John Brown's shortlived seizure of the federal
arsenal at Harper's Ferry in 1859, which was designed to
generate terror among slaveholders, was the first stage of a war
on slavery, and revealed the true intentions of Abolitionists.
Lyons captured the sense of surprised outrage and alarm to
which the Abolitionist attack gave rise: 'The extraordinary
excitement and alarm which exist in Virginia since the
Harper's Ferry affair, are not very confirmatory of the
confidence which the planters profess to feel in the "happy
and attached peasantry", by which euphonious appellation
they love to designate their slaves. There have been alarms and
movements of militia and volunteers almost daily.'[31] Fears of
an Abolitionist plot in Texas in late 1860 helped lead to
vigilante action and encouraged backing for secession.[32]

The outcome of the American Civil War (1861–5) and the
resulting fate of over four million American slaves were very
much a matter of chance, in the shape of the progress of the
conflict. Had the Confederacy won independence, slavery
might not only have been preserved, but might have expanded

or been sustained both in the West Indies and in areas contiguous with the Confederacy, principally parts of Mexico. Palmerston was concerned both that slavery would spread and that the slave trade would be revived either by the Confederates or by Southern adventurers establishing their own state in Mexico. He considered offering recognition of the South as an independent state in return for a promise to prevent the slave trade.[33]

By the autumn of 1862, when Robert E. Lee launched his first invasion of the North, Emperor Napoleon III of France and William Gladstone, the British Chancellor of the Exchequer, were pressing Palmerston to intervene and recognize the Confederacy. Especially given General George B. McClellan's maladroit previous performance, the Union victory at Antietam on 17 September 1862 was fortuitous, and depended in part on the accidental Union discovery of a copy of Lee's general orders just before the battle.

Initially, the Union had made no attempt to abolish slavery, both because Lincoln feared the impact of emancipation on sections of Northern opinion, especially in loyal slaveholding border states such as his native Kentucky, and because, like many others, he hoped that avoiding a pledge to support emancipation would weaken Southern backing for secession. In November 1862, the American envoy in Paris told the French foreign minister that 'neither principle nor policy will induce the United States to encourage a "servile war" or prompt the slave to cut the throat of his master or his master's family',[34] a clear reference to deep-seated racial anxieties.

After Antietam, in contrast, as part of the hardening of Union war goals and methods resulting from the sense that victory was more distant and conciliation not working, Lincoln heeded radical Republicans, and the Union became committed to the emancipation of the slaves in Confederate states, in other words not in the loyal border states of Delaware, Maryland, Kentucky and Missouri.[35] Although emancipation would clearly strengthen Southern resolve,[36] the new goal was seen as a way to weaken the Southern economy, and thus war effort, as well as providing a clear purpose to maintain Northern morale and a means to assuage the sin that was leading a wrathful God to punish America. The international law on war also influenced the Emancipation Proclamation.[37]

Moreover, the international audience was in Lincoln's mind. When, in April 1862, the Lincoln administration agreed to a treaty accepting a mutual right of search for ten years, a measure for which the British had long been pressing,[38] this pleased British opinion, including that of the government. The transatlantic Abolitionist cause rose to a height during the Civil War, with Abolitionists seeing their calling as a universal one. Thus, the prominent British Abolitionist George Thomas, who was very well received when he lectured in Massachusetts in September 1864 on behalf of the cause, wrote: 'On the side of the North the battle must be fought upon the very highest moral grounds and with the most uncompromising fidelity to the principles of equal absolute impartial, universal liberty.'[39] Such a universal quality was central to Christian ideas of political action because they were moralized as issues of the human condition. As with those Enlightenment strands that were more secular in character, the universalism was heavily qualified in practice, but it still remained highly important as a way to analyse the world.

Victory for the Union led to the end of slavery in the loyal as well as the Confederate states, with the Thirteenth Amendment to the Constitution, passed in 1865, resulting in the freeing of about four million slaves. The end of slavery in the USA made the earlier British emancipation appear brave and prescient, which was not how it had earlier appeared to British and American commentators focused on the difficulties it had given rise to.[40] Had slavery continued in the Confederacy, then this emancipation would have had a different significance.

The success of the Union also transformed the diplomatic position of the free-black states in the West Indies. Jefferson had refused to extend diplomatic recognition to Haiti when it won independence in 1804, in part due to his wish for friendly relations with France, but largely as a product of racism. A black state proved too much for the influential slaveholding interests, for black republicanism was perceived as a serious threat to the racial order in America. It was not until most of the American slave states had disenfranchised themselves by secession that the independence of Haiti and Liberia were recognized: in April 1862, Congress authorized the dispatch of American envoys. Opposition to recognition then was led by Senator Garrett Davis of Kentucky, who claimed to be able to imagine no sight so dreadful as that of 'a full-blooded negro' in Washington society. Diplomatic relations with the Dominican Republic followed in 1866.[41]

Moreover, the 1862 treaty with Britain took the protection of the American flag away from slavers and hit the slave trade to Cuba. The Civil War also led to the end of the provision of American capital for the slave trade.

The Civil War, therefore, was crucially significant to the fate of slavery throughout the New World, although it was not the sole cause of emancipation that decade. Portugal, the colonial power in Angola, Mozambique, Portuguese Guinea, the Cape Verde Islands, Madeira and the Azores, had embraced emancipation in 1861, followed, in 1863, by the Dutch, who still had a large plantation economy in Surinam, as well as islands in the Caribbean and a developing empire in the East Indies. Surinam bordered Brazil. Subsequently, Spain abolished slavery in its colonies, Puerto Rico in 1873 and Cuba in 1886: emancipation gradually began in 1870. These measures were taken by the Liberal governments that dominated the Spanish Restoration monarchy from 1874. The Liberals also introduced universal male suffrage in Spain in 1890. As in Britain in the early 1830s and France in 1848, support for the extension of the franchise was linked to abolition to slavery.

The end of slavery in Brazil

Meanwhile, emancipation in the USA left Brazil as the leading slave society, although its import of slaves had ended in 1850, to all intents and purposes. Longstanding British efforts to make Brazil enforce the observance of the treaties relating to the slave trade had greatly exacerbated relations. Brazil sought the repeal of the Aberdeen Act of 1845 under which British warships pursued slavers into Brazilian waters, an Act that compromised Brazilian sovereignty, but Palmerston strongly opposed repeal. Moreover, in 1860 William Christie, the British envoy, noted that there was no sign that the Brazilian government intended to end slavery.[42] British pressure for action[43] helped lead to a breach in diplomatic relations in 1863.

Yet, influential opinion in Brazil moved against slavery. Indeed, prior to 1888, the majority of black people in Brazil were already free, in part because of increased manumission under the Law of the Free Womb or Rio Branco law of 1871, which stated that all future children born to slave mothers would become free from the age of twenty-one (a clause that led to false registrations by owners); in addition, slaves were allowed to purchase their freedom. Slavery was regarded in influential circles, especially in the expanding cities, as a cause of unrest (which indeed increased in the 1880s) and a source of national embarrassment and relative backwardness. The Brazilian Society against Slavery was founded in 1880. As part of the process by which New World settler societies were culturally dependent on the Old World, the Brazilian elite looked to Europe to validate their sense of progress, and were affected by the extent to which slavery was increasingly presented as an uncivilized characteristic of barbaric societies and as incompatible with civil liberty. The British role was important here.

Moreover, the combination of the end of the slave trade with economic expansion meant that slavery was no longer able to supply Brazil's labour needs, including those in the

traditional centre of slavery, the north-east, and this situation
helped make slavery seem anachronistic. Not only was
quantity of labour an issue, but so was labour type, as a
growing need for artisans was not one that could be met from
the traditional Brazilian slave economy. The situation in
Brazil was an aspect of the degree to which modernization led
to the demise of slavery, not only culturally and ideologically,
but also for economic reasons. However, at the same time,
Western economic growth had helped provide the demand,
finance and technological innovation that kept slavery a major
option, and this is a reminder of the ambivalent relationship
between modernization and slavery. Nevertheless, as the role
of slavery in the Brazilian economy, and of slaves in net
capital, declined, so it seemed anachronistic. As a result,
slave-owners became increasingly isolated, with free labour
becoming more important, even in some plantation areas such
as São Paulo, although there was also a continued preference
for slave labour in others. The end of the slave trade had led
to higher slave prices and a concentration of ownership,[44] and
these factors reduced political support for slavery, which thus,
indirectly, was due to the end of the trade.

In 1884, two Brazilian provinces emancipated slaves,
creating free labour zones, and in 1885 all slaves over sixty
were freed. Furthermore, increased numbers of slaves fled,
many to the cities, such as Rio de Janeiro, so that by 1887 there
were fewer than one million slaves: only about 5 per cent of
the Brazilian population. There was considerable support for
slave flight, with much of the populace as well as the bulk of
the authorities unwilling to support the owners. This contrasted markedly with the situation in the antebellum USA, a
contrast that was very important to the subsequent history of
the two countries. Because, in Brazil the slave-owners were
without a mass domestic constituency, their eventual isolated
position was more similar to that of counterparts in the
Caribbean than those in the American South.

In Brazil, the military was not keen on hunting escaped

slaves, while there was no equivalent to the separatism based on slavery seen in the USA, a contrast that was important to the largely non-violent nature of Brazilian Abolitionism. There was no equivalent to the situation in Cuba, where the Ten Years War of 1868–78, an unsuccessful independence struggle against Spanish rule, had seen partial abolition in rebel areas, which encouraged the move for gradual abolition in the island as a whole. Whereas in the American South there was a stress on regarding white society as the people – an emphasis that was to encourage racial exclusion, whether slave-based or not, as a form and focus of Southern cultural identity – in Brazil the emphasis, in contrast, was on a multicultural society. In Brazil the 1888 Golden Law, passed by an overwhelming majority in Parliament, freed the remaining slaves, about three-quarters of a million people in total, without compensation to the owners. This law helped legalize the situation caused by large-scale flight, and has also been seen as an attempt to retain workers on the land,[45] rather like the system initially introduced in the British colonies as an aspect of emancipation.

The continuation of forced labour

The end of slavery in the Western world, however, did not completely transform labour relations, whether in Britain's colonies or in other former slave societies such as Haiti, Brazil and the American South.[46] Control over labour continued and did so irrespective of the racial situation. Most notably, in Haiti, the plantation economy producing for European markets survived black independence. Slavery had gone, but the black elite who ran the state used forced labour to protect their plantations from the preference of people to live as peasant proprietors. Thus, the pressures of the global economy and the attractions of cash crops selling into international markets triumphed over the potential consequences of independence.[47] At the same time, racism was seen in the hostile American response to Haiti from 1804 until the Civil War, and also played a role in France's harsh treatment of its former colony, with military and economic pressure employed to force an onerous compensation that hit living standards and social capital in Haiti. In turn, as the Abolitionist Stephen Cave noted in 1849, 'the miserable failure of emancipation in Haiti' was 'the favourite theme of all advocates of slavery'.[48]

In the British colonies, as elsewhere, many former slaves were pressed into continuing to work in sugar production.[49] Legal systems were employed in order to limit the mobility and freedom of former slaves, for example by restricting emigration and also what was presented as vagrancy, which, in practice, could mean a failure to engage in the world of work on approved terms. Rents were also used to control labour and to reduce labour costs. Resistance included strikes as well as workers leaving the plantations. The difficult situation for workers in the British colonies after 1838 undercuts any simple attempt to create a contrast between slavery and freedom,[50] although, on the other hand, very different notions of liberty were involved. Yet, the conditions of labour for slaves and ex-slaves reflected far more than the legal situation.[51] Across the world, for most former slaves, there was no sweeping change in their lives, and many remained dependent in some form or other on their ex-masters or on new masters, and could be treated brutally by the government and military, as in Cuba where black workers suffered disproportionately from government action and military repression.

Furthermore, despite the abolition of the slave trade and slavery, labour continued to flow to the colonies. Former slaves tended to take up small-scale independent farming, on provision grounds, rather than work on plantations, and this helped lead to demands for fresh labour in the colonies. In place of slaves, the British West Indies, especially Trinidad, British Guiana (now Guyana) and other colonies received plentiful cheap Indian indentured labour, although, despite the availability of this labour, sugar production declined.[52]

Moreover, the Indian Mutiny of 1857–9 led to the idea of transporting captured rebels in order to help cultivate sugar.[53] Critics claimed that the indentured labour systems, which were also employed in Mauritius, Surinam, Cuba and the French Caribbean, represented the continuation of the slave trade in its latter stages, not least due to the coercive character of these systems. In Cuba, indentured Chinese workers were treated harshly and found that, although 'free', they could not buy their way out of their contractual obligations. In the Pacific, the kidnap of islanders for slave labour involved brutality and killing, leading in 1872 to the Pacific Islanders' Protection (Kidnapping) Act.[54]

Meanwhile, the very flexibility of economic service, labour subjugation and social practices aided the continuation of systems of labour control. Moreover, as with slavery, these systems encompassed the movement of coerced labour. Thus, in India, where the British formally abolished slavery by the Indian Slavery Act of 1843, which was enforced by the Penal Code of 1861 making holding a slave a crime, it continued in a number of forms. Investigating the situation, the British concluded that slavery was not really in existence or at least, was not all that bad, which was politically convenient for them. In practice, there was unpaid labour, hereditary bond slaves and other forms of rural servitude, as well as children sold into slavery, girls sold (by dowry) into marriages that were little better than domestic servitude, girls sold to temples as *devadasis* (ritual dancers and prostitutes), and other forms of slavery.[55] Well into the nineteenth century, the servants of Europeans in India frequently included slaves, who were bought and sold, and left in legacies, although also commonly paid small amounts. Many were 'Portuguese', meaning Indian Christians and/or mixed-race migrants from Portuguese areas. Even among orthodox Muslims, the notion that slaves were properly secured by conquest alone remained very far from being observed.

In Russia, however, where, in 1861, Tsar Alexander II

emancipated the serfs, the continuation of practices of labour control was lessened by the opportunities opened up for workers by industrialization and urbanization. The emancipation of the serfs was seen by Abolitionists elsewhere as a key move in their struggle and led the Union during the Civil War to hope for Russian support.

The emphasis on liberty in the political ideology of the period made coercion, such as the kidnap of Pacific islanders, unacceptable; although if such violence was not employed and only the nature of the work was exploitative then the situation ceased to arouse such opprobrium. This change in response was related to that from the *ancien régime* system of estates, which could accommodate the legal condition of slavery, to a nineteenth-century situation, certainly in the West, in which increasingly universal (at least for male) rights were linked to a concept of classes which could not accept such a differentiation. In non-Western areas where the system of estates continued it was easier to explain the continuance of slavery.

The aftermath in the United States

Dependence on new or former masters was the case for many former slaves in the USA, although a new order had certainly been seen with and immediately after Union victory. Large numbers of slaves had escaped as the advance of Union forces brought disruption to the South, not least with General Sherman's advance across Georgia in 1864. The recruitment of all-black regiments for the Union army in the second half of the Civil War, numbering more than 120,000 men, was both a major operational help to the Union, and also a symbol of what to the Confederacy was indeed a total war. The symbolic power of black troops was shown in 1865 when the forces that occupied Charleston, the site of the outbreak of the war, included black troops recruited from former Carolina slaves.

Union victory in 1865 led initially to the overthrow of the previous system of exclusion, subordination and oppression.

In 1866, over the veto of President Andrew Johnson, who sought a rapid return to normality through the conciliation of the South, Congress passed the Civil Rights Act giving full citizenship to all born or naturalized in the United States, and voting rights to all male citizens. Black men thus gained legal equality. The provisions of this legislation became the Fourteenth Amendment, which was ratified in 1868. Thus the radicalizing nature of the war made it possible to envisage improvements on the provisions decreed by the Founding Fathers. Moreover, the Reconstruction Acts of 1867 dissolved the Southern state governments, which had passed racist 'black Codes' designed to limit the effect of slave emancipation; and, instead, reintroduced federal control, which gave the army the task of preserving this control against local opposition. Emancipation also affected the slaves owned by Native American tribes, such as the slave-owning Choctaw, which signed treaties with the Confederacy and fought for it.

The army, however, was confronted by the strength of white Southern belief in their own superiority, and the foundation of the Ku Klux Klan, a Confederate veterans' movement, in 1866, was followed by several thousand lynchings, although not all were by the Klan.[56] The military presence was modest, and the small army anyway was not in a position to support reconstruction once it was challenged by widespread violence against black people. By 1877, the Republican governments in the South had been overthrown, in part by the threat of mob violence, in every state bar Florida, Louisiana and South Carolina, and it was only in these states that the troops sent to support reconstruction remained. The situation was resolved as the result of a political compromise following the disputed presidential election of 1876. The returns from the three states were crucial, and the Republican candidate, Rutherford P. Hayes, won the election only in return for withdrawing the troops, which, in turn, led to the fall of the three Republican state governments.

Black people were left to celebrate Emancipation, not least

with 'Juneteenth', a holiday marking the day in 1865 when General Gordon Granger arrived in Galveston to deliver the news of the Emancipation Proclamation. They, however, were very much second-class citizens in political, social and economic terms, a situation that persisted until the 1950s and 1960s, only ending when federal pressure resumed. The black population suffered from the decision of many of the remaining Southern elite to maintain a smaller and poorer agricultural society with oppressive labour relations in which they remained at the top of the socio-economic pyramid,[57] rather than to join the new industrial order whose urbanization and mechanization would threaten their superiority in the South. This decision accentuated regional divisions in America and contrasted with the willingness of much of the Russian elite to accept industrialization and, therefore, social mobility and urbanization. A much blunter demonstration of white control in the South was provided by the disproportionate number of black people in prison and the widespread use of penal labour, notably for public construction, in the late nineteenth and early twentieth century but also thereafter.

Change in the West Indies

The abolition of slavery played a major role in the crisis of the British plantation societies, which was particularly marked in Jamaica. Labour availability and discipline were crucial to the ability of estates to hold down costs, but the end of the apprenticeship system in 1838 was followed by large numbers of former slaves leaving the plantations, notably in Jamaica, Trinidad and British Guiana, in order to seek unsettled land for their own where they followed subsistence agriculture. This option was not available in smaller colonies, such as Antigua and Barbados, which lacked free land, and the estate system remained effective there. However, in the larger colonies, emancipation led to a fall in estate productivity and profitability, as, despite the possibilities offered by the adoption of steam power in the shape of steam milling, sugar production continued to be labour intensive. Free labour proved more expensive and less reliable than slaves, greatly increasing the operating costs.

Despite the introduction of large numbers of Indian indentured workers, the former plantation societies of the West Indies and British Guiana became far less important to the British economy. This was a process accentuated by the equalization of the sugar duties in 1846, under the Sugar Duties Act, a Free Trade measure in accordance with which protection for British sugar was progressively reduced until all duties on imported sugar were equalized in 1851.[58] The Act encouraged sugar imports into Britain from Brazil and Cuba, which hit the British colonies, as did growing competition from imports of European sugar beet.

As the exports of the former British plantation economies declined, so they were less able to attract investment, afford imports from Britain and elsewhere, and develop social capital; this had an impact on the living standards of the bulk of the population of these colonies. In 1815, the West Indies had been the leading market for British exports, but, by 1840, they had been passed by India, Australia and Canada, in that order, and the role of the West Indies in British shipping needs also diminished. The decline of the plantation economies indeed helped ensure that the share of the empire in British trade fell, although the expansion of trade with other countries outside the empire was also important. In the former slave colonies, the problems centred on slavery had changed, not ended, as was to be made clear in Jamaica by the harsh (and illegal) suppression of the Morant Bay uprising in 1865.

Similarly, in Brazil, the end of slavery hit the sugar economy of the north-east as a crucial aspect of a more general agrarian depression that affected the old order in Brazil, weakening the imperial monarchy. As a key aspect of the end of the old order, Brazil became a republic in 1889.

Development in Africa

In West Africa, the end of the transatlantic slave trade greatly affected those kingdoms that had derived wealth from it, helping the European imperialist 'Scramble for Africa' in the second half of the century. However, the end of the transatlantic slave trade also led to the development of export agriculture in parts of Atlantic Africa, particularly Angola, which represented a response to labour availability in Africa, but also a shift in the terms of Western trade with Africa, away from a willingness to pay for labour in the shape of slaves, and towards one to pay for it in the form of products. There continued indeed to be multiple overlaps between servitude and trade in the Atlantic African economy. The Portuguese colonial government tried to make Angola into a smaller version of Brazil, producing sugar and coffee for export, a policy that relied (illegally) on surreptitious slaving, but this policy was a failure. The Portuguese also sought to use indentured servants to grow cocoa on São Tomé. The turn to barely concealed '*servicaes*' was similar to the Caribbean use of indentured Indians.

Just as African states were, eventually, affected by the greater military power of the West, so African economies were, earlier, hit by its new economic power projection. In contrast to the eighteenth century, Western goods, especially textiles and metals, became available in larger and cheaper quantities thanks to the economies of scale brought by the use of steamships, which hit African industries and led both to the growth of primary production focused on the European market, for example of palm oil, and also to a rise in the slave trade within Africa. The latter was exploited for the last stages of the Atlantic slave trade and also for the Arab slave trade. Similarly, in South-East Asia, new economic opportunities encouraged slavery, for example with Thai slaving into Laos in order to help produce goods for sale to China and Singapore. This was a key instance of the vitality of slavery in the region in this period.[59]

The slave trade particularly increased in East Africa, seriously affecting much of the interior of the continent,[60] as the Arab penetration of sub-Saharan Africa developed. For example, links with the kingdom of Buganda in modern Uganda developed from 1844, and it became a major exporter of slaves, a process eased by the importance of slavery already for internal purposes, including public works. Arab-Swahili slave traders, notoriously Tibbu Tib west of the Great Lakes from the mid-1870s, benefited from and developed a far-flung system dependent on the sale of slaves, and they became more effective because they were well armed with modern guns. Slaves were also required for the porterage encouraged by the exploitation of the interior, notably the ivory trade.

The increase in the slave trade in East Africa reflected the slave-based plantation systems that developed on Africa's Indian Ocean coast, producing for example cloves, the export of which boomed from the 1810s to the 1840s. Furthermore, the export of slaves to the Islamic world, notably Arabia and the Persian Gulf, continued. Kilwa was the leading port in East Africa, with a major trade from there to the Persian Gulf, much of it handled by Omani merchants. Their profits helped finance economic activity which, in turn, produced a need for slave labour. Slaves to Arabia, in contrast, were moved relatively short distances, particularly from the Red Sea ports of Suakin and Massawa, which were fed by slave trading into Sudan and Ethiopia. In 1877, the captain of HMS *Philomel* estimated that up to 45,000 slaves were moved annually from North Africa across the Red Sea.[61]

Slave labour in East Africa was largely, as in the New World, plantation labour, but the situation was different in Arabia and the Persian Gulf. This serves as a reminder of the economics of slavery, and the variety of slave conditions, and therefore the slave experience. Slaves in Arabia and the Persian Gulf were a mobile labour force that was appropriate to different needs and used for many activities, but there was no dominance by large-scale institutions of the plantation type, although slaves were used for date plantations for Oman.

As slaving was largely brought to an end in the Atlantic in the 1860s, so the British struggle against it in East African waters became more prominent, with the Cape Squadron being allocated to the task, and, in 1864, merged with the East Indies Squadron. This struggle with Arab slavers was presented in an heroic light and fully covered in British publications, both newspapers and magazines. The naval presence expanded with time, with a significant force in the Red Sea from the 1870s. Moreover, the slaves of Indian traders in East Africa were confiscated by the British consul in 1860 as the traders were British subjects. Empire thus served as a way to enforce British norms.

Opposition to slavery was not restricted to the oceans, seas and coasts, but also encouraged moral activism towards Africa, especially hostility to the slave trade in Central and East Africa. This hostility had a number of consequences, including the development of a British presence in Zanzibar,[62] and a strengthening of the determination to blaze the trail for Christian grace and morality that was seen in the actions of, and response to, David Livingstone. He helped secure British pressure through the Bartle Frere mission to persuade Barghash ibn Said, the Sultan of Zanzibar, to outlaw the slave trade in 1873. Zanzibar, long linked by common rule to Oman, was a key centre in the slave trade to the Persian Gulf. HMS *London*, an old ship of the line, was sent to Zanzibar to enforce this, and the acquisition from Germany of Zanzibar itself as a protectorate in 1890, in exchange for the island of Heligoland in the North Sea, led to the end of the trade. The previous year, resistance in East Africa (now Tanzania) to German control by the Arab leader Abushiri ibn Salim had been overcome when his main base at Pangani was bombarded and captured.

Colonies for free Africans, many of them freed slaves, also developed. Sierra Leone, established by the British in 1787, was the first. Both the Committee for the Relief of the Black Poor and key government supporters appear to have been motivated in founding this colony by humanitarianism springing from Christian convictions, gratitude towards black Loyalists from the former North American colonies, and Abolitionist sympathies; and the settlement explicitly forbade slavery. The great majority of newspaper items covering the expedition were sympathetic in tone. Together with intermarriage and the good public response to the appeal for money to help poor black people, this suggests that racial hostility may have been less common than has often been assumed.[63] Subsequently, slaves freed by the Royal Navy were taken to Sierra Leone. In 1798, the Romantic poet Robert Southey praised the aspirations involved in the new settlement:

> They come to bid injustice cease
> They come with science and with peace,
> To proffer happiness.[64]

The British were not alone. In 1849, the French founded Libreville in Gabon for freed slaves.

The American equivalent, Liberia, in contrast, was an independent republic, originally established by an anti-slavery group, the American Colonization Society (founded in 1816 by a group of white people), as a home for freed American slaves – a policy distrusted by many American black people as a means to strengthen slavery.[65] Indeed, for many white Americans, freedom for black people was only acceptable at a distance from America, and they supported repatriation accordingly.[66] Backing for racial removal could align Abolitionist sympathies with a hostility to multiculturalism. After a successful recommendation for support to the governor of the neighbouring British colony of Sierra Leone,[67] the first freed American black settlers in Liberia landed in 1821, although once established they treated the local Africans harshly. Colonists were taken to Liberia by American warships.

In Africa, the treatment of slaves held within native society became more problematic as, first European power and influence increased, and secondly as the Europeans became colonial rulers across most of the continent. European concern mounted as knowledge about the African interior increased thanks to the publications of explorers, for example John Duncan's *Travels in Western Africa in 1845 and 1846* (1847) – works that played a role in the mobilization of opinion against slavery. The books of Henry Morton Stanley about his expeditions, especially the trans-African expeditions of 1874–9, had a greater impact, not least in presenting European civilization as the means to resist the damaging hold on Africa of the Arab-Swahili slave trade.[68]

The Europeans were committed to Abolition as part of the civilizing mission used to justify imperialism as progressive, and this belief was underlined by the Congress of Berlin in 1885, and by the Brussels Conference of International Powers in 1889–90. In dealing with the competing interests of European powers in Africa, the Berlin Conference, under British influence, declared that the maritime slave trade was forbidden by international law, and also that those operations that provided slaves for it should similarly be regarded as forbidden. The Brussels Conference issued the General Act of the Slave Trade Conference which sought to deal with legal issues hindering the total suppression of the slave trade and slavery. Already, in 1877, British pressure had obliged Egypt to sign the Anglo-Egyptian Slave Trade Convention while General Charles Gordon appointed Governor-General of Sudan as the Khedive (ruler) of Egypt, sought to suppress the slave trade, only to resign in failure in 1879. British control of Egypt from 1882 led to more action, with Mahmud Tawfiq, the Khedive of Egypt signing a treaty that year,[69] and there were additional conventions in 1889 and 1895. Moreover, a convention with the Ottoman empire, which had had to turn to Britain in 1878 for protection against Russian expansionism, was concluded in 1880, although it was not ratified until 1883.[70] This convention prohibited the import and export of slaves into Ottoman territories, which included the crucial territory of the Hejaz on the Arabian coast of the Red Sea, a territory that included key routes between Sudan and the Middle East; already, in 1857, British pressure had led to an Ottoman *firman* abolishing the trade there.

This civilizing European mission, however, risked offending local vested interests that were seen as crucial to the stability of imperial control. Thus, pressure against slavery contributed to the overthrow of Egyptian control in Sudan by the Mahdists in the early 1880s, culminating in the killing of General George Gordon in 1885 when Khartoum, the capital, was stormed before a British relief expedition could arrive. Moreover, Emin Pasha (born Eduard Schnitzer), the Governor of the Equatorial (southern) province of Sudan, who had sought to end slavery there, had to be rescued by the Emin Pasha Relief Expedition (1887–9) organized by Henry Morton Stanley.

The suppression of the Mahdist movement in Sudan required a major military effort in which the British took the leading role, although there was also Egyptian participation. Khartoum was captured in the aftermath of General Kitchener's sweeping victory at Omdurman on 2 September 1898, and in November 1899 opposition was largely brought to an end when the Khalifa Abdullahi, the Mahdist leader, was defeated and killed by a British cavalry force at Umm Diwaykarat. This conquest was followed by action against the slave trade and slavery in an attempt to end both, with the Closed Districts Ordinance banning Arabs from the south.

Paradoxically, the slave trade and slavery therefore were ended, or at least curtailed as the ability of Western states to project power into the African interior became stronger. The French, for example, expanded their strength in the valley of the River Senegal from 1854, developing an effective chain of riverine forts linked by steamboats.[71] Having had their 1864 expedition wrecked by disease, the British in 1873–4 launched a successful punitive expedition against the Asante. Benefiting from superior weapons – Gatling guns, 7-pounder artillery and breech-loading rifles, as opposed to Asante muskets – they defeated the Asante at Amoafu (1874) and burned down the Asante capital, Kumasi. The assistance of other African peoples, especially the Fante, was also important in this campaign.[72] Victory over the Asante led to the emancipation of slaves on the Gold Coast by the British. Further north, the French also benefited from African support in conflict with Samory Touré, their major opponent, who they termed the 'Napoleon of the Sudan'. Thus, in 1887–8, King Tieba of Kénédougou sought French aid when attacked by Samory in modern Mali. The spread of European power also helped bring slavery to an end in New Zealand although, earlier, the rapid spread of Christianity there in the 1830s and 1840s was also important, as it was in the end of cannibalism. Moreover, the use of muskets in conflict between Maori groups meant that war parties killed the enemy rather than capturing them.

The demise of slavery and the slave trade thus prefigured the later, very different, case that Western colonialism receded after the Second World War, at a time when absolute Western military power reached a hitherto unprecedented level, again indicating the significance of ideas within the West. Slavery also came to an end when attitudes of racial superiority and Social Darwinism were becoming more clearly articulated, which underlines the complexities of linkage and causation. Thus, in his *Essai sur l'inégalité des races humaines* (1853–5), the French diplomat Arthur de Gobineau argued the importance of racial factors, backed slavery and influenced the work of Friedrich Nietzsche.

Local interests often wished to retain slavery, as in northern Nigeria where Britain established a protectorate in 1900. There were also concerns on the part of some colonial administrators, for example in Zanzibar, about the economic impact of Abolition. Nevertheless, slavery was largely ended, both by colonial policy and thanks to the slaves' attempts to seek advantage from their changing environment. The continuation of slave raiding was, in 1902, a pretext for war with the Sokoto caliphate in northern Nigeria and, rapidly victorious at Burmi in 1903,[73] Britain imposed an end to the practice. Similarly, the French conquest of Madagascar in 1894–5 was followed by the abolition of slavery there in 1896. In Indochina, the expansion of French control, for example in Cambodia from the 1860s, led to the end of the extensive slave trade there, as well as to measures to try to end slavery.

The French conquest of the Sahara and Morocco was particularly significant. A capacity to operate deep into the interior was displayed. Rabih az-Zubayr, the 'Black Sultan' who led resistance in Chad, was crushed as a result. In October 1899 he was seriously defeated at Kouno, to the south-east of Lake Chad, and in April 1900 was defeated and killed at Kousséri, to the south of the lake after his room for manoeuvre had been limited by converging French forces from Algeria, Congo and Niger. The submission of the Ahaggar Tuareg in 1905 ended effective resistance in the Sahara, but the further extension of French authority still involved military action. In 1909, Abéché, capital of Wadai in eastern Chad, was occupied and in 1910 Drijdjeli, the capital of Massalit. By 1912, the French had established a protectorate over most of Morocco, the rest becoming a Spanish protectorate. Faced by the Ottoman contacts of Ali Dinar, the Sultan of Darfur in western Sudan, the British conquered the sultanate, another Saharan slave society, in 1916.

In some cases, notably in German South-West and East Africa, the harsh response of the colonial power to opposition led to death rates among the African population that were more serious than those suffered as a result of most intra-African warfare, including the subsequent use of enslavement. In 1915–16, in the Volta-Bani war in West Africa, the French responded to opposition by deploying 5,000 men, mostly

West African troops, and by employing anti-societal warfare including the slaughter of men, women and children, and poisoning wells and killing animals, in order to destroy the environment among which their opponents operated. About 30,000 of the local population were killed in suppressing the rising. Moreover, even when large-scale violence was not used by the imperial powers, colonialism involved a degree of control that, while not slavery, was scarcely freedom. That of King Leopold II of the Belgians in the Congo Free State became a major scandal in the 1890s with the drive to secure rubber production accompanied by appalling atrocities.

As a reminder that we should not focus exclusively on Africa, similar treatment was visited on Korea by its Japanese rulers after it was occupied in 1905. Moreover, in 1915, Leslie Davis, the American consul in Erzurum, reported of the Turkish brutalization of the Armenians, 'The Turks have already chosen the most pretty from among the children and young girls. They will serve as slaves, if they do not serve ends that are more vile.' Noting the small number of Armenian men he saw, Davis assumed that the rest had been killed, and, indeed, the Turks did not seek a labour force.[74] This pattern continued a tendency which had been long established in the Ottoman empire, but more so than earlier because the state was now understood much more in terms of a nationalism based on ethnic exclusion. Thus, the military were now Turks rather than recruited from subject people. After the war, the Turks were to expel their Greek minority, and not to enslave them.

Western activism

The central theme in this chapter has been Western activism. Other narratives and analyses are possible, notably black resistance to slavery, but they are less credible. Instead, the focus is on Western action and that opens up debates about the intentionality underlining this action. The stress here is on an ideological approach. Moreover, this contrasts with the different attitude within the Islamic world of the nineteenth century. In the 1840s, Ahmad Bey, ruler of Tunisia, issued edicts to abolish the slave trade and emancipate the slaves, but these measures, the first by a Muslim ruler to end the trade, reflected his determination to establish Tunisia as a fully legitimate member of an international community organized on Western norms, and thus avoid the fate of Algiers, which had been invaded by France in 1830.

Slave raiding in, and by, the Islamic world continued to be common, but was reduced by Western action. The slave trade had long been important for the societies of the Caucasus, but it was banned by the Russian conquerors.[75] Uzbek slave raids on Persia in the 1860s and 1870s were a major issue for Britain and Russia as they sought to bring stability to Central Asia. When the Russians occupied the oasis of Khiva in 1873, they liberated 30,000 slaves, some of whom were Russians, although many were Persians, victims of the slave raiding by more nomadic societies on their more settled counterparts. The slave market at Bukhara continued to be fed with Afghan slaves, but the extension of Russian power lessened such activity. The Russian conquest of Tashkent in 1865, of Bukhara and Samarkand in 1868 and of Merv in 1884 were also significant for the ending of slavery. In the 1890s, in the British Parliament, there was considerable political pressure on the government over the continuing role in the slave trade of the sultanate of Zanzibar, which was a British protectorate, and in 1896 Hamid ibn Thuwaini, the Sultan of Zanzibar, was deposed. Two years later, Henry Newman presented recent events in Zanzibar in terms of 'the tide of deliverance . . . thus history kindles hope . . . In the zenith of power nations are proven, not by selfish ends or aims, but by their action towards weaker races.'[76]

Naval action against those smuggling slaves continued to be an important task in the Red Sea in the 1900s, and post-First World War disruption in Arabia, combined with its post-Ottoman Arab rulers tolerating slavery, led to a resumption in efforts against the slave trade there in the 1920s. Similarly, the extension of the power of the American state over Native Americans brought slavery to a close in the American West. Whatever their race, Comanche captives had been slaves, and that practice lasted well into the 1870s at least, but it was subsequently ended. A focus on Western action against slavery may not be a conclusion that suits modern ideological suppositions and commitments, but that is not the purpose of this work.

Slave survivals, as conventionally understood, continued during the colonial period[77] and beyond, and are a subject of current concern, notably about the situation in Sudan, but the scale of the problem had been transformed by 1910. Slavery was formally abolished in Korea in 1894, in Zanzibar in 1909, and in China in 1906 in a law that became effective in 1910 when all adult slaves became hired labourers, while freedom was decreed for young slaves when they reached twenty-five. The norms were clear. Ethiopia was only allowed to join the League of Nations in 1923 when it agreed to ban slavery and the slave trade, ending the legal source of slaves for the slave trade. Emperor Haile Sellassie was well on his way to eradicating slavery before the Italian invasion of 1935 and, with the invasion and Italian occupation (1935–41) and the coming of a money economy, slavery died out. It was not revived after the liberation from the Italians in 1941.[78]

The League sought international agreement on a range of issues, including the slave trade, drug control and disarmament, and in 1926 the ratification of the League of Nations' International Convention with the Object of Securing the Abolition of Slavery and the Slave Trade marked its abolition; although the drafting of the Convention had had to exclude forced labour and concubinage, the first a measure taken in order to avoid problems for imperial powers in their colonies. This activity was to be continued after the Second World War, with slavery condemned by the 1956 International Convention on the Abolition of Slavery, the Slave Trade and Practices

Similar to Slavery, and by the United Nations' Universal Declaration of Human Rights and the European Convention of Human Rights. Article Four of the Universal Declaration of Human Rights states 'No one shall be held in slavery or servitude; slavery and the slave trade shall be prohibited in all their forms.'

7

A TROUBLED PRESENT, 1930–2011

This time the slaves did not cower. They massacred everything.
Holden Roberto, leader of the National Liberation
Front of Angola when it launched its first guerrilla invasion
of the Portuguese colony, slaughtering colonists, 1961.

Almost one million bonded labourers in 4,000 brick kilns
across the country . . . Physical and sexual abuse, especially of
children, was common.
Human Rights Commission of Pakistan, 2006.[1]

The twentieth century was to witness a highpoint of slavery,
albeit not of the type that Abolitionists and governments had
struggled to suppress over the previous century, the type that
they found easier to define and confront. Instead, it was public
slavery that rose to a new peak. Moreover, this slavery was
seen in a continent, Europe, where slavery had not played a
central role for centuries. However, the discussion of slavery
in the period from the 1930s to the present is difficult, and it
is easy to appreciate why writers prefer to concentrate on the

conventional account of slavery in terms of enslavement, economic exploitation, racism and Abolitionism in the context of the Western-run Atlantic economy. Yet, to do so is not only to offer a misleading treatment of the period that ended in the late nineteenth century, but also to neglect the extent to which slavery played a major role in the twentieth century.

Into the twentieth century: genocidal slavery

Given the greater contentiousness of the recent past, it is very fortunate that there are few who would extenuate the vileness of Nazi rule from 1933 to 1945 over first Germany and then much of Europe. As a result, the discussion of the Nazi treatment of their victims in terms of enslavement is plausible to many readers, although this treatment was of course overshadowed by the genocidal intentions and policies of the regime. The habit of describing all the Nazi camps as concentration camps is unhelpful in this context, as there was a distinction between extermination camps, such as Betzec, Maly Trostenets, Sobibor and Treblinka, where the victims were promptly murdered, and concentration camps, where, although the long-term intention was very much the death of the prisoners, in the shorter term many were treated as an enslaved labour force.

This issue is discussed below, but no such agreement in approach is likely for the similar treatment of people by Communist regimes, ranging from Stalin's Soviet Union, Mao's China, Mengistu's Ethiopia and Pol Pot's Cambodia to the present-day situation in North Korea. Attempts to argue an equivalence between such regimes and that of Nazi Germany are often rejected, or at least qualified, while, aside from these regimes' treatment of those judged unacceptable, there is the contentious issue of whether the entire ideology of the regime in effect consigned the people to be the slaves of the government and of the historical process it saw as immutable. Indeed, leaving aside the question of whether the absence of civil rights is not quite the same as slavery, the idea of the people as slaves of the (Communist) Party is a troubling issue. [This is the case not only for the discussion of such regimes, but also because this idea spills over into political debate within and about countries that have democratic systems and, at least formally, practices as well as individual liberties affirmed in law, but where the assumptions, expectations and demands of government are such that these liberties, and with them freedom in general, are in practice greatly restricted. [Here, however, we are in danger of slippage into the territory of arguments about the supposed 'tyranny of the majority', or, more commonly, those that claim to represent them. The corollary of this is that everyone becomes actually, or potentially, a slave of this system, which is not a helpful way to discuss slavery; although, as a separate point, a focus on the lack of freedom of citizens and its description in terms of slavery may capture the power of life and death present in states obliging their citizens to military service. Thus, conscription, presented by its supporters as a burden of citizenship, is for its opponents a form of slavery.]

Leaving aside the question of the 'tyranny of the majority' in democratic societies, or indeed the *Road to Serfdom* (1944) discerned by the economist Friedrich Hayek (1899–1992), the 'father of monetarism', it became more common after the Second World War for all regimes, whatever their character, to proclaim a support for human rights for all even when the states themselves were dictatorships and the people treated as if at the disposal of the state. Thus, the *Green Book* that contained the thoughts of Colonel Gaddafi, leader of Libya from 1969, declared that 'Wealth, weapons and power lie with the people', but there was neither democracy nor free debate in the country. Hafez Assad, leader of Syria from 1970 (officially President from 1971) until his death in 2000, gained power as a result of a coup and relied heavily on oppressive secret police, but claimed to rule in accordance with the constitution and preserved a parliament; the governing Baath party in Syria was socialist and republican, but the reality of power was a dictatorship. The military dictators of Myanmar (Burma) refused to heed the election of 1990 and claimed to secure stability and development while brutally suppressing not only opposition but also the hopes and aspirations of a people treated as if slaves whose fate is of no consequence.[2] Although an Islamic dictatorship, the Sudanese government issued a new constitution in 1999 that promised freedom of religion, expression and association. Yet, chattel slavery is still practised in Sudan, while its president since 1993, Omar al-Bashir, has been indicted before the International Criminal Court for genocide and war crimes.

Communist China is a 'people's republic' and holds elections, but there is no alternative to the governing group. At present, China is an ardent supporter of capitalist growth, but under Mao Zedong, who seized power in 1949 with Communist victory in the Civil War and ruled until his death in 1976, the cause of progress led to an instrumentalism in which the entire population were subservient to the demands of change, as enunciated for example in the Sixteen Points adopted in 1966. Government policies led to the death of tens of millions, while many of those deemed in need of re-education were forced to move into the countryside and to become agricultural labourers, moved at the behest of the state and families split up. A similar policy, albeit with far higher death rates, was followed in Cambodia from 1976 to 1979 by the Khmer Rouge regime under Pol Pot.

Mao's affirmation of control over all included a rejection of the traditional Chinese notion of 'harmony between the heavens and humankind'. Instead, he proclaimed, 'Man must conquer nature.' In 1958, Mao declared, 'Make the high mountain bow its head; make the river yield the way', and, soon after, in a critique of an essay by Stalin stating that men could not affect natural processes such as geology, he claimed 'This argument is incorrect. Man's ability to know and change Nature is unlimited.' Indeed, for Mao, nature, like human-kind, was there to be forcibly mobilized in pursuit of the idea, a prospectus pushed with scant regard for human cost, scientific knowledge, rational analysis or environmental damage. The extent to which it is helpful to describe such attitudes in terms of enslavement is unclear, but the consequences were state control without constraints, and a lack of individual independence, combined with a situation in which critics were harshly punished. The justification of means by ends was a constant feature of control as in south-west Saxony in the Soviet occupation zone of eastern Germany (later East Germany), where forced labour, particularly of German political prisoners, and harsh conditions in the mines were the product of the search for uranium to support the Soviet atomic bomb programme in the late 1940s.[3] The processing of uranium was carried out without any concern about safety, and many of the workers lost fingers.

It is easy to understand why it is relatively simple to return from the complexities of modern governance and governments to the Nazis, whose vicious use of slave labour poses fewer problems of definition, analysis and judgement. When Auschwitz II (Birkenau) and Majdanek were established in 1942, they were both extermination camps and concentration camps. By then, it was clear that the war would not be rapidly settled with a German victory, as had seemed possible, and to optimists likely, in the autumn of 1941. Instead, Germany was now at war with a Soviet Union that had been capable of mounting a winter counter-offensive in 1941–2, as well as with the industrial might of the USA. This challenge suggested that the conflict would be attritional, which put a focus on industrial production and, thus, on labour.

Auschwitz had a major place in this new military and geopolitical prospectus because, unlike the other extermination camps, it was located in a key economic zone, that of coal-rich Upper Silesia. Aside from the coal mines, this was a major area of industrial activity and one that required a large slave labour force, not least because the Germans were increasingly conscripting their own men for the army.

Auschwitz, thus, acted as a nexus of the cooperation between Heinrich Himmler, Head of the SS, and Albert Speer, Minister for Armaments and Munitions from February 1942, that was to be so important to the German ability to sustain the conflict in the face of American and Soviet power.

The extensive plant of the major industrial concern I. G. Farben constructed near Auschwitz for the manufacture of synthetic rubber and oil was one of the largest German industrial projects. This Buna Works deliberately drew not just on local coal but also on the local slave labour which Himmler used to persuade the company to locate there.[4] Moreover, the exhausted nature of the workers, and specifically the impact of the daily march from Auschwitz II to the Buna Works, led the managers to have Auschwitz III constructed nearby in late 1942. The SS had not been keen on this additional facility, but they accepted this outcome, guarding what, in effect, was a private concentration camp. Workers who fell sick and did not recover speedily were sent to the gas chambers at Auschwitz II, and the arduous and cruel nature of work and life in such camps was such that many fell sick.

Jews were treated more viciously than the other forced labour on which Germany so heavily depended. Most of the cruelly treated Jews in these labour camps died as a result of serious malnutrition, physical violence and disease, or were killed. Aside from the harsh working conditions, the lack of sufficient and adequate food, clothing, bedding and shoes, and the frequent epidemics, there were brutal punishments, including public floggings and hangings for minor infractions of arbitrary rules. The SS assumed anyway that most prisoners would die in these conditions in under three months, and they were frequently correct. At Auschwitz, those deemed unable to work hard were gassed on arrival, while fit men and women selected for labour were sent to crowded barracks with a serial number tattooed on their forearm, subsequently an emblem of the suffering.[5]

If Auschwitz represented the culmination of Nazi extermination policies, the use of slave labour there was the end result in another narrative of the brutal treatment of Jews. Forced labour had become an important theme from 1938, not least because in Germany Nazi persecution, in seizing Jewish businesses and closing down Jewish employment opportunities, made it possible to direct Jewish labour. Having made Jews unemployed, they were given state welfare only on condition that they accepted employment in difficult and demeaning conditions that were designed to remove them from fellow Germans. Thus, Jews were made to work on processing rubbish or in projects in which they were segregated in camps.

From 1939, this programme expanded, in response to the need for non-Jewish German manpower for the army. The Reich Labour Office recruited Jews for skilled work, a process that continued to be important, and not under SS control, until large-scale deportations from Germany occurred in 1941. Even after that some Jewish workers were retained in Germany by influential employers, for example the armaments division of the army, until they were finally all seized for deportation in February 1943.

At the Wansee conference in January 1942, Reinhard Heydrich, the Head of the Reich Security Main Office, announced that all European Jews were to be deported to the East and worked to death. Already, the Jews of Poland, which had been conquered by Germany in 1939, had been moved into ghettos and forced-labour camps. All Jewish men between twelve and sixty were placed under an obligation for forced labour. Thus, the Lódź ghetto, established in April 1940, specialized in uniforms for the army and other military supplies. Large numbers of Jews were used for forced labour under labour agencies that were not under SS control, for example the Organisation Todt, the key construction agency for the war machine, but this SS control became dominant as the 'Jewish question' moved towards the Final Solution, with the allocation of Jews for slaughter or work a central means and display of SS power.[6]

In some respects, as with the slaughter, forced labour was a continuum that did not only include Jews. Taking forward small-scale attempts in the First World War which had included the brutal seizure in 1916–17 of 60,000 Belgians for work in Germany, millions of foreign workers, especially Soviet, Polish and French, were brought to Germany, while, elsewhere in occupied Europe, workers were forced to work in their home countries in order to produce resources for Germany. Aside from prisoners of war, 5.7 million foreign workers were registered in the Greater German Reich in August 1944; combined with the prisoners of war, they provided half the workforce in agriculture and in the manufacture of munitions.[7]

The need for the labour of prisoners led the Germans to cease being so murderous to Soviet prisoners of war in October 1941, although their working conditions, which, from 1944, included fewer than 1,000 calories of food daily (in comparison to the official German civilian ration of 2,100 calories), were such as to lead to high death rates, and knowingly so. In 1942–3, for example, about 120,000 Jews, Soviet prisoners and Ukranian forced labourers were made to work on the projected road from Lvov to Stalino and in supporting quarries, with many being killed after they had been worked to exhaustion. In addition, German prisoners categorized as asocial or social misfits were allocated to the SS from 1942 and deliberately worked to death. Many were petty thieves, the work-shy, tramps and alcoholics. Aside from those to be moved to work, German colonization plans for European Russia and much of Eastern Europe entailed leaving a labour force of slaves in place.[8]

Germany's ally Japan also used large-scale forced labour, notably from Korea, China, the Dutch East Indies (Indonesia) and Burma. Most of this labour was for construction and economic activity,[9] although sexual slavery was also a major issue. Post-war Japan was very reluctant to acknowledge this conduct and in many respects still is. There are no reliable statistics for the 'comfort women', enforced prostitutes for the Japanese military, used to staff their brothels, but they are estimated at over 100,000, mostly Koreans and many quite young.[10] In 1993, Kōno Yōhei, the Chief Cabinet Secretary, admitted and apologized for the military's role in coercing women into prostitution, while, in 1995, the Asian Women's Fund was established in Japan to provide financial compensation. In 2007, however, Abe Shinzō, the Prime Minister, tried to introduce qualifications by arguing that there was no proof that women were coerced, leading to a serious controversy. Moreover, although wartime forced labour, mostly Chinese and Korean, was frequently treated in a murderous fashion, attempts to seek compensation were rejected in 2007 by the High Court in Sapporo.

The deliberate and deadly neglect of Jewish workers by the Germans was a particular characteristic of their treatment and, as such, the use of the term slave labour is problematic as it can be made to imply a comparison with other systems of slavery, notably those of African slaves in the European, Islamic and African worlds. Such a comparison, however, is of limited value as these slaves had a clear financial value expressed in sale and purchase and, for that reason, as well as to fulfil productive tasks, it was important to keep them alive. Indeed, in marked contrast to Nazi conduct towards Jews, there could be added value from slaves having children, and castration of slaves was only normal in the Islamic world. The equating of the Atlantic slave trade to an African Holocaust also underrates the major role of African agency in the slave trade, and, conversely, the extent to which the Holocaust was an aspect of the savage reordering of the racial geography of conquered territory. It is interesting that some racists, such as the Nazi Manfred Sell in his *Die Schwarze Völkerwanderung* (*The Black Migration*, 1940), opposed the slave trade because of the possibilities it offered for intermarriage and deracination.

A more direct linkage has been drawn between the allegedly genocidal nature of Western colonialism, particularly, but not only by Germany in Africa, and Nazi policies. This linkage, however, has been contested, as has the parallel.[11] Other roots have been emphasized for Nazi violence, not least the impact of defeat in the First World War and subsequent fantasies of reshaping Europe.[12] A comparison of Nazi policy with governmental control systems in the twentieth century, notably those of Communist states, is also relevant but only up to a point. There was a shared focus on forced labour, with both (unlike the Atlantic slavery) emphasising productivism, not capitalism, and goods, not profit; but in the case of Nazi policy towards Jews there was a distinct genocidal intent. In contrast, although there was also the murderous deportation of national groups such as the Crimean Tatars, Communist action focused on entire social categories.[13] The *kulak* (peasant proprietors) deportees were sent in the early 1930s with their whole families to the special settlements, about two million people in total. Murderous punishment was a key element in the system,[14] but the very large numbers imprisoned in the Soviet *gulags*, about 2.3 million in 1941, played a major role in the Soviet economy and, in particular, in opening up the north in the 1930s, notably with construction, mining and forestry. Soviet demographic displacement can be related to earlier practices of imperial and colonial penal transportation, including of Russians to Siberia prior to the Revolution, but under Stalin the scale was far greater and the cruelty more pronounced.

The large numbers of political prisoners used as labour provided a model for Soviet occupation regimes and Communist states elsewhere. In 1939–40, 1.17 million people were deported from Soviet-occupied Poland to Soviet labour camps,[15] and in 1940 about 127,000 more were deported from the occupied Baltic states. Many others who were not deported were slaughtered. The cruelty of Soviet treatment of dissidents was captured by the novelist Alexander Solzhenitsyn, who had been imprisoned for making critical remarks about the Soviet dictator Joseph Stalin. In his novel *The First Circle* (1968), which won the Nobel Prize for Literature in 1970, Solzhenitsyn described the dehumanizing practices of the police state: 'Will they stop his correspondence for years on end, so that his family thinks he is dead? . . . Will he die of dysentery in his cattle truck? Or die of hunger because the train does not stop for six days and no rations are issued?' The total power of the Soviet state was tyrannical, and the consequences for individuals was that they became slaves of its power.[16]

Chattel slavery and its continuation in Africa

Such power still exists around the world, although it affects fewer people than in the 1960s. There has also been a decline in chattel slavery. In 1936, Ibn Sa'ūd, the ruler of Saudi Arabia, had promulgated a slave law, restating the Qur'anic teachings, as well as requiring the registration of slaves and licensing slave traders, but in 1962 slavery was made illegal. Moreover, slaves were freed in Bahrain in 1937, Kuwait in 1949, Qatar in 1952, and Oman in 1970.

Such chattel slavery remains a factor in parts of Africa, notably Sudan and Mauritania, but far less so than a century ago. Aside from such long-term slavery, the other major forms of slavery in Africa are the kidnapping of children to use as soldiers and sex slaves, and trafficking in people to sell as slaves. In Uganda, the rebel Lord's Resistance Army kidnapped children in the 2000s for use as soldiers and sex slaves. Similar practices were seen in Congo, Liberia, Sierra Leone, Ivory Coast and Sri Lanka.

An ethnic and religious dimension pertains in many cases and especially in Mauritania and Sudan, with ancient paths of exploitation followed in both cases and unequal relations between the descendants of former masters and of former slaves kept alive. About one million slaves are held in Mauritania as inheritable property, out of a total population of 3.2 million in 2007. Slavery was abolished in Mauritania by the French colonial rulers, and again in the independence constitution of 1960 and in 1980 and 2008, but the minority light-skinned Bidan Moors continue to dominate the state and many of the majority Harratin black Moors remain dependants of their former masters. Slaves are black people largely from the country's south-west near Senegal.[17] In September 2007, human rights activists demonstrated in the capital, Nouakchott, against both the failure to enforce the law prohibiting slavery, and the ability of feudal lords to seize the property of former slaves,[18] which served as a way to discourage those seeking freedom.

Slavery returned in Sudan as a side-effect of the civil wars between north and south from 1961 to 1972 and 1983 and 2005, civil wars which destabilized the relationship between tribes. Militias from the north raided the south for cattle and killed many civilians, especially men. They took mainly women and children back north with them, using them principally as domestic slaves and to tend to the cattle. This practice was denied by the Sudanese government but was documented by a committee of the national university after 1983 and was confirmed by missionaries working in southern Sudan and by American journalists. Ethnic tensions continue to play a major role, as in the very harsh treatment of black people in Darfur in west Sudan in the 2000s. A standard practice is for villages to be surrounded, houses burned, men slaughtered, and the women and children taken as slaves for household and sexual reasons. There is a religious and racial dimension, with the slavers being Muslim Arabs. Alongside violence, slaves are obtained as a result of debt, with poor parents selling their children in order to provide a form of indentured labour that in practice becomes slavery.

The government of Sudan does nothing about slavery, and Mali, where there are thousands of slaves in the Saharan north, does little, but other governments take action, such as that of Senegal in 2010. Moreover, although Africa remains exposed to very harsh pressures, as seen in the warfare in Rwanda and

Congo in the 1990s and 2000s, widespread slavery on the earlier scale is not a consequence.[19] For example, in Niger, there are at least 43,000 slaves out of a total population of 14.9 million in 2007. The ratio would certainly have been higher 150 years ago and rulers then would scarcely have said, as that of Niger did in 2008, that it had done all it could to end slavery. Nevertheless, although legislation to that end was passed in 2003, little has been done to enforce it. In Niger, slaves are not on the electoral role.[20]

Economic pressures in Africa, however, have led to an emigration that has some echoes of the slave trade, with the crucial difference that the would-be migrants are not slaves. Much of the movement is to Europe, rather than the New World, and a key means is crossing in open boats to the Canary Islands, a Spanish possession, where they seek asylum. As with the slave boats, these boats are very crowded, and a certain number die in the crossing. As with the slave trade, money is being made from transportation under inhumane conditions. In the year from August 2005 to August 2006, 20,000 African refugees arrived in the Canaries and up to 3,000 are thought to have died. The sight of these Africans being intercepted by the Spanish Navy in an attempt to keep them from the European economy invites attention to the varied relationship between globalization and movement for work, which is a theme throughout the history of the slave trade.

Sex trafficking and child slavery

The relationship between globalisation and movement for work is also seen with the large-scale sex trade, in which women and children are trafficked, against their will, to work as prostitutes, generally in harsh conditions. This trade reflects the continuing brutal side to exploitation and entrepreneurialism and also the differences in employment, opportunity and prosperity around the world that provide a basis for such a trade. The 2005 Trafficking in Persons Report by the US State Department estimated that 80 per cent of the 600,000–800,000 people trafficked across international borders annually were women and children. Such trades can be seen across the world, for example about 35,000 women and children go from the Philippines to Japan each year. Women are trafficked from poor areas in Eastern Europe into Western Europe by particular criminal networks, notably Albanian and Russian ones. Once in Western Europe, the women are frequently brutalized, and sometimes put on narcotic drugs in order to control them. The confiscation of passports is another form of dependence.

The large-scale and growing imbalance between male and female children in East and South Asia, due to selective abortion and infanticide, notably in India and Pakistan, and the abandonment of female babies (often for adoption outside Asia, notably Chinese girls by Americans), is likely to lead to a further development of this form of slavery and slave trade. Attitudes to women are closely linked to slavery, with the ratio of men to women being a key factor. The harsh, often murderous, treatment of female babies and girls that helps lead to this ratio is then replicated by an exploitative treatment of their older counterparts. Already, there is the large-scale sale in South-East and South Asia of poor children who are then used as prostitutes, domestics and workers. The sex tourist industry rests in large part on slavery, with debt bondage and the exploitation of children both being factors.

The children of the poor are a major source of slaves across the world, with, for example, children enslaved in Cameroon and Togo and sold in Nigeria, and in Benin, Togo, Nigeria and Cameroon for sale in Gabon. Countries such as Nigeria are sources as well as destinations and transit points for children trafficked as slaves, which serves as a reminder of the complexities of earlier patterns in the slave trade. Similar points can be made about Angola, Benin, Burkina Faso, Burundi, Cameroon, Congo, Ghana, Guinea, Ivory Coast, Mali, Mauritius, Mozambique, Rwanda, Senegal, Sierra Leone, South Africa, Tanzania and other African countries.[21] The range of occupations for slave children is very extensive, including for example the fishing industry in Ghana and cocoa harvesting in the Ivory Coast. In Brazil in 2010 the number of child prostitutes is estimated at a quarter of a million (out of a population of 191.3 million), some of them sold into prostitution by impoverished parents. At a very different scale, the occasional self-immolation of widows and the more frequent murder of wives whose dowries were deemed inadequate in India are the most dramatic sign of a widespread subordination of women there that has features akin to slavery.

Indeed, it is a comment on demographic, economic and social changes that, whereas slavery for much of history focused on arduous productive work in economies short of labour, especially for agriculture, now, alongside the continued use of slaves in agriculture and industry especially in South Asia, much of slavery is more focused on a service economy dealing with the needs of individual consumers. Yet, in Western Europe and the USA, migrant labour, exploited and controlled by 'gang masters', is frequently involved in crop picking, for example of tomatoes in Florida, and often in construction. As with sex trafficking, these migrant workers are generally brought into the country illegally and are thus dependent on the gangs, although the terms for subsequent working and living conditions vary. The confiscation of passports is used to keep pliant men and women who have been illegally moved across international borders, as well as those who have moved legally but are under the control of the gangs.[22]

The emphasis on the service economy can be taken further if slavery is extended to include 'wage slavery', for much of the recent expansion of low-paid jobs classically done by recent immigrants is in the care sector. Thus, medical assistants, physician assistants, home health aides and physical therapist assistants were among the ten fastest-growing occupations in America listed by the American Labor

Department. Again, this definition of work as slavery takes us away from slavery understood as a form of coerced labour. The latter was still all too present in 2011, but more obviously so among the population of North Korea or the *Dalits* (Untouchables) of India trapped in debt bondage, than among those classified by the American Labor Department.

8

LEGACIES AND CONCLUSIONS

I have had hardly a day in office that has not been dominated by this all-embracing struggle – this conflict between those who love freedom and those who would lead the world back into slavery and darkness.

President Harry Truman, Farewell Address, 15 January 1953.

'Virginia is alive and well, and Virginia was built on the backs of slaves, and Virginia's economy boomed because of slavery, and it is Virginia that ought to apologise.' Donald E. McEachin, a descendant of slaves, was in no doubt when, in January 2007, as a member of the House of Delegates, he sponsored a proposal for an expression of state contrition for slavery. This, however, was not a unanimous view: Frank Hargrove, a Republican Delegate whose ancestors were French Huguenots who had come to America in search of religious freedom, remarked, 'The present Commonwealth [Virginia] has nothing to do with slavery ... Nobody living today had anything to do with it. It would be far more appropriate in my view to apologise to the Upper Mattaponi and the Pamunkey [Native Americans who lost their lands]. I personally think that our black citizens should get over it. By golly, we're living in 2007.' This, however, was very much a minority view and one for which Hargrove was greatly criticized. The following month, 'profound regret', but not apology, was voted in a resolution noting that government-sanctioned slavery 'ranks as the most horrendous of all depredations of human rights and violation of our founding ideals in our nation's history'. This controversy overlapped with the celebrations of the four-hundredth anniversary of the Jamestown settlement by the English, and McEachin also called on Queen Elizabeth II to 'express regret'. She did not do so, but on 4 May 2007, at a Special Joint Session of the General Assembly at Richmond, the Queen noted the difference between her visit in 2007 and that in 1957, for the three-hundred-and-fiftieth anniversary, when there had been no pressure for an apology, concluding, 'It is right that we continue to reassess the meaning of historical events in the changing context of the present.'

The present, indeed, sees many forms of slavery including debt bondage, penal labour and sexual slavery. In Brazil today, slave-like conditions, in which debt bondage is linked to the seizure of identity papers and to the cruel treatment of workers by armed guards, can be seen, for example in the pig-iron industry around Maraba. Yet, coming to terms with slavery is a challenge, instead, that is frequently historicized by discussing it in terms of how best to consider the Atlantic slave trade. The legacy of the latter in terms of different and often competing public narratives proves part of this story, but the inherent issue is how to confront the past. The role of this past in contemporary culture wars is a central aspect of the discussion of slavery in the modern USA.[1]

As suggested in this book, however, such an account, while important, is less than the whole story, and is indeed in part an evasion of it. This incompleteness arises from the failure to note the role of public slavery in the history of enslavement, while evasion stems from the unwillingness to consider the extent to which forms of public and private slavery still exist today. Instead, it is easier to apologize for the past, and such apology became a major theme in the 2000s at and before the time of the bicentenary of the abolition of the British slave trade. The descendants of those active were prominent. Liverpool made a public apology in 1994 for its role in the slave trade, while, in 2006, John Hawkins' descendant Andrew and a group of twenty friends locked themselves in chains in Gambia in order to demonstrate their sense of sorrow before being forgiven by the country's Vice-President. The General Synod of the Church of England followed suit in apologizing in 2006, while British Prime Minister Tony Blair expressed deep sorrow.

British imperialism and racism are key issues in the cult of apology, while the discussion of slavery and the slave trade is also an aspect of the longstanding critique of their alleged role in the development of capitalism and Western power.[2] Thus, the treatment of slavery is at the same time historicized and part of modern debates, if not 'culture wars', about British identity.

Slavery also plays a key part in the discussion of American history, serving as it does to emphasize distinctive developments, thus challenging ideas of cultural syncretism, let alone benign American exceptionalism.[3] Slavery in particular proved a way to discuss the South, presenting its heritage as 'un-American' or 'anti-American', while, in contrast, charges of exploitation and historic wrongs were rejected in the 'White South', which has its own aggressive and self-righteous sense of historical grievance. In 1990, Virginia elected America's first black governor, Douglas Wilder, a grandson of slaves. Yet, at the same time, there was considerable resistance in parts of the South, for example Mississippi, to abandoning the Confederate flag and other symbols of deference and defiance – symbols that, to critics, contributed to the intimidation of black people. In 1998, David Beasley lost his post as Governor of South Carolina for supporting the removal of the flag from the statehouse.

These issues drew some of their energy from the role of Civil Rights and its association with a particular strand in the Democratic Party. In his 'I have a dream' speech, delivered on the steps of the Lincoln Memorial in Washington on 28 August 1963, Martin Luther King Jr declared that, despite the Emancipation Proclamation, 'One hundred years later, the life of the Negro is still sadly crippled by the manacles of segregation and the chains of discrimination.' Indeed, in the USA, as in Brazil, the poor remain to this day disproportionately black, and the black disproportionately poor. The percentage of black people below the poverty line in the USA was 35.7 in 1983, 22.5 in 2000, and 24.7 in 2004, compared to percentages for non-Hispanic whites of eight to nine. The percentage of white people in the population, however, ensured that the number of white people below the poverty line was greater than that of black people. At the national level, in the early 2000s, black mothers were twice as likely as their white counterparts to give birth to a low-weight baby, and their children were twice as likely to die before their first birthday. Furthermore, black people are disproportionately numerous in the prison population, which itself is enormous, with between 2.3 million Americans behind bars in 2010, about 748 per 100,000 Americans, a rate five times that of Britain.

The extent to which such issues can be traced to slavery is contentious, but the assertion of African identity by some of the black rights movement is directly pertinent. W. E. B. Du Bois (1868–1963), one of the founders in 1909 of the National Association for the Advancement of Colored People, and as an historian the author of *The Suppression of the African Slave Trade* (1896) and the highly critical *The World and Africa* (1947), which argued a parallel between the treatment of Africa and Nazi policies, emigrated in 1960 to Ghana, where he supported the idea of an *Encyclopaedia Africana*. The assertion of African identity was a particular issue for black separatism. In a speech at Detroit in 1965, given a week before he was assassinated, Malcolm X declared: 'One of the things that made the Black Muslim movement grow was its emphasis upon things Africa. This was the secret to the growth of the Black Muslim movement. African blood, African origin, African culture, African ties ... we discovered that deep within the subconscious of the black man in this country, he is still more African than he is American.'

Slavery and the slave trade were, and are, intertwined as issues with other aspects of public history, which reflects the extent to which they have long been used to assert identity and to advance grievances. Thus, Alessandro Manzoni (1785–1873), a Milanese poet and novelist who supported liberal causes and national independence for Italy from foreign rule, depicted, in his tragedy *Adelchis* (1822), a society in which Romans were enslaved by the Lombards who invaded Italy from 568 CE. To Manzoni, this story symbolized the plight of modern Italians before the *Risorgimento* (movement of Italian unification), and thus paralleled Giuseppe Verdi's use, in his opera *Nabucco* (1842), of the plight of the Hebrew slaves in Babylon. In practice, the extent of slavery under the Lombards can be queried.

French public culture has repeatedly demonstrated the uses of Abolition, not least as a sign of republican virtue in contrast to the *ancien régime*. Thus, the Revolutionaries ended the slave trade, only for Napoleon to restore and then (at the close of his career) abolish it. As far as slavery is concerned, it was the Second Republic which replaced the Orléans monarchy in 1848 that passed the Abolition Act that year. The continued resonance of Abolitionism chimes with left-wing French thought, and it was under a Socialist government that, in 1993, the remains of the Abbé Henri Grégoire (1750–1831), a radical priest opposed to the slave trade, were moved into the Panthéon in Paris. The positive and large-scale contribution of African soldiers from the colonies to the defence of France and French interests, notably in both World Wars but also and more generally, helped contribute to a more positive attitude to black people. The lasting legacy of slavery, however, became more contentious in the 2000s, as a result of racial discontent in France, as well as controversy over the future of the ex-colonial *Départements d'Outre-mer*, notably Guadeloupe and Martinique.

The situation among former slave trading and owning states varies greatly, but with a consistent contrast between a lack of interest, and certainly contrition, on the part of Islamic states and a sense of guilt on that of many Western ones. Rowan Williams, the Archbishop of Canterbury, told the General Synod of the Church of England in 2006 that apology for the Church's role in the slave trade was 'necessary', adding:

> The body of Christ is not just a body that exists at any one time; it exists across history and we therefore share the shame and the sinfulness of our predecessors and part of what we can do, with them and for them in the body of Christ is prayerful acknowledgement of the failure that is part of us not just of some distant 'them'.

In practice, the slave trade and slavery was a less prominent issue in Catholic Europe, while, among the Protestant states, it was less significant in the Netherlands than in Britain. This is even more the case in Denmark, which offers the interesting perspective of a relatively minor slave trading and owning country, although relatively minor would not have been much consolation for the approximately 74,000 Africans transported by the Danes in the eighteenth century. The Danes had slave bases on the African Gold Coast and slave plantations on their island colonies in the West Indies.[4] Yet, the overseas colonies never had a prominent place on the Danish political agenda, nor in Danish collective memory. The colonies were small, and very few Danes actually had any direct contact with them. Only a small part of the population of the Danish West Indies (since 1917 the American Virgin Islands) were Danes, most of the planters being British or Dutch, so connections with Denmark and the memories of Danish rule soon vanished. Like many Western countries, immigration is a major issue in Denmark, but, unlike Britain or France, large numbers of immigrants do not come from areas that used to be Danish colonies, and thus there is no direct link between Denmark's colonial past and her present-day problems with immigration. Denmark's 'take' on slavery is as valid as that of Britain, just as Canada's is as valid as that of the USA, or that of Ethiopia and Kenya as valid as that of Ghana and Dahomey, and it is necessary to remember these very different perspectives when considering the character of the legacy of slavery and the slave trade, and the nature of public memory.

Thus, the practice of, and pressure for, apology varies greatly, while the theme of apology provides only a very partial guide to the past. In particular, in the calls for apology there is an emphasis on European agency which downplays the active role of others. In short, the demand for European apology, paradoxically, is an aspect of the very Eurocentric practice of history about which complaints are frequently made. Leaving aside the important role of other slave traders out of Africa, as well as of slave societies elsewhere, this account underplays the role of Africans. As such, it contributes to, and draws on, the symbolic role of the slave trade as the nadir of black abasement. Indeed, the trade frequently stands for black weakness and for exploitation by others, as when Archbishop Desmond Tutu referred to the arms trade as the new slave trade.[5] Exploitation and victimization are seen as, at once, commodification and racism. However, a contrary emphasis on African agency in the slave trade emerges ever more clearly as Europe's relative weakness in Africa prior to the late nineteenth century is understood. The theme of Europe's relative weakness seen in this book is an important one arising from work on military history which, hitherto, has not been adequately integrated into consideration of the slave trade at the public level. Any such integration makes it clear that discussion of African vulnerability is misplaced, indeed woefully so.

This emphasis also accords with the post-colonial re-evaluation of pre-colonial African history which directed attention to powerful civilizations and states, for example medieval Mali. Earlier attempts to explain such African civilizations as the work of Mediterranean peoples moving south, the theory advanced in Harry Johnston's *History of the Colonisation of Africa by Alien Races* (1899) and C. G. Seligman's *Races of Africa* (1930), were rejected. This was in accord with academic arguments, but also fitted the new political mood with its stress on African achievement, and thus on the absence of need for European intervention. In a related process, research indicated that the notion of tribes advanced in works such as Samuel Johnson's *History of the Yorubas* (1921) was, in large part, an aspect of Western classification that was designed to aid comprehension, if not control, and, due to the pejorative connotations of tribalism, to demean African society. Instead, a more complex account of ethnogenesis was offered.[6] Interpretations stressing African political maturity paradoxically underlined African agency in the slave trade, although this agency was downplayed in the post-independence rethinking of the colonial period which led, instead, to a greater emphasis on resistance to colonial rule, a resistance linked to anti-colonialism.

Moreover, owing to the nature of the sources, the direction of scholarship and, even more, public commemoration, there has been an underplaying of conflict between Africans and its role in producing captives for slavery. For example, the link between African Americans and Africa was fostered by interest in roots and pathways, most prominently by Alex Haley's popular book *Roots* (1967), but there was a lack of awareness about tensions within African society and, even more, about rival ethnic groups, although within Africa there are continuing tensions between the descendants of slave traders and slaves, for example in both Ghana and Nigeria. When warfare within Africa was discussed, it was generally attributed to the pressures and opportunities of European slave trading, although, in practice, this warfare was not necessarily dependent on these opportunities. For example, the scale and bitterness of the *Mfecane* wars in southern Africa caused by the rise of the Zulu empire in the early nineteenth century and by competition for resources cannot be readily linked to the slave trade, nor indeed attributed to exogenous pressure in the shape of European actions. As with the case of the provision of weapons in modern conflicts, such pressures did play a role, but they were instrumental rather than causative.

More contentiously, despite the estimate that, due to slavery Western Africa lost a little over 10 per cent of its population between 1680 and 1860,[7] it is unclear what percentage of its population Africa as a whole lost. It is also unclear whether this loss was replaced by higher rates of reproduction, and whether, irrespective of this factor, the creation of an African diaspora, however involuntary and painful, should, in the long term, be regarded as a disaster.

If blame is to be heaped on the Europeans and, even more, if wild and inappropriate talk of genocide is to be employed, then it is more pertinent to consider the Western impact on the native population of the Americas in this light, as the percentage killed there as a result of European contact was higher. In part, this fatality rate was a result of disease, but the inroads of the latter were furthered as a consequence of the disruption caused by European conquest, which proved far more total than the later European conquest of Africa.

Slavery and the slave trade were acute issues for native peoples in the early stages of European conquest of the Americas, at a period in which the transatlantic slave trade was still relatively modest. Even when the transatlantic trade became far more important, slave raiding continued in the Americas, although it tends to be downplayed, not only because of its smaller scale but also because it was characteristic of Spanish and, even more, Portuguese America, rather than of British America, although it was still significant there.[8] Moreover, this slave raiding does not have much resonance in the world of modern culture wars or the politics of apology.

Critical views of the slave trade and slavery are not lessened by the large degree of African, Arab and, indeed, Native American agency, but slavery and the slave trade can be better understood if the variations in circumstances and contexts are probed. Moreover, the perspective changes somewhat if it is broadened to consider the widespread and diverse nature of coerced labour. This range is rather overlooked in the Americas because indentured white labour in North America was, on the whole, far less dire than slavery, not least because white people could move to the open frontier of opportunity. The situation is less comfortable, however, if the treatment of Native American labour in Latin America is considered, and comparison with European serfdom can be underscored by considering the scale and frequency of peasant uprisings in both. There were over 100 risings in the Andes in 1742–82 alone, although major rebellions were rare.[9] Labour control depended ultimately on the availability of force, the support of law and the nature of social norms. As such, public and private slavery were each part of a continuum, and rigid distinctions and definitions are unhelpful.

This approach can be underlined by considering the extent to which the economic, ideological and moral underpinnings of both Abolitionism and continued slave trading and slavery not only took on meaning with reference to the other, but also interacted and were shaped in a dynamic fashion that was caused by their relationship. The emphasis in my study is on cultural and ideological factors, especially religion, in Abolition, as opposed to economic determinism. At the same time, despite the great achievements represented by Abolition, there were many limitations and unforeseen consequences, ranging from the persistence of slave trading and new forms of coerced labour, to the often cynical merger of anti-slavery with imperialism. It is therefore easy to present the period covered in chapters 6 and 7 within a tradition of writing critical of the West, but this is a simplistic stance that indeed tells us more about present than past. Moreover, the crude anti-Western account of slavery needs to take note of the disillusionment that affected many Africanist historians as optimism about independence from European colonial rule in the late 1950s and 1960s gave way to a more pessimistic account based on a grimmer reality. Moving to the present, recent and current developments in Sudan and Zimbabwe, including their relationship with their prime foreign sponsor, China, provide a way, however ahistorical, to understand the African basis of the pre-modern slave trade, a basis that included widespread slavery in Africa itself. Irrespective of their constitutional pretensions, the number of dictatorial and authoritarian states in modern Africa is also notable. In 2010, West Africa included democracies, notably Ghana, but also authoritarian regimes such as Mauritania, Guinea-Bissau, Ivory Coast, Togo, Cameroon, Equatorial Guinea, Gabon and Angola.

In fact, the abolition of the slave trade was a distinctive feature of the nineteenth-century West, a point that raises the issues of anti-Western bias in some of the modern popular literature about slavery, as well as materialist versus idealist interpretations of Abolitionism, and the uniqueness of the West. The last is more distinctive because it contrasted with the very different position in other societies, notably in the Muslim world, which, unwilling to abolish the trade, indeed had to be pressed, if not coerced, into line. An emphasis on the role of slavery in other cultures and periods also underlines the extent to which it was not simply a pathogen of the rise of Western capitalism, an approach taken in part of the public debate. Moreover, the abolition of slavery and the slave trade cannot be seen simply as a consequence of a particular stage in the Western economy, not least a shifting of the factors of production and profitability, with the clear implication that self-interest led to Abolitionism.

Instead, it is necessary to look to a different genesis for Abolitionism, namely a religious and moral one, while, at the same time, accepting that this had materialist aspects. An emphasis on cultural-ideological factors in causing and sustaining Abolitionism is also in accord with the general thrust of much historical work in recent decades, one away from patterns of materialist determinism in which motives are explained in terms of economic self-interest.

The lessons that Abolitionism offers for today are also suggestive, in that they outline the possibility of advancing progressive moral vistas and helping ensure that they influence government policy. That these vistas were focused on, and by, the leading world power, Britain, however, entails a major difference between the nineteenth century and the present age. In the former, there was no approximation of world government or forum for cooperation comparable to the United Nations and the other institutions and treaties created under American auspices to further a new world order after the Second World War. As a result, moral suasion at the international level was, in diplomatic terms, essentially bilateral, rather than multilateral, and attempts at a multilateral level – as by the British at the Congress of Verona in 1822 – to persuade other European powers to participate in more than declamatory diplomacy against the slave trade achieved very little. However, although the mixed commission courts, which were responsible for adjudicating on the fate of captured slave ships, were established on the basis of bilateral agreements, they had a multilateral element in so far as British appointees could serve coterminously on several such courts, for example in Freetown, Sierra Leone. Some American legal historians now regard the mixed commission courts as the first human rights courts; although the courts were concerned with ships rather than individuals (the slaves they carried), thousands of the latter were liberated. In contrast to the situation in the nineteenth century, not least the centrality of bilateral relations then and Britain's role in seeing itself as the progenitor of international improvement, the modern, multi-lateral and far more insistent nature of international moral suasion creates many problems for the leading world power, the USA,[10] problems accentuated by the decline in American 'soft power' both in the 1960s and more recently.[11] Further-more, the weak purchase of internationalism in American popular politics leads to difficulties for any attempt to anchor American moral suasion in international structures such as the United Nations.

The protean character of slavery in the human imagination is indicated by the extent to which modern opposition to slavery has taken another form in science fiction, which has provided possibilities for imaginative engagement with issues of control, otherness, and labour issues that developments in cloning may take out of the field of fiction. A sense of the dehumanizing effects of slavery and the fear of slaves that might take power could be seen with humanoids, as in films such as *Metropolis* (1926) and *The Terminator* (1984), and in many of the stories of the television series *Doctor Who*, notably those involving the Daleks and the Cybermen. In addition, these humanoids could, in turn, make humans into slaves as in the *Doctor Who* episode 'The Final Experiment' of 21 April 2007, in which Daleks based in Manhattan turned humans into pig-slaves in a 'transgenic' laboratory. The fear posed by slaves extended to super-intelligent computers that seized control, as in the films *2001: A Space Odyssey* (1968) and *The Forbin Project* (1970). In the British television series *Mission 2110* (2010), humankind had been mostly destroyed by rebellious robot slaves. Science fiction became reality in the development of robotics, and, by the end of 1999, 750,000 robots were in use in manufacturing around the world, their distribution reflecting the dominance of technology by the developed world, with not a single country in Africa, Latin America or South Asia in the list of the twenty countries with the most robots. Concern over robots entailed issues of employment and control, and reflected some longstanding facets of discussion about controlled labour as well as raising new ones.

The potential challenges posed by the use of robotic labour looks more to the future, but, leaving it aside, to present slavery as a feature of the past is to underplay the extent not only to which it continues, but also could revive, albeit in particular forms. In light of this challenge, it is valuable to be reminded of the vileness of the control and vulnerability that slavery reflects, but it is also important not to be bounded by past episodes, definitions and grievances. The curse of the past lies not in what happened, terrible as that is, but rather in an inability to look clearly at the present and to the future.

NOTES

Preface

1. *The Free Lance-Star*, 18 Apr. 2010, section D, p. 4
2. H. Innlick and R. Murphey (eds), *The History of Mehmet the Conqueror* by Tursun Beq (Minneapolis, MN, 1978), p. 44. See also C. T. Riggs (ed.), *History of Mehmet the Conqueror* by Kritovoulus (Princeton, NJ, 1954), p. 155.

Chapter 1

1. *Africa Research Bulletin, Political Series*, 45/10 (Oct. 2008), p. 17733.
2. D. Eltis and D. Richardson (eds), *Extending the Frontiers: Essays on the New Transatlantic Slave Trade Database* (New Haven, CT, 2008), www.slavevoyages.org
3. M. C. Gomez-Geraud and S. Yerasimos (eds), *Dans l'empire de Soliman le Magnifique* (Geneva, 1989), p. 83.
4. *The Times*, 5 Mar. 2005.
5. M. Finley, 'Between Slavery and Freedom', *Comparative Studies in Society and History*, 6 (1964), pp. 233–49.
6. A. Walker, *Ideas Suggested on the Spot in a Late Excursion* (London, 1790), p. 108.
7. E. Yates, *A. Letter to the Women on Slavery in the Southern States of America* (London, 1863), p. 66.

8. 'Englishwoman', *A Letter to those Ladies Who Met at Stafford House* ... (London, 1853), pp. 15–16, 18, 20, 22.

9. I have benefited from the advice of Joe Miller on this point.

10. E.g. A. R. Ekrich, *Bound for America: The Transportation of British Convicts to the Colonies, 1718–1775* (Oxford, 1987).

11. M. Finley, 'Slavery', in D. L. Sills (ed.), *International Encyclopedia of the Social Sciences*, 14 (1968), pp. 307–13.

12. P. Dubois, 'Slavery', in G. Boys-Stones, B. Graziosi and P. Vasunia (eds), *The Oxford Handbook of Hellenic Studies* (Oxford, 2009), pp. 321–2.

13. *London Journal*, 17 Nov. 1722; *Whitehall Journal*, 19 Feb. 1723.

14. J. Thomson, *Alfred: a Masque* (London, 1740), Act II.

15. W. Cowper, 'The Timepiece', *The Task* (London, 1785) Act II.

16. John to Richard Tucker, 19 Apr. 1748, Oxford, Bodleian Library, Department of Western Manuscripts, MS. Don. C. 110 fol. 13.

17. J. Guilmartin, *Gunpowder and Galleys: Changing Technology and Mediterranean Warfare at Sea in the Sixteenth Century* (Cambridge, 1974); P. W. Bamford, 'The Procurement of Oarsmen for the French Galleys, 1660–1748', *American Historical Review*, 65 (1959), pp. 31–49.

Chapter 2

1. T. Nelson, 'Slavery in Medieval Japan', *Monumenta Nipponica*, 59 (2004), p. 488.

2. J. Fisch, *Burning Women: A Global History of Widow-Sacrifice from Ancient Times to the Present* (Oxford, 2006).

3. http://projectsx.dartmouth.edu/history/bronzeage/lessons/les/25.html.

4. I. Mendelsohn, *Slavery in the Ancient Near East* (Oxford, 1949).

5. I. Shaw, 'Egypt and the Outside World', in I. Shaw (ed.), *The Oxford History of Ancient Egypt* (Oxford, 2000), pp. 322–4.

6. S. Barton, *A History of Spain* (2nd edn, Basingstoke, 2009), p. 3.

7. F. D. Miller, 'Naturalism', in C. Rowe and M. Schofield (eds), *The Cambridge History of Greek and Roman Political Thought* (Cambridge, 2000), pp. 332–5.

8. V. D. Hanson, *The Other Greeks: The Family Farm and the Agrarian Roots of Western Civilization* (New York, 1995).

9. M. Finley, *Ancient Slavery and Modern Ideology* (New York, 1980).

10. P. Hunt, *Slaves, Warfare and Ideology in the Greek Historians* (Cambridge, 1998).

11. S. R. Joshel and S. Murnaghan (eds), *Women and Slaves in Greco-Roman Culture: Differential Equations* (London, 1998).

12. L. E. Tise, *Proslavery: A History of the Defense of Slavery in America, 1701–1840* (Athens, GA, 1988).

13. Letter from Claude Sintes, Director of the Museum, 21 June 2010.

14. M. Finley, *Economy and Society in Ancient Greece* (London, 1981).

15. K. Hopkins, *Conquerors and Slaves: Sociological Studies in Roman History* (Cambridge, 1978).

16. Aristotle, *The Politics*, edited by H. Rackham (London, 1932), pp. 29, 31; P. Garnsey, *Ideas of Slavery from Aristotle to Augustine* (Cambridge, 1996).

17. Polybius, *History of Rome*, 16.30–4, 15.21–4.

18. I have benefited greatly from the advice of Art Eckstein on this section.

19. Polybius, *The Histories*, edited by W. R. Paton (6 vols, London, 1925), IV, 143.

20. Y. Garlan, *Slavery in Ancient Greece* (Ithaca, NY, 1998).

21. M. Finley, *The Ancient Economy* (Berkeley, CA, 1973).

22. P. A. Brunt, *Italian Manpower, 225 BC–AD 14* (Oxford, 1971).

23. D. Eley, *The Epic Film: Myth and History* (London, 1980); M. M. Winkler (ed.), *Gladiator: Film and History* (Oxford, 2004) – for a defence of historical filmmaking see the essay by K. M. Coleman, 'The Pedant Goes to Hollywood: The Role of the Academic Consultant'; J. Richards, *The Ancient World on Screen* (London, 2008).

24. M. Finley, *A History of Sicily: Ancient Sicily to the Arab Conquest* (New York, 1968), pp. 139–44.

25. K. R. Bradley, *Slavery and Rebellion in the Roman World, 140 BC–70 BC* (Bloomington, IN, 1989).

26. This situation prefigured later relationships between African kingdoms and European in the age of the Atlantic slave trade.

27. E. G. Pulleyblank, 'The Origins and Nature of Chattel Slavery in China', *Journal of the Economic and Social History of the*

Orient, 1 (1958), pp. 185–220; J. A. G. Roberts, *A History of China* (2nd edn, Basingstoke, 2006), p. 5.

28. T. Nelson, 'Slavery in Medieval Japan', *Monumenta Nipponica*, 59 (2004), pp. 463–92.

29. This approach has also been taken up by cinema. Thus, in Alejandro Amenábar's film *Agora* (2009), the slave, Davus, falls in love with his mistress, Hypatia of Alexandria, a Greek scholar, but is torn between her and the upsurge of Christianity.

30. J. R. Willis (ed.), *Slaves and Slavery in Muslim Africa. I: Islam and the Ideology of Enslavement* (London, 1985).

31. C. Freeman, *A New History of Early Christianity* (New Haven, CT, 2009), p. 99.

32. This idea, however, could also be found in Roman law before the Christian period.

33. R. Y. Rotman, *Byzantine Slavery and the Mediterranean* (Cambridge, MA, 2009).

34. E. F. Toledano, *As If Silent and Absent: Bonds of Enslavement in the Islamic Middle East* (New Haven, CT, 2007).

35. S. Kidwai, 'Sultans, Eunuchs and Domestics: New Forms of Bondage in Medieval India', in U. Patnaik and M. Dingwaney (eds), *Chains of Servitude: Bondage and Slavery in India* (Madras, 1985); K. S. Lal, *The Muslim Slave System in Medieval India* (New Delhi, 1994).

36. G. E. von Grunebaum, *Medieval Islam* (2nd edn, Chicago, 1953), p. 210.

37. A. Tinniswood, *Pirates of Barbary* (London, 2010), pp. 168, 185.

38. J. Schacht, *An Introduction to Islamic Law* (Oxford, 1964), p. 130.

39. S. Vryonis, 'Seljuk Gulams and Ottoman Divşirme', *Der Islam*, 41 (1965), pp. 224–52; C. Imber, *The Ottoman Empire* (2nd edn, Basingstoke, 2009), p. 118.

40. P. Jackson, *The Delhi Sultanate* (Cambridge, 1999).

41. P. Crone, *Slaves on Horseback: The Evolution of the Islamic Polity* (Cambridge, 1980).

42. D. Bracken, 'Rome and the Isles: Ireland, England and the Rhetoric of Orthodoxy', in J. Graham-Campbell and M. Ryan (eds), *Anglo-Saxon/Irish Relations Before the Vikings* (Oxford, 2009), pp. 76–7.

43. V. Achim, *The Roma in Romanian History* (Budapest, 2004).

44. A. P. Smyth, *Scandinavian Kings in the British Isles* (Oxford, 1977), pp. 154–68; P. H. Sawyer, *Kings and Vikings* (London, 1982), pp. 39–42; R. Karras, *Slavery and Society in Medieval Scandinavia* (New Haven, CT, 1988); S. Brink (ed.), *The Viking World* (London, 2008), pp. 49–56.

45. D. Wyatt, *Slaves and Warriors in Britain and Ireland, 800–1200* (Leiden, 2009).

46. M. Bloch, *Slavery and Serfdom in the Middle Ages* (Berkeley, CA, 1975); W. Davis, 'On Servile Status in the Early Middle Ages', in M. L. Bush (ed.), *Serfdom and Slavery: Studies in Legal Bondage* (London, 1996), pp. 225–46; D.A.E. Pelteret, *Slavery in Early Medieval England* (Woodbridge, 1995), pp. 251–6.

47. A. L. Poole, *From Domesday Book to Magna Carta* (Oxford, 1955), p. 40.

48. A. Smith, *An Inquiry into the Nature and Wealth of Nations* (London, 1776; Oxford edn, 1979), p. 386.

49. J. Hatcher, *English Tin Production and Trade before 1550* (Oxford, 1973), p. 17.

50. C. Verlinden, *L'Esclavage dans l'Europe médiévale* (2 vols, Ghent, 1955–77); J. Heers, *Esclaves domestiques au Moyen Age dans le monde méditerranéen* (Paris, 1981).

51. J. Vogt, *Portuguese Rule on the Gold Coast, 1469–1682* (Athens, GA, 1979).

52. V. Rau, 'The Madeiran Sugar Cane Plantations', in H. B. Johnson, Jr (ed.), *From Reconquest to Empire: The Iberian Background to Latin American History* (New York, 1970), pp. 71–84.

53. K. Seaver, *The Frozen Echo: Greenland and the Exploration of North America c. 1000–1500* (Stanford, CA, 1966), pp. 178–9, 206. I have benefited from the advice of Peter Fleming and Michael Bennett.

54. A. Korhonen, 'Washing the Ethiopian White: Conceptualising Black Skin in Renaissance England', in T. F. Earle and K. J. P. Lowe (eds), *Black Africans in Renaissance Europe* (Cambridge, 2005), p. 111.

55. G. E. von Grunebaum, *Medieval Islam* (2nd edn, Chicago, 1953), pp. 209–11.

56. M. Newitt, *A History of Portuguese Overseas Expansion, 1400–1668* (Abingdon, 2005), p. 45.

57. J. Black, *European Warfare, 1494–1660* (London, 2002); J. Black, *Beyond the Military Revolution: War in the Seventeenth Century World* (London, 2011).

58. A. W. Lawrence, *Trade Castles and Forts of West Africa* (London, 1963).

59. D. Burwash, *English Merchant Shipping, 1460–1540* (Toronto, 1947); I. Friel, *The Good Ship: Ships, Shipbuilding and Technology in England, 1200–1520* (London, 1995).

60. S. M. Greenfield, 'Madeira and the Beginning of New World Sugar Cane Cultivation and Plantation Slavery', in V. D. Rubin and A. Tuden (eds), *Comparative Perspectives on Slavery in New World Plantation Societies* (New York, 1977), pp. 536–52.

Chapter 3

1. T. Nelson, 'Slavery in Medieval Japan', *Monumenta Nipponica*, 59 (2004), pp. 465–6.

2. G. Condominas (ed.), *Formes extrêmes de dépendance: contributions à l'étude de l'esclavage en Asie du Sud-Est* (Paris, 1998).

3. J. Thornton, 'The Slave Trade in Eighteenth Century Angola: Effects on Demographic Structures', *Canadian Journal of African Studies*, 14 (1980), pp. 417–27.

4. P. Lane and D. Johnson, 'The Archaeology and History of Slavery in South Sudan in the Nineteenth Century', in A. C. S. Peacock (ed.), *The Frontiers of the Ottoman World* (London, 2009), p. 513.

5. R. A. Austen, *African Economic History: Internal Development and External Dependency* (Portsmouth, NH, 1987), p. 275; R. A. Austen, 'The 19th Century Islamic Slave Trade from East Africa: A Tentative Census', in W. G. Clarence-Smith (ed.), *The Economics of the Indian Ocean Slave Trade in the Nineteenth Century* (London, 1989), pp. 21–44.

6. G. Knaap, 'Headhunting, Carnage and Armed Peace in Amboina, 1500–1700', *Journal of the Economic and Social History of the Orient*, 46 (2003), pp. 165–92.

7. C. Imber, *The Ottoman Empire* (2nd edn, Basingstoke, 2009), pp. 123–7.

8. J. Blum, *Lord and Peasant in Russia from the Ninth to the Nineteenth Century* (Princeton, NJ, 1961); R. C. Hoffmann,

Land, Liberties, and Lordship in a Late Medieval Countryside. Agrarian Structures and Change in the Duchy of Wroclaw (Philadelphia, PA, 1989).

9. R. Hellie, *Slavery in Russia, 1450–1725* (Chicago, 1982).

10. R. J. Pym, *The Gypsies of Early Modern Spain, 1425–1783* (Basingstoke, 2007). For another group seen as vagrants, C. S. L. Davies, 'Slavery and Protector Somerset: The Vagrancy Act of 1547', *Economic History Review*, 1–3 (1966), pp. 533–49.

11. R. Pike, *Penal Servitude in Early Modern Spain* (Madison, WI, 1983).

12. R. Garfield, *A History of São Tomé Island, 1470–1655: The Key to Guinea* (San Francisco, CA, 1992); T. J. Coates, *Convicts and Orphans: Forced and State-Sponsored Colonizers in the Portuguese Empire, 1550–1755* (Stanford, CA, 2001).

13. A. Crosby, *The Columbian Exchange: Biological and Cultural Consequences of 1492* (Westport, CT, 1969); N. D. Cook, *Demographic Collapse: Indian Peru, 1520–1620* (Cambridge, 1981); S. A. Alchon, *A Pest in the Land: New World Epidemics in a Global Perspective* (Albuquerque, NM, 2003).

14. A. M. Stevens-Arroyo, 'The Inter-Atlantic Paradigm: The Failure of Spanish Medieval Colonization of the Canary and Caribbean Islands', *Journal of Comparative Studies in Society and History*, 35 (1993), p. 521.

15. J. M. Monteiro, 'From Indian to Slave: Forced Native Labour and Colonial Society in São Paulo during the Seventeenth Century', *Slavery and Abolition*, 9 (1988), pp. 105–27.

16. R. A. Williams, *The American Indian in Western Legal Thought: The Discourses of Conquest* (New York, 1990).

17. J. H. Elliott, *Spain, Europe and The Wider World, 1500–1800* (New Haven, CT, 2009), p. 165.

18. L. B. Simpson, *The Encomienda in New Spain: the Beginning of Spanish Mexico* (3rd edn, Berkeley, CA, 1966); W. L. Sherman, *Forced Native Labor in Sixteenth-Century Central America* (Lincoln, NB, 1979); O. N. Bolland, 'Colonization and Slavery in Central America', in P. E. Lovejoy and N. Rogers (eds), *Unfree Labour in the Development of the Atlantic World* (Ilford, 1994), pp. 11–25.

19. A. Hess, *The Forgotten Frontier: A History of the Sixteenth-Century Ibero-African Frontier* (Chicago, 1978).

20. P. Gerhard, 'A Black Conquistador in Mexico', *Hispanic American Historical Review*, 58 (1978), pp. 451–9; M. Restall, 'Black Conquistadors: Armed Africans in Early Spanish America', *The Americas*, 57 (2000), pp. 171–206.

21. F. A. Scarano, 'Spanish Hispaniola and Puerto Rico', in R. L. Paquette and M. M. Smith (eds), *The Oxford Handbook of Slavery in the Americas* (Oxford, 2010), p. 28.

22. F. Bowser, *The African Slave in Colonial Peru, 1524–1650* (Stanford, CA, 1974); C. A. Palmer, *Slaves of the White Gods: Blacks in Mexico, 1570–1650* (Cambridge, MA, 1976).

23. L. Felipe de Alencastro, 'The Apprenticeship of Colonization', in B. L. Solow (ed.), *Slavery and the Rise of the Atlantic System* (Cambridge, 1991), pp. 168–9.

24. M. W. Lewis and K. E. Wigen, *The Myth of Continents: A Critique of Metageography* (Berkeley, CA, 1997).

25. T. Seijas, 'The Portuguese Slave Trade to Spanish Manila, 1580–1640', *Itinerario*, 32 (2008), pp. 19–38.

26. T. Nelson, 'Slavery in Medieval Japan', *Monumenta Nipponica*, 59 (2004), pp. 463–94.

27. K. F. Hall, *Things of Darkness: Economies of Race and Gender in Early Modern England* (Ithaca, NY, 1995); M. Sherwood, 'Blacks in Tudor England', *History Today*, 53/10 (Oct. 2003), pp. 40–2; I. Habib, *Black Lives in the English Archives, 1500–1677: Imprints of the Invisible* (Farnham, 2008).

28. R. Unwin, *The Defeat of John Hawkins* (London, 1960).

29. J. W. Blake, 'English Trade with the Portuguese Empire in West Africa, 1581–1629', *Quarto Congreso do Mundo Português*, 6 (1940), pp. 313–41.

Chapter 4

1. BL Maps K.A.r. (38).

2. P. K. Crossley, *Orphan Warriors* (Princeton, NJ, 1991).

3. P. M. Torbert, *The Ch'ing Imperial Household Department* (Cambridge, MA, 1977).

4. G. E. Aylmer, 'Slavery Under Charles II: The Mediterranean and Tangier', *English Historical Review*, 144 (1999), pp. 378–88.

5. R. C. Davis, *Christian Slaves, Muslim Masters: White Slavery in*

the Mediterranean, the Barbary Coast, and Italy, 1500–1800 (Basingstoke, 2004).

6. T. Gray, 'Turkish Piracy and Early Stuart Devon', *Transactions of the Devonshire Association*, 121 (1989), pp. 159–71; C. R. Pennell, *Piracy and Diplomacy in Seventeenth-Century North Africa* (Rutherford, NJ, 1989); N. Matar, *Britain and Barbary, 1589–1689* (Gainesville, FL, 2005).

7. L. Voigt, *Writing Captivity in the Early Modern Atlantic: Circulations of Knowledge and Authority in the Iberian and English Atlantic Worlds* (Chapel Hill, NC, 2009); C. R. Pennell (ed.), *Piracy and Diplomacy in Seventeenth-Century North Africa: The Journal of Thomas Baker, English Consul in Tripoli, 1677–85* (Cranbury, NJ, 1989).

8. R. Matthee, 'Exotic Substances: The Introduction and Global Spread of Tobacco, Coffee, Cocoa, Tea, and Distilled Liquor, Sixteenth to Eighteenth Centuries', in R. Porter and M. Teich (eds), *Drugs and Narcotics in History* (Cambridge, 1995), pp. 38–46; J. Walvin, *Fruits of Empire: Exotic Produce and British Taste, 1660–1800* (London, 1997); M. Norton, *Sacred Gifts, Profane Pleasures: A History of Tobacco and Chocolate in the Atlantic World* (Ithaca, NY, 2008); S. W. Mintz, *Sweetness and Power: The Place of Sugar in Modern History* (London, 1985).

9. A. L. Butler, 'Europe's Indian Nectar: The Transatlantic Cacao and Chocolate Trade in the Seventeenth Century' (M. Litt., Oxford, 1993).

10. R. J. Ferry, 'Encomienda, African Slavery, and Agriculture in Seventeenth-Century Caracas', *Hispanic American Historical Review*, 61 (1981), pp. 620–36.

11. J. R. Ward, 'The Profitability of Sugar Planting in the British West Indies, 1650–1834', *Economic History Review*, 2nd series, 31 (1978), p. 208.

12. A. E. Smith, *Colonists in Bondage: White Servitude and Convict Labor in America, 1607–1776* (Chapel Hill, NC, 1947).

13. D. Hancock (ed.), *The Letters of William Freeman, London Merchant, 1678–1685* (London, 2002), p. xl.

14. E. Vila Vilar, *Hispanoamérica y el comercio de esclavos: Los asientos portugueses* (Seville, 1977).

15. J. and L. Thornton, *Central Africans, Atlantic Creoles, and the Foundation of the Americas, 1585–1660* (Cambridge, 2007).

16. C. R. Boxer, *Salvador da Sá and the Struggle for Brazil and Angola 1602–1686* (London, 1952) and *The Dutch in Brazil, 1624–1654* (Oxford, 1957).

17. G. J. Ames, 'Pedro II and the Estado da India: Braganzan Absolutism and Overseas Empire, 1668–1683', *Luso-Brazilian Review*, 34 (1997), pp. 9–10; E. Van Veen, *Decay or Defeat? An Enquiry into the Portuguese Decline in Asia, 1580–1645* (Leiden, 2000).

18. A. S. Szarka, 'Portugal, France, and the coming of the War of the Spanish Succession' (PhD, Ohio State, 1975), p. 125.

19. M. Vink, '"The World's Oldest Trade": Dutch Slavery and the Slave Trade in the Indian Ocean in the Seventeenth Century', *Journal of World History*, 14 (2003), pp. 131–77.

20. N. Zahedieh, 'Trade, Plunder, and Economic Development in Early English Jamaica, 1655–89', *Economic History Review*, 2nd series, 39 (1980), pp. 205–22. The 1956–7 Hollywood television series *The Buccaneers* had the hero freeing slaves from slave ships, but that spoke more to contemporary values than those of the seventeenth century. See also the films *The Crimson Pirate* (1952) and *Swashbuckler* (1976).

21. D. H. Akenson, *If the Irish Ran the World: Montserrat, 1630–1730* (Montréal, 1997).

22. H. Beckles, 'The Economic Origins of Black Slavery in the British West Indies, 1640–1680: A Tentative Analysis of the Barbados Model', *Journal of Caribbean History*, 16 (1982), pp. 36–56, esp. pp. 52–4.

23. H. Beckles, *White Slavery and Black Servitude in Barbados, 1627–1715* (Knoxville, TN, 1989); L. Gragg, '"To Procure Negroes": The English Slave Trade to Barbados, 1627–60', *Slavery and Abolition*, 16 (1995), pp. 70, 74.

24. H. Beckles and A. Downes, 'The Economics of Transition to the Black Labor System in Barbados, 1630–1680', *Journal of Interdisciplinary History*, 18 (1987), pp. 246–7.

25. T. Burnard, 'Who Bought Slaves in Early America? Purchasers of Slaves from the Royal African Company in Jamaica, 1674–1708', *Slavery and Abolition*, 17 (1996), p. 88.

26. V. A. Shepherd, 'Livestock and Sugar: Aspects of Jamaican Agricultural Development from the Late Seventeenth to the Early Nineteenth Century', *Historical Journal*, 34 (1991), pp. 627–43.

27. R. Law, 'The First Scottish Guinea Company, 1634–9', *Scottish Historical Review*, 76 (1997), pp. 185–202.

28. Sir George Downing, envoy to the United Provinces, to Henry, Lord Arlington, Secretary of State, 14, 22 Aug. 1664, NA SP 84/171; R. Ollard, *Man of War: Sir Robert Holmes and the Restoration Navy* (London, 1969).

29. P. E. Lovejoy, 'The Volume of the Atlantic Slave Trade: A Synthesis', *Journal of African History*, 23 (1982), p. 481.

30. A .M. Carlos and J. B. Kruse, 'The Decline of the Royal African Company: Fringe Firms and the Role of the Charter', *Economic History Review*, 2nd series, 49 (1996), pp. 291–313; K. Morgan (ed.), *The British Transatlantic Slave Trade. II: The Royal African Company* (London, 2003).

31. D. Geggus, 'The French Slave Trade: An Overview', *William and Mary Quarterly*, 58 (2001), p. 120.

32. F. Guerra, 'The Influence of Disease on Race, Logistics and Colonization in the Antilles', *Journal of Tropical Medicine and Hygiene*, 69 (1966), pp. 33–5.

33. T. Burnard, '"The Countrie Continues Sicklie": White Mortality in Jamaica, 1655–1780', *Social History of Medicine*, 12 (1999), pp. 45–72, esp. 55–6, 71.

34. E. S. Morgan, 'The First American Boom: Virginia 1618 to 1630', *William and Mary Quarterly*, 3rd series, 28 (1971), pp. 169–98, esp. 197.

35. P. N. Moogk, 'Reluctant Exiles: The Problems of Colonisation in French North America', *William and Mary Quarterly*, 46 (1989), pp. 463–505.

36. J. Michel, *La Guyane sous l'Ancien Régime* (Paris, 1989).

37. R. Menard, 'The Tobacco Industry in the Chesapeake Colonies, 1617–1730: An Interpretation', *Research in Economic History*, 5 (1980), pp. 109–77, esp. 153–5.

38. R. Menard, 'From Servants to Slaves: The Transformation of the Chesapeake Labor System', *Southern Studies*, 16 (1977), pp. 355–90, esp. p. 389.

39. R. McColley, 'Slavery in Virginia, 1619–1660: A Reexamination', in R. H. Abzug and S. E. Maizlish (eds), *New Perspectives on Race and Slavery in America* (Lexington, KT, 1986), pp. 11–24; J. Horn, *Adapting to a New World: English Society in the Seventeenth-Century Chesapeake* (Chapel Hill, NC, 1994).

40. O. Patterson, 'Slavery and Slave Revolts: A Socio-Historical Analysis of the First Maroon War, Jamaica, 1655–1740', *Social and Economic Studies*, 19 (1970), pp. 289–325; M. Craton, 'The Passion to Exist: Slave Rebellions in the British West Indies, 1650–1832', *Journal of Caribbean History*, 13 (1980), p. 4; R. Price (ed.), *Maroon Societies: Rebel Slave Communities in the Americas* (2nd edn, Baltimore, MD, 1996).

41. M. Restall (ed.), *Beyond Black and Red: African-Native Relations in Colonial Latin America* (Albuquerque, NM, 2005).

42. A. T. Vaughan, 'The Origins Debate: Slavery and Racism in Seventeenth-Century Virginia', *Virginia Magazine of History and Biography*, 97 (1989), p. 353.

43. R. S. Dunn, 'The English Sugar Islands and the Founding of South Carolina', *South Carolina Historical Magazine*, 72 (1971), pp. 81–93, esp. 85, 92–3.

44. R. C. Nash, 'South Carolina and the Atlantic Economy in the Late Seventeenth and Eighteenth Centuries', *Economic History Review*, 45 (1992), pp. 677–702.

45. W. Rodney, 'African Slavery and Other Forms of Social Oppression on the Upper Guinea Coast in the Context of the Atlantic Slave Trade', *Journal of African History*, 7 (1966), pp. 431–43; J. D. Fage, 'African Societies and the Atlantic Slave Trade', *Past and Present*, 125 (1989), pp. 97–115; E. W. Evans and D. Richardson, 'Hunting for Rents: The Economics of Slaving in Pre-Colonial Africa', *Economic History Review*, 2nd series, 48 (1995), pp. 665–86.

46. P. Manning, *Slavery and African Life: Occidental, Oriental and African Slave Trades* (Cambridge, 1990).

47. J. Thornton, *Africa and Africans in the Making of the Atlantic World, 1400–1800* (2nd edn, Cambridge, 1998); Y. Peron, *Atlas de la Haute-Volta* (Paris, 1975), pp. 20–1; P. Pélissier, *Atlas du Sénégal* (Paris, 1980), pp. 22–5.

48. L. M. Heywood, 'Slavery and its Transformation in the kingdom of the Kongo, 1491–1800', *Journal of African History*, 50 (2009), pp. 17–18.

49. J. Thornton, *Africa and Africans in the Making of the Atlantic World, 1400–1800* (2nd edn, Cambridge, 1998), pp. 98–125 and *Warfare in Atlantic Africa, 1500–1800* (London, 1999), esp. pp. 127–39.

50. R. Law, '"Here is No Resisting the Country": The Realities of Power in Afro-European Relations on the West African "Slave Coast"', *Itinerario*, 18 (1994), pp. 50–64, esp. 52–7; W. St. Clair, *The Grand Slave Emporium: Cape Coast Castle and the British Slave Trade* (London, 2006).

51. G. Nováky, *Handelskompanier och kompanihandel. Svenska Afrikakompaniet 1649–1663* (Uppsala, 1990), English summary, pp. 241, 244.

52. R. Law and K. Mann, 'West Africa in the Atlantic Community: The Case of the Slave Coast', *William and Mary Quarterly*, 56 (1999), pp. 307–34.

53. K. Y. Daaku, *Trade and Politics on the Gold Coast, 1600–1700* (Oxford, 1970), pp. 96–114.

54. J. Thornton, 'Cannibals, Witches, and Slave Traders in the Atlantic World', *William and Mary Quarterly*, 60 (2003), pp. 274–5.

55. S. E. Smallwood, 'African Guardians, European Slave Ships, and the Changing Dynamics of Power in the Early Modern Atlantic', *William and Mary Quarterly*, 64 (2007), pp. 679–716.

56. Thornton, 'Warfare, Slave Trading and European Influence: Atlantic Africa 1450–1800', in J. Black (ed.), *War in the Early Modern World* (London, 1999), p. 141.

57. E. van den Boogaart and P.C. Emmer, 'The Dutch Participation in the Atlantic Slave Trade, 1596–1650', in H. A. Gemery and J. S. Hogendorn (eds), *The Uncommon Market: Essays in the Economic History of the Atlantic Slave Trade* (New York, 1979), p. 367; K. G. Davies, *The Royal African Company* (London, 1957), p. 292.

58. J. C. Miller, 'Some Aspects of the Commercial Organization of Slaving at Luanda, Angola, 1760–1830', in H. A. Gemery and J. S. Hogendorn (eds), *The Uncommon Market: Essays in the Economic History of the Atlantic Slave Trade* (New York, 1979), p. 104.

59. M. Craton, *Sinews of Empire: A Short History of British Slavery* (New York, 1974), pp. 194–5.

60. A. Pagden, 'Europe and the Wider World', in J. Bergin (ed.), *The Seventeenth Century* (Oxford, 2001), pp. 207–9.

61. R. Law, 'Individualising the Atlantic Slave Trade: The Biography of Mahommah Gardo Baquaqua of Djougou', *Transactions of the Royal Historical Society*, 6th series, 12 (2002), pp. 133–40.

62. S. W. Mintz and R. Price, *The Birth of African-American Culture: An Anthropological Perspective* (Boston, MA, 1976); A. J. R. Russell-Wood, *The Black Man in Slavery and Freedom in Colonial Brazil* (London, 1982); K.M. de Queirós Mattoso, *To Be a Slave in Brazil* (New Brunswick, NJ, 1989); C. H. Lutz, *Santiago de Guatemala, 1541–1773: City, Caste, and the Colonial Experience* (Norman, OK, 1994); R. D. Cope, *The Limits of Radical Domination: Plebeian Society in Colonial Mexico City, 1660–1720* (Madison, WI, 1994); J. Landers, *Black Society in Spanish Florida* (Urbana, IL, 1999); H. L. Bennett, *Africans in Colonial Mexico: Absolutism, Christianity, and Afro-Creole Consciousness, 1570–1640* (Bloomington, IN, 2003); M. L. Conniff and T. J. Davis, *Africans in the Americas: A History of the Black Diaspora* (New York, 1994).

63. J. H. Elliott, *Empires of the Atlantic World: Britain and Spain in America 1492–1830* (New Haven, CT, 2000), p. 107.

64. A. J. R. Russell-Wood, 'Black and Mulatto Brotherhoods in Colonial Brazil: A Study in Collective Behaviour', *Hispanic American Historical Review*, 54 (1974), pp. 567–602, esp. 581–2; R. C. Rath, 'African Music in Seventeenth-Century Jamaica: Cultural Transit and Transmission', *William and Mary Quarterly*, 3rd series, 50 (1993), pp. 700–26.

Chapter 5

1. W. Macaulay, *Memoranda Respecting the French Slave Trade in 1820* (London, 1820), pp. 29–30.

2. M. S. Anderson, 'Great Britain and the Barbary States in the Eighteenth Century', *Bulletin of the Institute of Historical Research*, 29 (1956), pp. 87–107.

3. Voltaire, *Candide* (1759), translated by J. Butt (London, 1947), pp. 85–6; J. M. Postma, *The Dutch in the Atlantic Slave Trades* (Cambridge, 1990).

4. R. Horton, 'African Conversion', *Africa*, 41 (1971), pp. 85–108.

5. S. Cave, *A Few Words, on the Encouragement Given to Slavery . . . by the Sugar Bill of 1846* (London, 1849), p. 6.

6. P. E. Lovejoy, 'The Volume of the Atlantic Slave Trade: A Synthesis', *Journal of African History*, 23 (1982), p. 478, but see upward revision in volume of slave exports from 1700 to 1810 by 8 per cent in D. Richardson, 'Slave Exports from West and

West-Central Africa, 1700–1810: New Estimates of Volume and Distribution', *Journal of African History*, 30 (1989), pp. 1–22.

7. K. Banks, 'The Illicit Slave-Trade out of Martinique, 1718–1756', in P. A. Coclanis, *The Atlantic Economy during the Seventeenth and Eighteenth Centuries: Organization, Operation, Practice, and Personnel* (Columbia, SC, 2005).

8. G. Scelle, 'The Slave-Trade in the Spanish Colonies of America: the Asiento', *American Journal of International Law*, 4 (1910), pp. 612–61.

9. C. A. Palmer, *Human Cargoes: The British Slave Trade to Spanish America, 1700–1739* (Urbana, IL, 1981).

10. R. Austen, 'Dutch Trading Voyages to Cameroon, 1721–1759: European Documents and African History', *Annales de la Faculté des Lettres et Sciences Humaines, Université de Yaounde*, 6 (1975), pp. 5–27; J. Postma, 'A Reassessment of the Dutch Atlantic Slave Trade', in Postma and V. Enthoven (eds), *Riches from Atlantic Commerce; Dutch Transatlantic Trade and Shipping, 1585–1817* (Leiden, 2003), p. 137.

11. R. Ross, *Cape of Torment: Slavery and Resistance in South Africa* (London, 1983).

12. S. E. Green-Pedersen, 'The History of the Danish Negro Slave Trade, 1733–1807', *Revue française d'histoire d'outre-mer*, 62 (1975), p. 209; S. E. Green-Pedersen, 'The Scope and Structure of the Danish Negro Slave Trade', *Scandinavian Economic History Review*, 19 (1971), pp. 149–97.

13. P. D. Curtin, *The Atlantic Slave Trade: A Census* (Madison, WI, 1969).

14. R. Stein, 'Measuring the French Slave Trade, 1713–1792/3', *Journal of African History*, 19 (1978), pp. 520–1; D. Geggus, 'The French Slave Trade: An Overview', *William and Mary Quarterly*, 58 (2001), pp. 119–38.

15. R. Stein, 'The French Sugar Business in the Eighteenth Century: A Quantitative Study', *Journal of Business History*, 22 (1980), p. 14.

16. J. Dupâquier (ed.), *Histoire de la population française, II: De la Renaissance à 1789* (Paris, 1988), pp. 127–8; G. Martin, *Nantes au XVIIIe siècle: L'ère des négriers, 1714–1774* (Paris, 1931); H. Robert, 'Les traffics coloniaux du port de La Rochelle au

XVIIIe siècle, 1713–1789', *Bulletin de la Société des Antiquaires de l'Ouest* (1949), pp. 135–79; J. Tarrade, *Le Commerce colonial de la France à la fin de l'Ancien Régime* (Paris, 1972), II, p. 759; P. Butel, *Les négociations bordelais, l'Europe et les Iles au XVIIIe siècle* (Paris, 1974); G. Debien, *Les Esclaves aux Antilles Française: XVII–XVIII siècle* (Basse-Terre, Guadeloupe, 1974); R.L. Stein, *The French Slave Trade in the Eighteenth Century: An Old Regime Business* (Madison, WI, 1979); W.B. Cohen, *The French Encounter with Africans: White Response to Blacks, 1530–1888* (Bloomington, IN, 1980); E. Saugéra, *Bordeaux port négrier. XVIIIe–XIXe siècles. Chronologie, économie, idéologie* (Paris, 1995); A. Roman, *Saint-Malo au temps des négriers* (Paris, 2001); P. Røge, '"Legal Despotism" and Enlightened Reform in the Îles du Vent: The Colonial Governments of Chevalier de Mirabeau and Mercier de la Rivière, 1754–1764', in G. Paquette (ed.), *Enlightened Reform in Southern Europe and its Atlantic Colonies, c. 1750–1830* (Farnham, 2009), p. 170.

17. E. Alpers, 'The French Slave Trade in East Africa, 1721–1810', *Cahiers d' Études Africaines*, 37 (1970), pp. 80–124.

18. C. Shammas, 'The Eighteenth-Century English Diet and Economic Change', *Explorations in Economic History*, 21 (1984), pp. 254–69.

19. Evelyn journal, BL Evelyn papers, vol. 49 fol. 37; NA SP 89/59 fol. 115.

20. T. Burnard, '"Prodigious Riches": The Wealth of Jamaica before the American Revolution', *Economic History Review*, 54 (2001), pp. 506–24.

21. D. J. Hamilton, *Scotland, the Caribbean and the Atlantic world 1750–1820* (Manchester, 2005), p. 181.

22. Diary of Sir Dudley Ryder, Attorney-General, 6 Jan. 1744, Sandon Hall, Harrowby papers, Ryder diary. *Old England*, 18 Feb. 1744.

23. R. B. Sheridan, 'The Molasses Act and the Market Strategy of the British Sugar Planters', *Journal of Economic History*, 17 (1957), pp. 62–83; A. J. O'Shaughnessy, 'The Formation of a Commercial Lobby: The West India Interest, British Colonial Policy and the American Revolution', *Historical Journal*, 40 (1997), pp. 71–95.

24. C. C. Goslinga, *The Dutch in the Caribbean and in the Guianas 1680–1791* (Assen, 1985).

25. K. Ward, *Networks of Empire: Forced Migration in the Dutch East India Company* (Cambridge, 2009); U. Bosma and R. Raben, *Being 'Dutch' in the Indies: A History of Creolisation and Empire, 1500–1920* (Athens, OH, 2008).

26. I. Chatterjee, 'Colouring Subalternity: Slaves, Concubines and Social Orphans under the East India Company', *Subaltern Studies*, 10 (1999), pp. 49–97 and *Gender, Slavery and Law in Colonial India* (Delhi, 1999).

27. African Company memoranda, 13, 28 Feb., 4, 18 Dec. 1724, 18 Mar. 1725, 18 Mar. 1726, Charles, Second Viscount Townshend, Secretary of State for the Northern Department, to William Finch, envoy in The Hague, 10 June 1726, African Company to Burchett, Secretary of the Admiralty, 28 May, 6 June, 3 Aug. 1728, NA SP 35/48, 54, 55, 61, 84/290, ADM 1/3810; James, Lord Waldegrave, envoy in Paris, to Thomas, Duke of Newcastle, Secretary of State for the Southern Department, 29 Mar. 1733, BL Add. 32781; Couraud to Waldegrave, 25 June 1733, enclosing 'Observations Relating to the Gum Trade', Chewton Mendip, Chewton House, Waldegrave papers; Chavigny, French envoy in London, to Chauvelin, French Foreign Minister, 24 Dec. 1735, AE CP Ang. 392; Sir Charles Wager, First Lord of the Admiralty, to Newcastle, 18 Nov. 1736, Amelot, French envoy in London, to Cambis, French Foreign Minister, 16 Feb. 1738, NA SP 42/21, 107/21.

28. Memorandum, 14 Aug., Evan Nepean to William Fraser, 18 Aug. 1784, NA FO 27/12 fols 262–4.

29. Robert Walpole, envoy in Lisbon, to William, Lord Grenville, Foreign Secretary, 13 July, 13 Aug., Grenville to Walpole, 28 June 1791, NA FO 63/14; Cabinet minute, 28 July 1791, BL Add. 59306 fol. 3.

30. William Murray to Newcastle, 7 Sep. 1754, BL Add. 32736 fol. 438.

31. Reporting William Pitt the Elder, Viry, Sardinian envoy to Charles Emmanuel III of Sardinia, 13 June 1758, Turin, Archivio di Stato, Lettere Ministri Inghilterra 63.

32. BL Add. 36797 fol. 1.

33. M. Pelletier, 'La Martinique et La Guadeloupe au lendemain du Traité de Paris, l'oeuvre des ingénieurs géographes', *Chronique d'histoire Maritime*, 9 (1984), pp. 22–30.

34. A. J. O'Shaughnessy, *An Empire Divided: The American Revolution and the British Caribbean* (Philadelphia, PA, 2000), p. 166.

35. L. W. Bergad, *Slavery and the Demographic and Economic History of Minas Gerais, 1720–1888* (Cambridge, 1999).

36. NA SP 89/30 fol. 164.

37. K. Schultz, 'The Crisis of Empire and the Problem of Slavery: Portugal and Brazil, c. 1700–1820', *Common Knowledge*, 11 (2005), pp. 273–4.

38. P. Vergier, *Flux et reflux de la traite des nègres entre le golfe de Benin et Bahia de Todos os Santos du 17e et 18e siècles* (The Hague, 1968).

39. S. B. Schwartz, *Sugar Plantations in the Formation of Brazilian Society: Bahia, 1550–1835* (Cambridge, 1985), p. 182.

40. J. C. Miller, *Way of Death: Merchant Capitalism and the Angolan Slave Trade, 1730–1830* (Madison, WI, 1988); J. C. Miller, 'A Marginal Institution on the Margin of the Atlantic System: The Portuguese Southern Atlantic Trade in the Eighteenth Century', in B. L. Solow (ed.), *Slavery and the Rise of the Atlantic System* (Cambridge, 1991), pp. 120–50; P. Mark, *'Portuguese' Style and Luso-African Identity: Precolonial Senegambia, Sixteenth-Nineteenth Centuries* (Bloomington, IN, 2002).

41. P. Caraman, *The Lost Paradise: An Account of the Jesuits in Paraguay, 1607–1768* (London, 1975); D. Sweet, 'Native Resistance in Eighteenth-Century Amazonia: The "Abominable Muras" in War and Peace', *Radical History Review*, 53 (1992), p. 58.

42. E. Piñero, 'The Cacao Economy of the Eighteenth-Century Province of Caracas and the Spanish Cacao Market', *Hispanic American Historical Review*, 68 (1988), p. 92.

43. J. R. Booker, 'Needed but Unwanted: Black Militiamen in Veracruz, Mexico, 1760–1810', *Historian*, 55 (1993), p. 259; R. J. Singh, *French Diplomacy in the Caribbean and the American Revolution* (Hicksville, NY, 1977), p. 122; K. Maxwell, *Pombal: Paradox of the Enlightenment* (Cambridge, 1995), p. 120.

44. N. Zahedieh, *The Capitol and the Colonies: London and the Atlantic Economy, 1660–1700* (Cambridge, 2010); D. Richardson, 'The Eighteenth-Century British Slave Trade: Estimates of its Volume and Coastal Distribution in Africa', *Research in Economic History*, 12 (1989), pp. 151–196.

45. D. Richardson (ed.), *Bristol, Africa and the Eighteenth-Century Slave Trade to America: II, The Years of Ascendancy, 1730–1745* (Gloucester, 1987).

46. D. Richardson, 'The British Empire and the Atlantic Slave Trade, 1660–1807', in P. J. Marshall (ed.), *The Oxford History of the British Empire, II: The Eighteenth Century* (Oxford, 1998), p. 446; J. E. Inikori, *Africans and the Industrial Revolution in England: A Study in International Trade and Economic Development* (Cambridge, 2002), esp. pp. 479–82.

47. M. Dresser, *Slavery Obscured: The Social History of the Slave Trade in an English Provincial Port* (London, 2001).

48. D. Richardson, 'The British Empire and the Atlantic Slave Trade, 1660–1807', in P. J. Marshall (ed.), *The Oxford History of the British Empire, II: The Eighteenth Century* (Oxford, 1998), p. 442; D. Richardson and M. M. Schofield, 'Whitehaven and the Eighteenth-Century British Slave Trade', *Transactions of the Cumberland and Westmorland Antiquarian and Archaeological Society*, 102 (1992), pp. 183–204, esp. p. 195.

49. W. Minchinton, 'Characteristics of British Slaving Vessels, 1698–1775', *Journal of Interdisciplinary History*, 20 (1989), pp. 53–81, esp. p. 74.

50. For the French equivalent, R. Lemesle, *Le Commerce colonial triangulaire: XVIIIe–XIXe siècles* (Paris, 1998).

51. R. B. Sheridan, 'The Commercial and Financial Organization of the British Slave Trade, 1750–1807', *Economic History Review*, 2nd series, 11 (1958–9), pp. 249–63, esp. p. 263; J. A. Rawley, *London: Metropolis of the Slave Trade* (Columbia, MO, 2003).

52. N. Tatterfield, *The Forgotten Trade, Comprising the Log of the Daniel and Henry of 1700 and Accounts of the Slave Trade from the Minor Ports of England, 1698–1725* (London, 1991); M. Elder, *The Slave Trade and the Economic Development of Eighteenth-Century Lancaster* (Preston, 1992).

53. R. A. Austen and W. D. Smith, 'Private Tooth Decay as Public Economic Virtue: The Slave–Sugar Triangle, Consumerism, and European Industrialization', *Social Science History*, 14 (1990), pp. 95–115.

54. D. Armitage and M.J. Braddick (eds), *The British Atlantic World, 1500–1800* (Basingstoke, 2002), p. 247. See also E. Mancke and C. Shammas (eds), *The Creation of the British Atlantic World* (Baltimore, MD, 2005).

55. J. Clark, *La Rochelle and the Atlantic Economy during the Eighteenth Century* (London, 1982).

56. G. Daudin, 'Comment calculer les profits de la traite?', *Outre-Mer*, 89 (2002), pp. 43–62; G. Daudin, 'Profitability of Slave and Long-Distance Trading in Context: The Case of Eighteenth-Century France', *Journal of Economic History*, 64 (2004), pp. 144–71.

57. G. M. Ostrander, 'The Making of the Triangular Trade Myth', *William and Mary Quarterly*, 30 (1973), pp. 635–44; J. Coughtry, *The Notorious Triangle: Rhode Island and the African Slave Trade, 1700–1807* (Philadelphia, PA, 1981); A. Jones, 'The Rhode Island Slave Trade: A Trading Advantage in Africa', *Slavery and Abolition*, 2 (1981), pp. 225–44.

58. D. Eltis and S. L. Engerman, 'Fluctuations in Age and Sex Ratios in the Transatlantic Slave Trade, 1663–1864', *Economic History Review*, 2nd series, 46 (1993), p. 321.

59. J. E. Inikori, 'Market Structure and the Profits of the British African Trade in the Late Eighteenth Century', *Journal of Economic History*, 41 (1981), pp. 745–76, esp. pp. 774–5. For the argument that there was a reasonable rate of return, W. Darity, Jr, 'Profitability of the British Trade in Slaves Once Again', *Explorations in Economic History*, 26 (1989), pp. 380–4. A clear summary is offered by K. Morgan, *Slavery, Atlantic Trade and the British Economy, 1660–1800* (Cambridge, 2000), pp. 36–48.

60. J. C. Appleby, '"A Business of Much Difficulty": A London Slaving Venture, 1651–1654', *The Mariner's Mirror*, 71, 1 (1995), pp. 3–14; A. Yacou, *Journaux de bord et de traite de Joseph Crassous de Médeuil: de La Rochelle à la côte de Guinée et aux Antilles, 1772–1776* (Paris, 2001); R. Harris, *The Diligent: A Voyage through the Worlds of the Slave Trade* (New York, 2002), re. a French ship that in 1731–2 sailed from Vannes

to Africa and then Martinique before returning to Vannes; R. Damon, *Joseph Crassous de Médeuil: 1741–1793, marchand, officier de la Marine royale et négrier* (Paris, 2004).

61. K. Morgan (ed.), *The Royal African Company* (London, 2003).

62. H. S. Klein and S. L. Engerman, 'Slave Mortality on British Ships, 1791–1797', in R. Anstey and P. E. H. Hair (eds), *Liverpool, the African Slave Trade and Abolition* (Liverpool, 1976), pp. 113–25; H. S. Klein, S. L. Engerman, R. Haines and R. Schlomowitz, 'Transoceanic Mortality: The Slave Trade in Comparative Perspective', *William and Mary Quarterly*, 58 (2000), p. 113.

63. S. D. Behrendt, 'The Captains in the British Slave Trade from 1785 to 1807', *Transactions of the Historic Society of Lancashire and Cheshire*, 140 (1991), p. 115; C. M. MacInnes, *Bristol and the Slave Trade* (Bristol, 1963), pp. 10–11.

64. R. L. Roberts, *Warriors, Merchants, and Slaves: The State and the Economy in the Middle Niger Valley, 1700–1914* (Stanford, CA, 1987); S. P. Reyna, *Wars Without End: The Political Economy of a Precolonial African State* (Hanover, NH, 1990).

65. J. Thornton, *The Kingdom of Kongo: Civil War and Transition, 1641–1718* (Madison, WI, 1983).

66. L. M. Heywood, 'Slavery and its Transformation in the kingdom of Kongo, 1491–1800', *Journal of African History*, 50 (2009), p. 22.

67. J. K. Fynn, *Asante and its Neighbours, 1700–1807* (London, 1971); R. A. Kea, 'Firearms and Warfare on the Gold and Slave Coasts from the Sixteenth to the Nineteenth Centuries', *Journal of African History*, 12 (1971), pp. 185–213.

68. J. C. Miller, 'Worlds Apart: Africans' Encounters and Africa's Encounters with the Atlantic in Angola, before 1800', *Actas do Seminário Encontro de Povos e Culturas em Angola* (1995), p. 274; D. Richardson, 'Prices of Slaves in West and West-Central Africa: Toward an Annual Series, 1698–1807', *Bulletin of Economic Research*, 43 (1991), pp. 21–56, esp. p. 47.

69. D. Eltis and D. Richardson, 'Productivity in the Transatlantic Slave Trade', *Explorations in Economic History*, 32 (1995), pp. 465–84, esp. p. 480; H. A. Gemery, J. S. Hogendorn and M. Johnson, 'Evidence on English–African Terms of Trade in the Eighteenth Century', *Explorations in Economic History*, 27 (1990), pp. 157–78, esp. p. 170.

70. J. E. Inikori, 'The Import of Firearms into West Africa', *Journal of African History*, 18 (1977), pp. 339–68; W. Richards, 'The Import of Firearms into West Africa in the Eighteenth Century', *Journal of African History*, 21 (1980), pp. 43–59; R. S. Smith, *Warfare and Diplomacy in Pre-Colonial West Africa* (2nd edn, London, 1989).

71. R. Law, 'Warfare on the West Africa Slave Coast, 1650–1850', in R. B. Ferguson and N. L. Whitehead (eds), *War in the Tribal Zone: Expanding States and Indigenous Warfare* (Santa Fe, NM, 1992), pp. 103–26; R. Law, '"Here is No Resisting the Country". The Realities of Power in Afro-European Relations on the West African "Slave Coast"', *Itinerario*, 18 (1994), pp. 55–6.

72. J. P. Smaldone, *Warfare in the Sokoto Caliphate* (Cambridge, 1977); R. Law, *The Oyo Empire c. 1600-c.1836: A West African Imperialism in the Era of the Atlantic Slave Trade* (Oxford, 1977); J. P. Smaldone, *The Horse in West African History: The Role of the Horse in the Societies of Pre-Colonial West Africa* (London, 1980); and 'The Horse in Pre-Colonial West Africa', in G. Pezzoli (ed.), *Cavalieri dell'Africa* (Milan, 1995), pp. 175–84.

73. G. Cornwallis-West, *The Life and Letters of Admiral Cornwallis* (London, 1927), pp. 50–1.

74. R. Law, 'King Agaja of Dahomey, the Slave Trade, and the Question of West African Plantations: The Mission of Bulfinch Lambe and Adomo Tomo to England, 1726–32', *Journal of Imperial and Commonwealth History*, 19 (1991), pp. 138–63.

75. P. E. Lovejoy and D. Richardson, 'Trust, Pawnship and Atlantic History: The Institutional Foundations of the Old Calabar Slave Trade', *American Historical Review*, 104 (1999), pp. 333–55; R. Law (ed.), *The Operation of the Slave Trade in Africa* (London, 2003); S. D. Behrendt, A. J. H. Latham and D. Northrup (eds), *The Diary of Antera Duke, an Eighteenth-Century African Slave Trader* (Oxford, 2010).

76. G. E. Brooks, *Eurafricans in Western Africa: Commerce, Social Status, Gender, and Religious Observance from the Sixteenth to the Eighteenth Century* (Oxford, 2003).

77. J. F. Searing, *West African Slavery and Atlantic Commerce: The Senegal River Valley, 1700–1860* (Cambridge, 1993); D. R.

Wright, *The World and a Very Small Place in Africa* (Armonk, NY, 1997).

78. S. A. Diouf (ed.), *Fighting the Slave Trade: West African Strategies* (Athens, OH, 2003).

79. W. Macaulay, *Memoranda Respecting the French Slave Trade in 1820* (London, 1820), p. 30.

80. D. Richardson, 'Shipboard Slave Revolts, African Authority, and the Atlantic Slave Trade', *William and Mary Quarterly*, 58 (2001), p. 74; E. R. Taylor, *If We Must Die: Shipboard Insurrections in the Era of the Atlantic Slave Trade* (Baton Rouge, LA, 2006).

81. E. J. Christopher, *Slave Ship Sailors and their Captive Cargoes* (Cambridge, 2006).

82. E. de Vattel, *The Laws of Nations* (Philadelphia, PA, 1861, translation of 1758 original), p. 361.

83. M. Mullin, *Africa in America: Slave Acculteration and Resistance in the American South and the British Caribbean, 1736–1831* (Urbana, IL, 1994).

84. S. J. Hornsby, *British Atlantic, American Frontier: Spaces of Power in Early Modern British America* (Lebanon, NH, 2005), p. 193.

85. R. R. Rea, 'Urban Problems and Responses in British Pensacola', *Gulf Coast Historical Review*, 3 (1987), p. 56.

86. D. R. Egerton, *Gabriel's Rebellion: The Virginia Slave Conspiracies of 1800 and 1802* (Chapel Hill, NC, 1997); J. Sidbury, *Ploughshares into Swords: Race, Rebellion, and Identity in Gabriel's Virginia, 1730–1810* (Cambridge, 1997).

87. H. L. Root, *Peasants and King in Burgundy: Agrarian Foundations of French Absolutism* (Berkeley, CA, 1987); W. te Brake, *Shaping History: Ordinary People in European Politics, 1500–1700* (Berkeley, CA, 1998); H. Beckles and K. Watson, 'Social Protest and Labour Bargaining: The Changing Nature of Slaves' Responses to Plantation Life in Eighteenth-Century Barbados', *Slavery and Abolition*, 8 (1987), pp. 272–93, esp. p. 275.

88. J. Lean and T. Burnard, 'Hearing Slave Voices: The Fiscal's Reports of Berbice and Demerara-Essequebo', *Archives*, 27 (2002), p. 123.

89. R. Soulodre-La France, 'Socially Not So Dead! Slave Identities in Bourbon Nueva Granada', *Colonial Latin American Review*,

10/1 (2001), pp. 87–103; A. A. Sio, 'Marginality and Free Colored Identity in Caribbean Slave Society', *Slavery and Abolition*, 8 (1987), pp. 166–82.

90. P. D. Morgan, *Slave Counterpoint: Black Culture in the Eighteenth-Century Chesapeake and Lowcountry* (Chapel Hill, NC, 1998).

91. R. Law, 'Individualising the Atlantic Slave Trade: The Biography of Mahommah Gardo Baquaqua of Djougou', *Transactions of the Royal Historical Society*, 6th series, 12 (2002), p. 116.

92. Quotation from R.B. Sheridan, 'The Condition of the Slaves in the Settlement and Economic Development of the British Windward Islands, 1763–1775', *Journal of Caribbean History*, 24 (1990), p. 131; T. Burnard, *Mastery, Tyranny, and Desire: Thomas Thistlewood and His Slaves in the Anglo-Jamaican World* (Chapel Hill, NC, 2004); K. Mason, 'The World an Absentee Planter and his Slaves Made: Sir William Stapleton and his Nevis Sugar Estate, 1722–1740', *Bulletin of the John Rylands University Library of Manchester*, 75 (1993), pp. 103–31, esp. p. 131. See also Klein, *Slavery in the Americas: A Comparative Study of Virginia and Cuba* (Chicago, 1967).

93. R. and S. Price (eds), *Stedman's Surinam: Life in an Eighteenth-Century Slave Society* (Baltimore, MD, 1992), pp. xxxii–xxxiii, 21.

94. J. Lean and T. Burnard, 'Hearing Slave Voices: The Fiscal's Report of Berbice and Demerara-Essequebo', *Archives*, 27 (2002), pp. 125–6.

95. J. E. Chaplin, *An Anxious Pursuit: Agricultural Innovation and Modernity in the Lower South, 1730–1815* (Chapel Hill, NC, 1993).

96. D. H. Usner, *Indians, Settlers and Slaves in a Frontier Exchange Economy: The Lower Mississippi Valley before 1783* (Chapel Hill, NC, 1992).

97. G. S. Rousseau, 'Le Cat and the Physiology of Negroes', *Studies in Eighteenth-Century Culture* (1973), pp. 369–86.

98. F. Felsenstein (ed.), *English Trader, Indian Maid: Representing Gender, Race, and Slavery in the New World: An Inkle and Yarico Reader* (Baltimore, MD, 1999).

99. J. R. Hertzler, 'Slavery in the Yearly Sermons Before the Georgia Trustees', *Georgia Historical Quarterly*, 59 (1975), pp. 118–26.

100. W. J. Fitzpatrick, *Suggestions on the Slave Trade for the Consideration of the Legislature of Great Britain* (London, 1797), pp. 45–6, 7 (quote).

101. Cited in D. Dabydeen, 'References to Blacks in William Hogarth's *Analysis of Beauty*', *British Journal for Eighteenth-Century Studies*, 5 (1982), p. 93.

102. J. M. Hartley, *A Social History of the Russian Empire, 1650–1825* (Harlow, 1999), pp. 67–8.

103. B. M. Saunderson, 'The *Encyclopédie* and Colonial Slavery', *British Journal for Eighteenth-Century Studies*, 7 (1984), pp. 15–37, esp. p. 37.

104. H. J. Lüsebrink and M. Tietz (eds), *Lectures de Raynal: L'Histoire des deux Indes en Europe et en Amérique au XVIIIe siècle* (Oxford, 1991).

105. G. W. Mullin, 'Rethinking American Negro Slavery from the Vantage Point of the Colonial Era', *Louisiana Studies*, 12 (1973), pp. 398–422; S. S. Hughes, 'Slaves for Hire: The Allocation of Black Labor in Elizabeth City County, Virginia, 1782 to 1810', *William and Mary Quarterly*, 35 (1978), pp. 260–86.

106. Silhouette to Amelot, 7 Sep. 1741, NA SP 107/49.

107. W. T. Hutchinson et al. (eds), *The Papers of James Madison* (Chicago, 1962), Vol. I, pp. 129–30, 153; G.S. McCowen, *The British Occupation of Charleston, 1780–1782* (Columbia, SC, 1972), p. 99.

108. A. A. Lawrence, *Storm over Savannah* (Athens, GA, 1951), p. 73.

109. J. Nagler, 'Achilles' Heel. Slavery and War in the American Revolution', in R. Chickering and S. Förster (eds), *War in an Age of Revolution, 1775–1815* (Cambridge, 2010), p. 296.

110. W. Cobbett (ed.), *Parliamentary History of England from the Norman Conquest 1066 to the year 1803* (36 vols, London, 1806–20), vol. 20, columns 1061–2.

111. M. Mullin, 'British Caribbean and North American Slaves in an Era of War and Revolution, 1775–1807', in J. J. Crow and L. E. Tise (eds), *The Southern Experience in the American Revolution* (Chapel Hill, NC, 1978), pp. 235, 240–1.

112. B. Quarles, *The Negro in the American Revolution* (Chapel Hill, NC, 1961); G.S. McCowen, *The British Occupation of*

Charleston, 1780–1782 (Columbia, SC, 1972), pp. 100–3; J. L. Malcolm, *Peter's War: A New England Slave Boy and the American Revolution* (New Haven, CT, 2009).

113. A. Zilversmit, *The First Emancipation: The Abolition of Slavery in the North* (Chicago, 1967).

Chapter 6

1. Cockburn to Kindelen, 13 Feb. 1815, NA War Office papers, 1/144. The island was Cumberland Island.

2. Exhibited in the National Gallery in Edinburgh.

3. Russell to Duke of Somerset, First Lord of the Admiralty, 7 Sep., NA PRO 30/22/30, Palmerston to Russell, 13 Aug. 1862, 30/22/22 fol. 92.

4. E.g. D. Laven, *Venice and Venetia under the Habsburgs, 1815–1835* (Oxford, 2002).

5. P. J. Marshall, *The Making and Unmaking of Empires: Britain, India, and America c. 1750–1783* (Oxford, 2005), p. 195.

6. E. Gøbel, 'The Danish Edict of 16th March 1792 to Abolish the Slave Trade', in J. Parmentier and S. Spanoghe (eds), *Orbis et orbem: Liber amicorum Jan Everaert* (Ghent, 2001), pp. 251–63. More generally, see D. Eltis and J. Walvin (eds), *The Abolition of the Atlantic Slave Trade: Origins and Effects in Europe, Africa, and the Americas* (Madison, WI, 1981).

7. A. Sens, 'Dutch Debates on Overseas Man and his World, 1770–1820', in B. Moore and H. van Nierop (eds), *Colonial Empires Compared: Britain and the Netherlands, 1750–1850* (Aldershot, 2003), pp. 86–7.

8. M. Postlethwayt, *The Universal Dictionary of Trade and Commerce* (4th edn, 2 vols, London, 1774), I, no pagination, entry for Africa.

9. C. L. Brown, *Moral Capital: Foundations of British Abolitionism* (Chapel Hill, NC, 2006).

10. T. Gray, *Devon and the Slave Trade: Documents on African Enslavement, Abolition and Emancipation from 1562 to 1867* (Exeter, 2007), pp. 166–8. For the situation in Scotland, I. Whyte, *Scotland and the Abolition of Black Slavery, 1756–1838* (Edinburgh, 2006).

11. S. Farrell, M. Unwin and J. Walvin (eds), *The British Slave Trade: Abolition, Parliament and People*, a special issue of *Parliamentary History* (Edinburgh, 2007).

12. Captain William Mackintosh to Henry Dundas, Secretary for War, 15 Apr. 1799, NA PRO 30/8/154 fol. 241.

13. Library of Congress, Washington, British caricature collection 2–575.

14. R. E. Close, 'Toleration and its Limits in the Late Hanoverian Empire: The Cape Colony 1795–1828', in S. Taylor, R. Connors and C. Jones (eds), *Hanoverian Britain and Empire* (Woodbridge, 1998), p. 303.

15. M. Dorigny and B. Gainot, *Atlas des Esclavages* (Paris, 2006), pp. 50–1.

16. M. Dorigny and B. Gainot, *La Société des Amis des Noirs, 1788–1799. Contributions à l'histoire de l'abolition de l'esclavage* (Paris, 1998).

17. *Archives parlementaires de 1790 à 1860: Recueil complet des débats législatifs et politiques des chambers françaises* (127 vols, Paris, 1879–1913), XXXVII, p. 152.

18. D. Geggus, 'Racial Equality, Slavery and Colonial Secession during the Constituent Assembly', *American Historical Review* (1989), pp. 1290–1308; J. J. Pierce, 'The Struggle for Black Liberty: Revolution and Emancipation in Saint Domingue', *Consortium on Revolutionary Europe. Selected Papers, 1997*, pp. 168–79.

19. C. Fink, *The Making of Haiti: The Saint Domingue Revolution from Below* (Knoxville, TN, 1991); L. Dubois, *A Colony of Citizens: Revolution and Slave Emancipation in the French Caribbean, 1787–1804* (Chapel Hill, NC, 2004).

20. R. N. Buckley, *Slaves in Red Coats: The British West India Regiments, 1795–1815* (New Haven, CT, 1979).

21. P. R. Girard, 'Liberté, Égalité, Esclavage: French Revolutionary Ideals and the Failure of the Leclerc Expedition to Saint-Domingue', *French Colonial History*, 6 (2005), pp. 67–8.

22. J. Adélaide-Merlande, R. Bélénus and F. Régent, *La Rébellion de la Guadeloupe, 1801–1802* (Gourbeyre, 2002).

23. J. R. McNeill, *Mosquito Empires: Ecology and War in the Greater Caribbean, 1620–1914* (Cambridge, 2010), p. 259.

24. M. Mason, *Slavery and Politics in the Early American Republic* (Chapel Hill, NC, 2006)

25. B. Marshall, 'Slave Resistance and White Reaction in the British Windward Islands, 1763–1833', *Caribbean Quarterly*, 28/3 (1982), pp. 39–40.

26. K. R. Maxwell, *Conflicts and Conspiracies: Brazil and Portugal, 1750–1808* (Cambridge, 1973), p. 222.

27. A. Hochschild, *Bury the Chains: The British Struggle to Abolish Slavery* (London, 2005).

28. E. Williams, *Capitalism and Slavery* (Chapel Hill, NC, 1944).

29. S. H. H. Carrington, *The Sugar Industry and the Abolition of the Slave Trade, 1775–1810* (Gainesville, FL, 2002).

30. D. B. Ryden, *West Indian Slavery and British Abolition, 1783–1807* (Cambridge, 2009), p. 252.

31. S. Drescher, *Econocide: British Slavery in the Era of Abolition* (London, 1977).

32. R. Anstey, 'Capitalism and Slavery: a Critique', *Economic History Review*, 2nd series, 21/2 (1968), p. 320.

33. K. Jacoby, 'Slaves by Nature? Domestic Animals and Human Slaves', *Slavery and Abolition*, 15 (1994), pp. 96–7.

34. S. Drescher, 'Whose Abolition? Popular Pressure and the Ending of the British Slave Trade', *Past and Present*, 143 (1994), pp. 136–66, esp. pp. 165–6.

35. William Hutton to Castlereagh, 11 Sep. 1812, in the papers of Henry, Third Earl Bathurst, Secretary of State for War and the Colonies, BL., Department of Manuscripts, Loan 57, vol. 21 no. 100.

36. J. Reich, 'The Slave Trade at the Congress of Vienna – A Study in English Public Opinion', *Journal of Negro History*, 53 (1968), pp. 129–43.

37. J. Pedro Marques, *The Sounds of Silence: Nineteenth-Century Portugal and the Abolition of the Slave Trade* (Oxford, 2006).

38. A. Burton, 'British Evangelicals, Economic Warfare and the Abolition of the Atlantic Slave Trade, 1794–1810', *Anglican and Episcopal History*, 65 (1996), pp. 197–225, esp. p. 223.

39. C. J. Bartlett and G. A. Smith, 'A "Species of Milito-Nautico-Guerrilla-Plundering Warfare". Admiral Alexander Cochrane's Naval Campaign against the United States, 1814–1815', in J. Flavell and S. Conway (eds), *Britain and America Go to War: The Impact of War and Warfare in Anglo-America, 1754–1815* (Gainesville, FL, 2004), pp. 187–90; John Harriott to Sidmouth, 7 May 1814, Exeter, Devon Record Office, Sidmouth papers, 152M/C1814/OF13. See also 152M/C1813/OF3 and NA War Office papers 1/141, pp. 63–7.

40. Foreign and Commonwealth Office Historians, History Note number 17, *Slavery in Diplomacy. The Foreign Office and the Suppression of the Transatlantic Slave Trade* (London, 2007), p. 11.

41. D. Eltis, 'The British Contribution to the Nineteenth-Century Transatlantic Slave Trade', *Economic History Review*, 2nd series, 32 (1979), pp. 211–27.

42. L. C. Jennings, 'French Policy towards Trading with African and Brazilian Slave Merchants', *Journal of African History*, 17 (1976), pp. 515–28; J. C. Dorsey, *Slave Traffic in the Age of Abolition: Puerto Rico, West Africa, and the Non-Hispanic Caribbean, 1815–1859* (Gainesville, FL, 2003).

43. J. Cobbing, 'The Mfecane as Alibi: Thoughts on Dithakong and Mbolompo', *Journal of African History*, 29 (1998), pp. 487–519.

44. E.g. J. D. Omer-Cooper, 'Has the Mfecane a Future? A Response to the Cobbing Critique', *Journal of Southern African Studies*, 19 (1993), pp. 273–94.

45. E. A. Eldredge, 'Sources of Conflict in Southern Africa, c. 1800–30: The Mfecane Reconsidered', *Journal of African History*, 23 (1992) pp. 1–35, esp. pp. 34–5.

46. S. Cave, *A Few Words, on the encouragement given to Slavery and the Slave Trade by Recent Measures, and Chiefly by the Sugar Bill of 1846* (London, 1849).

47. H. Klein and S. Engerman, 'Shipping Patterns and Mortality in the African Slave Trade to Rio de Janeiro, 1825–1830', *Cahiers d'Études Africaines*, 15 (1975), pp. 385–7.

48. K. O. Dike, *Trade and Politics in the Niger Delta 1830–1885* (Oxford, 1956), pp. 68–9.

49. K. Arhin, 'The Structure of Greater Ashanti (1700–1824)', *Journal of African History*, 8 (1967), pp. 65–85; K. Arhin, 'The Financing of Ashanti Expansion, 1700–1820', *Africa*, 37 (1967), pp. 283–91.

50. D. Ross, 'Mid-Nineteenth Century Dahomey: Recent Views vs. Contemporary Evidence', *History in Africa*, 12 (1985), pp. 307–23.

51. G. Campbell, 'Madagascar and the Slave Trade, 1810–1895', *Journal of African History*, 23 (1981), pp. 203–27; G. Campbell, 'The East African Slave Trade, 1861–1895: The "Southern Complex"', *International Journal of African Historical Studies*, 22 (1989), pp. 1–26.

52. M. Mason, 'The *Jihad* in the South: An Outline of the Nineteenth-Century Nupe Hegemony in North-Eastern Yorubaland and Afenmai', *Journal of the Historical Society of Nigeria*, 5 (1970), pp. 193–209; R. S. O'Fahey, 'Slavery and the Slave Trade in Darfur', *Journal of African History*, 14 (1973), pp. 29–43.

53. C. A. Bayly, *The Birth of the Modern World 1780–1914: Global Connections and Comparisons* (Oxford, 2004), pp. 404–5.

54. J. C. Dorsey, *Slave Traffic in the Age of Abolition: Puerto Rico, West Africa, and the Non-Hispanic Caribbean, 1815–1859* (Gainesville, FL, 2003).

55. M. Tadman, *Speculators and Slaves: Masters, Traders, and Slaves in the Old South* (Madison, WI, 1996); W. Johnson, *Soul By Soul: Life inside the Antebellum Slave Market* (Cambridge, MA, 1999); J. D. Martin, *Divided Mastery: Slave Hiring in the American South* (Cambridge, MA, 2004).

56. C. O. Paullin, *Atlas of the Historical Geography of the United States* (Washington, 1932); D. B. Dodd, *Historical Atlas of Alabama* (Tuscaloosa, AL, 1974); R. D. Gastil, *Culture Regions of the United States* (Seattle, MA, 1975).

57. J. Mokyr, *The Enlightened Economy: An Economic History of Britain 1700–1850* (New Haven, CT, 2009), p. 162.

58. J. Ashworth, *Slavery, Capitalism, and Politics in the Antebellum Republic. I: Commerce and Compromise, 1820–1850* (Cambridge, 1996).

59. J. Williamson, *New People: Miscegenation and Mullatoes in the United States* (Baton Rouge, LA, 1995).

60. S. Wilentz, 'Jeffersonian Democracy and the Origins of Political Antislavery in the United States: The Missouri Crisis Revisted', *Journal of the Historical Society*, 4 (2004), p. 392.

61. R. P. Forbes, *The Missouri Compromise and Its Aftermath: Slavery and the Meaning of America* (Chapel Hill, NC, 2007).

62. Stratford Canning to Viscount Castlereagh, Foreign Secretary, 6 Mar. 1820, 22 Apr. 1823, NA FO 5/166 fol. 196, 5/176 fol. 103.

63. G. Zellar, *African Creeks* (Norman, OK, 2007).

64. G. S. Graham, *Great Britain and the Indian Ocean: A Study of Maritime Enterprise, 1810–1850* (Oxford, 1967), pp. 106–7.

65. Palmerston to Russell, 21 July 1862, NA PRO 30/22/14C fol. 256.

66. Palmerston to Russell, 13 Aug. 1862, NA PRO 30/22/22 fol. 93.

67. Russell to Earl Cowley, envoy in Paris, 15 Apr. 1865, NA PRO 30/22/106 fol. 119.

68. K. A. Hamilton and P. Salmon (eds), *Slavery, Diplomacy and Empire: Britain and the Suppression of the Slave Trade, 1807–1975* (Brighton, 2009).

69. M. Dorigny and B. Gainot, *Atlas des Esclavages* (Paris, 2006), pp. 64–5.

70. W. J. Fitzpatrick (ed.), *Correspondence of Daniel O'Connell* (2 vols, London, 1888), II, pp. 207–10; E. D. Adams, *British Interests and Activities in Texas* (Gloucester, MA, 1963).

71. G. M. Brooke, 'The Role of the United States Navy in the Suppression of the African Slave Trade', *American Neptune*, 21 (1961), pp. 28–41; D. L. Canney, *Africa Squadron: The U.S. Navy and the Slave Trade, 1842–1861* (Dulles, VA, 2006).

72. C. H. Gilliland, *Voyage to a Thousand Cares: Master's Mate Lawrence with the African Squadron, 1844–1846* (Annapolis, MD, 2004).

73. Henry Fox, British envoy, to Aberdeen, 12 Dec. 1842, NA FO 5/377 fols 199–200, Lord Lyons, British envoy, to John, Lord Russell, Foreign Secretary, 6 Dec. 1859, 23 Jan., 5 Mar., 10 Apr. 1860, NA PRO 30/22/34 fols 63, 101, 118, 126–9.

74. C. Gillis, *Roman Catholicism in America* (Boulder, CO, 1999), p. 58.

75. W. L. Mathieson, *Great Britain and the Slave Trade, 1839–65* (London, 1929).

76. R. Conrad, *World of Sorrow: The African Slave Trade to Brazil* (Baton Rouge, LA, 1986).

77. Palmerston to Russell, 3 Mar., Buxton to Palmerston, 2 Mar. 1861, NA PRO 30/22/21 fols 444–6.

78. L. Bethell, *The Abolition of the Brazilian Slave Trade* (Cambridge, 1970).

79. A. F. Corwin, *Spain and the Abolition of Slavery in Cuba, 1817–1886* (Austin, TX, 1967); D. R. Murray, *Odious Commerce: Britain, Spain and the Abolition of the Cuban Slave Trade* (Cambridge, 1980).

80. Palmerston to Russell, 31 July 1863, Russell to Sir John Crampton, envoy in Madrid, 8 Aug. 1861, 12 June 1862, 23 Jan., 30 Mar. 1863, NA PRO 30/22/22 fol. 221, 30/22/115 fols 26, 43, 53, 55.

81. P. M. Kielstra, *The Politics of Slave Trade Suppression in Britain and France, 1814–48: Diplomacy, Morality and Economics* (Basingstoke, 2000).

82. C. N. Parkinson, *Edward Pellew, Viscount Exmouth, Admiral of the Red* (London, 1934), pp. 419–72.

83. S. J. Shaw, 'The Origins of Ottoman Military Reform: The Nizam-I Cedid Army of Sultan Selim III', *Journal of Modern History*, 37 (1965), pp. 291–5.

84. J. Waley-Cohen, *Exile in Mid-Qing China: Banishment to Xinjiang, 1758–1820* (New Haven, CT, 1991).

85. D. Northrup, 'The Compatibility of the Slave and Palm Oil Trades in the Bight of Biafra', *Journal of African History*, 17 (1976), p. 357.

86. S. Rees, *Sweet Water and Bitter: The Ships that Stopped the Slave Trade* (London, 2009), p. 308; Elliott journal reported on in *The Times*, 12 July 2006.

87. C. D. Kaufmann and R. A. Pape, 'Explaining Costly International Action: Britain's Sixty-Year Campaign Against the Atlantic Slave Trade', *International Organization*, 53 (2003), pp. 634–7.

88. Palmerston to Russell, 31 July 1863, NA PRO 30/22/22 fol. 221.

89. J. E. Thomson, *Mercenaries, Pirates, and Sovereigns: State-Building and Extraterritorial Violence in Early Modern Europe* (Princeton, NJ, 1994).

90. J. S. Mansfield, *Remarks on the African Squadron* (London, 1851), p. 21.

91. A.A. Boahen, *Britain, the Sahara and the Western Sudan, 1788–1861* (Oxford, 1964).

92. Stevenson to Liverpool, 1 Feb. 1812, Exeter, Devon County Record Office, 152H/C1812/OF27.

93. K. Gleadle, *Borderline Citizens: Women, Gender, and Political Culture in Britain, 1815–1867* (Oxford, 2009).

94. Palmerston to Russell, 21 July, 13 Aug. 1862, NA PRO 30/22/14C fols 255–6, 30/22/22 fol. 94.

95. N. Thompson, *Earl Bathurst and the British Empire* (Barnsley, 1999), pp. 167–8.

96. P. Lane and D. Johnson, 'The Archaeology and History of Slavery in South Sudan in the Nineteenth Century', in A. C. S. Peacock (ed.), *The Frontiers of the Ottoman World* (London, 2009), pp. 516–18.

97. J. J. Ewald, *Soldiers, Traders and Slaves: State Formation and Economic Transformation in the Greater Nile Valley, 1700–1885* (Madison, WI, 1990).
98. R. Adams, *A Narrative of Robert Adams* (London, 1816), pp. 39–40, 62.
99. M. Crowder and S. Miers, 'The Politics of Slavery in Bechuanaland: Power Struggles and the Plight of the Basarwa', in S. Miers and R. Roberts (eds), *The End of Slavery in Africa* (Madison, WI, 1988), pp. 175–6.

Chapter 7

1. Z. Macauley, *The Slave Colonies of Great Britain* (London, 1826), p. 115.
2. Palmerston to Russell, 24 Sep. 1861, NA PRO 30/22/21 fol. 563.
3. A. J. Barker, *Slavery and Antislavery in Mauritius, 1810–33: The Conflict between Economic Expansion and Humanitarian Reform under British Rule* (London, 1996); B. W. Higman, *Slave Populations of the British Caribbean, 1807–1834* (Baltimore, MD, 1984).
4. J. R. Ward, *British West Indian Slavery, 1750–1834: The Process of Amelioration* (London, 1988).
5. T. S. Winn, *A Speedy End to Slavery in our West India Colonies* (London, 1825), p. 105.
6. M. Turner, *Slaves and Missionaries: The Disintegration of Jamaican Slave Society, 1787–1834* (Urbana, IL, 1982); E. V. d'Costa, *Crowns of Glory, Tears of Blood: The Demerara Slave Rebellion of 1823* (New York, 1994).
7. C. Petley, *Slaveholders in Jamaica* (London, 2009), pp. 119–20; G. Mathews, *Caribbean Slave Revolts and the British Abolitionist Movement* (Baton Rouge, LA, 2006).
8. M. D. Childs, *The 1812 Aponte Rebellion in Cuba and the Struggle against Atlantic Slavery* (Chapel Hill, NC, 2006).
9. Winn, *Speedy End*, p. 109.
10. T. R. Young, 'The United States Army and the Institution of Slavery in Louisiana, 1803–1835', *Louisiana Studies*, 13 (1974), pp. 209–13; S. Hadden, *Slave Patrols: Law and Violence in Virginia and the Carolinas* (Cambridge, MA, 2001).
11. R. A. Gross (ed.), 'Forum: The Making of a Slave Conspiracy', *William and Mary Quarterly*, 58 (2001), pp. 913–76, 59 (2002),

pp. 135–202; R. L. Paquette, 'From Rebellion to Revisionism: The Continuing Debate about the Denmark Vesey Affair', *Journal of the Historical Society*, 4 (2004), pp. 291–334.

12. J. D. Milligan, 'Slave rebelliousness and the Florida Maroon', *Prologue*, 6 (spring 1974), pp. 4–18.

13. J. J. Reis, *Slave Rebellion in Brazil: The Muslim Uprising of 1835 in Bahia* (Baltimore, MD, 1993).

14. *Second Report of the Committee of the Society for the Mitigation and Gradual Abolition of Slavery* . . . (London, 1825), p. 115.

15. M. C. Karasch, *Slave Life in Rio de Janeiro, 1808–1850* (Princeton, NJ, 1987); B. J. Barickman, *A Bahian Counterpoint: Sugar, Tobacco, Cassava, and Slavery in the Recôncavo, 1780–1860* (Stanford, CA, 1998).

16. *Third Report of the Committee of the Society for the Mitigation and Gradual Abolition of Slavery* . . . (London, 1826), p. 20.

17. R. Newton, *Eighteenth Century Exeter* (Exeter, 1984), p. 143.

18. N. Draper, *The Price of Emancipation: Slave-Ownership, Compensation and British Society at the End of Slavery* (Cambridge, 2009), p. 272.

19. M. Ennaji, *Serving the Master: Slavery and Society in Nineteenth-Century Morocco* (New York, 1999).

20. S. Drescher, *The Mighty Experiment: Free Labor versus Slavery in British Emancipation* (Oxford, 2002).

21. B. Fladeland, *Men and Brothers: Anglo-American Antislavery Cooperation* (Urbana, IL, 1972).

22. S. Drescher, *From Slavery to Freedom: Comparative Studies in the Rise and Fall of Atlantic Slavery* (New York, 1999).

23. Russell to Sir John Crampton, envoy in Madrid, 12 July 1862, NA PRO 30/22/115 fol. 43.

24. L. Dubois, 'The Road to 1848: Interpreting French Anti-Slavery', *Slavery and Abolition*, 22 (2001), pp. 150–7.

25. M. A. Morrison, 'The Westward Curse of Empire: Texas Annexation and the American Whig Party', *Journal of the Early Republic*, 10 (1990), pp. 221–49.

26. Clarendon to Sir John Crampton, 4 Jan. 1846, Bod. MS Clar. Dep C. 135 p. 37.

27. J. G. Dawson, 'Jefferson Davis and the Confederacy's "Offensive-Defensive Strategy" in the U.S. Civil War', *Journal of Military History*, 73 (2009), p. 595.

28. B. Rauch, *American Interest in Cuba, 1848–1855* (New York, 1948); R. E. May, *The Southern Dream of a Caribbean Empire, 1854–1861* (Baton Rouge, LA, 1973); Sir Henry Bulwer, British envoy in Washington, to Palmerston, 27 Jan. 1851, NA FO 5/527 fols 90–1.

29. Lyons to Russell, 5 Mar. 1860, NA PRO 30/22/34 fol. 119.

30. Lyons to Russell, 6 Dec. 1859, NA PRO 30/22/34.

31. Lyons to Russell, 22 Nov. 1859, NA PRO 30/22/34 fol. 54; R. E. McGlone, *John Brown's War against Slavery* (New York, 2009).

32. D. E. Reynolds, *Texas Terror: The Slave Insurrection Panic of 1860 and the Secession of the Lower South* (Baton Rouge, LA, 2007).

33. Palmerston to Russell, 14 Apr. 1861 NA PRO 30/22/21 fols 464–5.

34. NA FO 5/877 fol. 149.

35. A. C. Guelzo, *Lincoln's Emancipation Proclamation: The End of Slavery in America* (New York, 2004).

36. Lyons to Russell, 2 Jan. 1863, NA PRO 30/22/37 fol. 1.

37. B. M. Carnaham, *Act of Justice: Lincoln's Emancipation Proclamation and the Law of War* (Lexington, KT, 2007).

38. Lyons to Russell, 21 Feb., 25, 31 Mar., 8, 22, 25 Apr. 1862, NA PRO 30/22/36 fols 48–9, 56, 58, 63, 70–1, 83.

39. Thomas to Elizabeth Peace, 19 Sep. 1864, Manchester, John Rylands Library, REAS/2/4/25.

40. D. B. Davis, 'Slavery, Emancipation, and Progress', *Historically Speaking*, 8/6 (July/August 2007), p. 14.

41. E. L. Pierce (ed.), *Memoirs and Letters of Charles Sumner, 1860 to Death* (London, 1893), pp. 68–9.

42. Christie to Russell, 20 Aug. 1859, 21 Sep. 1860, 24 Aug. 1861, NA PRO 30/22/48 fols 9, 33–4, 71.

43. Palmerston to Russell, 13 Aug. 1862, 4 May, 31 July 1863, NA PRO 30/22/22 fols 94–5, 168–70, 221.

44. S. Drescher, 'Brazilian Abolition in Comparative Perspective', *Hispanic American Historical Review*, 68 (1988), p. 433.

45. R. B. Toplin, *The Abolition of Slavery in Brazil* (New York, 1972); R. Conrad, *The Destruction of Brazilian Slavery, 1850–1888* (Berkeley, CA, 1972); P. A. Howard, *Changing History: Afro-Cuban Cabildos and Societies of Color in the Nineteenth Century* (Baton Rouge, LA, 1998).

46. S. Miers, *Slavery in the Twentieth Century: The Evolution of a Global Problem* (Walnut Creek, CA, 2003).

47. A. Dupuy, *Haiti in the World Economy: Class, Race, and Under-development since 1700* (Boulder, CO, 1989).

48. S. Cave, *A Few Words on the Encouragement Given to Slavery . . . by the Sugar Bill of 1846* (London, 1849), p. 8.

49. O. N. Bolland, 'Systems of Domination after Slavery: The Control of Land and Labor in the British West Indies after 1838', *Comparative Studies in Society and History*, 23 (1981), pp. 591–619, esp. 612–17.

50. W. Kloosterboer, *Involuntary Labour Since the Abolition of Slavery* (Leiden, 1960); D. Eltis (ed.), *Coerced and Free Migration: Global Perspectives* (Stanford, CA, 2002).

51. P. Morgan, 'Work and Culture: The Task System and the World of Lowcountry Blacks, 1700 to 1880', *William and Mary Quarterly*, 3rd series, 39 (1982), pp. 563–99.

52. M. Kale, *Fragments of Empire: Capital, Slavery and Indian Indentured Labor Migration in the British Caribbean* (Philadelphia, PA, 1998).

53. M. Carter and C. Bates, 'Empire and Locality: A Global Dimension to the 1857 Indian Uprising', *Journal of Global History*, 5 (2010), pp. 58–60.

54. L. Yun, *The Coolie Speaks: Chinese Indentured Laborers and African Slaves of Cuba* (Philadelphia, PA, 2008); J. M. T. Carter, *Painting the Islands Vermilion: Archibald Watson and the Brig 'Carl'* (Melbourne, 1999); N. Thomas, *Islanders: The Pacific in the Age of Empire* (New Haven, CT, 2010), pp. 192–9.

55. G. Prakash, *Bonded Histories: Genealogies of Labour Servitude in Colonial India* (Cambridge, 1990).

56. A. W. Trelease, *White Terror: The Ku Klux Klan Conspiracy and Southern Reconstruction* (New York, 1971).

57. R. Ransom and R. Sutch, *One Kind of Freedom?: The Economic Consequences of Emancipation* (Cambridge, 1977); S. Decarrio, 'Productivity and Income Distribution in the Postbellum South', *Journal of Economic History*, 34 (1974), pp. 422–46.

58. W. A. Green, 'The Planter Class and British West Indian Sugar Production Before and After Emancipation', *Economic History Review*, 2nd series, 26 (1973), pp. 448–63, esp. pp. 462–3.

59. K. Bawil, 'Slavers in nineteenth-century Northern Thailand', in E. P. Durrenberger (ed.), *State Power and Culture in Thailand* (New Haven, CT, 1996), pp. 100–38.

60. A. Sheriff, *Slaves, Spices and Ivory in Zanzibar* (London, 1987); T. Ricks, 'Slaves and Slave Traders in the Persian Gulf, 18th and 19th Centuries: An Assessment', in W. G. Clarence-Smith (ed.), *The Economics of the Indian Ocean Slave Trade in the Nineteenth Century* (London, 1989), pp. 60–70; A. Moore-Harell, 'Economic and Political Aspects of the Slave Trade in Ethiopia and the Sudan in the Second Half of the Nineteenth Century', *International Journal of African Historical Studies*, 32 (1999), pp. 407–21.

61. A. L. P. Burdett (ed.), *The Slave Trade to Arabia 1820–1973*, I (Slough, 2006), p. vi, fn. 5.

62. R. Coupland, *The Exploitation of East Africa, 1856–90: The Slave Trade and the Scramble* (London, 1939).

63. S. J. Braidwood, *Black Poor and White Philanthropists: London Blacks and the Foundation of the Sierra Leone Settlement, 1786–1791* (Liverpool, 1994).

64. K. O'Brien, 'Colonial Emigration, Public Policy, and Tory Romanticism, 1783–1830', in D. Kelly (ed.), *Lineages of Empire: The Historical Roots of British Imperial Thought* (Oxford, 2009), p. 172; D. Coleman, *Romantic Colonization and British Anti-Slavery* (Cambridge, 2005).

65. J. Sidbury, *Becoming African in America: Race and Nation in the Early Black Atlantic* (New York, 2007).

66. E. S. Vansickle, 'A Transnational Vision for African Colonization: John H.B. Latrobe and the Future of Maryland in Liberia', *Journal of Transatlantic Studies*, 1 (2003), pp. 214–32.

67. Stratford Canning, British envoy in Washington, to Castlereagh, 5 Feb. 1821, NA FO 5/157 fol. 78.

68. T. Jeal, *Stanley: The Impossible Life of Africa's Greatest Explorer* (London, 2007).

69. R. Mowafi, *Slavery, Slave Trade and Abolition Attempts in Egypt and the Sudan, 1820–1882* (Lund, 1985).

70. D. Robinson-Dunn, *The Harem, Slavery and British Imperial Culture: Anglo-Muslim Relations in the Late-Nineteenth Century* (Manchester, 2006); E.R. Toledano, *The Ottoman Slave Trade and its Suppression, 1840–1890* (Princeton, NJ, 1982); and

Slavery and Abolition in the Ottoman Middle East (Seattle, WA, 1998).

71. D. Robinson, *The Holy War of Umar Tel: The Western Sudan in the Mid-Nineteenth Century* (Oxford, 1985), p. 330.

72. C. I. Wilks, *Asante in the Nineteenth Century* (Cambridge, 1975).

73. R. H. Dusgate, *The Conquest of Northern Nigeria* (London, 1985).

74. G. Chaliand and Y. Ternon, *Le génocide des Arméniens* (Brussels, 1984), p. 112.

75. L. Kurtynova-D'Herlugnan, *The Tsar's Abolitionists: The Slave Trade in the Caucasus and its Suppression* (London, 2010).

76. H. Newman, *Banani: The Transition from Slavery to Freedom in Zanzibar and Perma* (London, 1898), pp. vi, 200.

77. J. Grace, *Domestic Slavery in West Africa, with particular reference to the Sierra Leone Protectorate, 1896–1927* (London, 1975).

78. S. J. Coleman, 'Gradual Abolition or Immediate Abolition of Slavery? The Political, Social and Economic Quandry of Emperor Haile Selassie I', *Slavery and Abolition*, 29 (2008), pp. 65–82.

Chapter 8

1. M. Lombardo, 'Bonded Labour in Pakistan', in D. Smith (ed.), *Slavery Now and Then* (Eastbourne, 2007), p. 112.

2. E. Larkin, *Everything is Broken: The Untold Story of Life under Burma's Military Regime* (London, 2010).

3. D. S. Painter, 'Oil, Resources, and the Cold War, 1945–1962', in M. P. Leffler and O.A. Westad (eds), *The Cambridge History of the Cold War* (3 vols, Cambridge, 2010), I, p. 488.

4. P. Hayes, *Industry and Ideology: I. G. Farben in the Nazi Era* (Cambridge, 1987); M.T. Allen, *The Business of Genocide: The SS, Slave Labor, and the Concentration Camps* (Chapel Hill, NC, 2002).

5. F. Piper, *Auschwitz Prison Labour: The Organisation and Exploitation of Auschwitz Concentration Camp Prisoners as Labourers* (Oswiecim, 2002).

6. W. Gruner, *Jewish Forced Labor under the Nazis: Economic Needs and Racial Aims, 1938–1944* (Cambridge, 2006).

7. U. Herbert, *Hitler's Foreign Workers: Enforced Labor in Germany under the Third Reich* (Cambridge, 1977).

8. T. P. Mulligan, *The Politics of Illusion and Empire: German Occupation Policy in the Soviet Union, 1942–1943* (London, 1988).

9. W. D. Smith, 'Beyond the Bridge on the River Kwai: Labor Mobilization in the Greater East Asia Co-Prosperity Sphere', *International Labor and Working Class History*, 58 (2000), pp. 219–38.

10. G. Hicks, *The Comfort Women: Japan's Brutal Regime of Enforced Prostitution in the Second World War* (New York, 1994); Y. Yoshimi, *Comfort Women: Sexual Slavery in the Japanese Military During World War II* (New York, 2000); Y. Tanaka, *Japan's Comfort Women: Sexual Slavery and Prostitution during World War II and the US Occupation* (London, 2002).

11. B. Madley, 'From Africa to Auschwitz: How German South West Africa Included Ideas and Methods Adopted and Developed by the Nazis in Eastern Europe', *European History Quarterly*, 33 (2005), pp. 429–64; J. Zimmerer, 'The Birth of the "Ostland" out of the Spirit of Colonialism: A Postcolonial Perspective on Nazi Policy of Conquest and Extermination', *Patterns of Prejudice*, 39 (2005), pp. 197–219.

12. R. Gerwarth and S. Malinowski, 'Hannah Arendt's Ghosts: Reflections on the Disputable Path from Windhoek to Auschwitz', *Central European History*, 42 (2009), pp. 279–300.

13. S. Courtois (ed.), *The Black Book of Communism: Crimes, Terror, Repression* (Cambridge, MA, 1999).

14. N. Werth, *Cannibal Island: Death in the Siberian Gulag* (Princeton, NJ, 2007); N. M. Naimark, *Stalin's Genocides* (Princeton, NJ, 2010), pp. 59–66.

15. K. R. Jolluck, *Exile and Identity: Polish Women in the Soviet Union during World War II* (Pittsburgh, PA, 2003).

16. A. Applebaum, *Gulag: A History* (London, 2003); O. V. Klevniuk, *The History of the Gulag: From Collectivization to the Great Terror* (New Haven, CT, 2004).

17. *Africa Research Bulletin, Political Series*, 17/7 (July 1980), p. 5757, 18/1 (Jan. 1981), p. 6267.

18. *Africa Research Bulletin, Political Series*, 44/9 (Sep. 2007), p. 17246.

19. Special issue, 'Esclavage moderne ou modernité de l'esclavage?', *Cahiers d'Études Africaines*, 179 (2005).

20. *Africa Research Bulletin, Political Series*, 45/10 (Oct. 2008), p. 17733, 42/3 (Mar. 2005), p. 16164.

21. US State Department, *Trafficking in Persons Report* (June 2005); *Africa Research Bulletin, Political Series*, 42/8 (Aug. 2005), pp. 16341–4.

22. K. Bales, *Disposable People: New Slavery in the Global Economy* (Berkeley, CA, 1999).

Chapter 9

1. J. O. and L. E. Horton (eds), *Slavery and Public History: The Tough Stuff of American Memory* (New York, 2006).

2. E. Williams, *Capitalism and Slavery* (Chapel Hill, NC, 1944).

3. S. W. Mintz and R. Price, *The Birth of African American Culture: An Anthropological Perspective* (Boston, MA, 1992).

4. S. E. Green-Pedersen, 'The Scope and Structure of the Danish Negro Slave Trade', *Scandinavian Economic History Review*, 19 (1971), pp. 149–97.

5. *Independent*, 13 Sep. 2006.

6. T. Ranger, 'The Invention of Tradition in Colonial Africa', in E. Hobsbawn and T. Ranger (eds), *The Invention of Tradition* (Cambridge, 1983), pp. 211–62; C. Lentz and P. Nugent (eds), *Ethnicity in Ghana: The Limits of Invention* (Basingstoke, 2000); J. D. Y. Peel, *Religious Encounter and the Making of the Yoruba* (Bloomington, IN, 2000).

7. P. Manning, *Slavery and African Life: Occidental, Oriental, and African Slave Trades* (Cambridge, 1990).

8. A. Gallay, *The Indian Slave Trade* (New Haven, CT, 2002).

9. A. McFarlane, 'Rebellions in Late Colonial Spanish America: a Comparative Perspective', *Bulletin of Latin American Research*, 14 (1995), p. 313; S. J. Stern, 'The Age of Andean Insurrection, 1742–1782', in S. J. Stern (ed.), *Resistance, Rebellion and Consciousness in the Andean Peasant World: 18th to 20th Centuries* (Madison, WI), p. 35.

10. J. Fonte, 'Liberal Democracy vs. Transnational Progressivism: The Ideological War Within the West', *Orbis*, 46 (2002), pp. 449–67.

11. J. Kurlantzick, *Charm Offensive: How China's Soft Power is Transforming the World* (New Haven, CT, 2007).

SELECTED FURTHER READING

The extensive and excellent literature on this subject grows annually. To suggest a small number of works is therefore difficult. In line with the likely readership, the emphasis here is on English-language works and recent literature, as earlier studies can be followed up through the footnotes of this book and those cited in this list. A searchable online version of Joseph Miller's slavery bibliography can be found at http://www2.vcdh.virginia.edu/bib/

Bales, K., *Understanding Global Slavery* (2005).
Blackburn, R., *The Making of New World Slavery* (1997).
Brown, C. L., *Moral Capital: Foundations of British Abolitionism* (2006).
Conrad, R., *The Destruction of Brazilian Slavery* (1972).
Davis, D. B., *The Problem of Slavery in Western Culture* (1966).
Davis, D. B., *Slavery and Human Progress* (1984).
Davis, D. B., *Inhuman Bondage: The Rise and Fall of Slavery in the New World* (2006).
Davis, R. C., *Christian Slaves, Muslim Masters: White Slavery in the Mediterranean, the Barbary Coast, and Italy, 1500–1800* (2004).

Drescher, S., *The Mighty Experiment: Free Labor versus Slavery in British Emancipation* (2002).

Drescher, S., *Abolition. A History of Slavery and Antislavery* (2009).

Dunn, R. S., *Sugar and Slaves: The Rise of the Planter Class in the English West Indies* (1972).

Eltis, D. (ed.), *Coerced and Free Migration: Global Perspectives* (2002).

Eltis, D. and Richardson, D. (eds), *Extending the Frontiers: Essays on the New Transatlantic Slave Trade Database.* (2008).

Engerman, S. L., *Slavery, Emancipation, and Freedom: Comparative Perspectives* (2007).

Ettis, D. and Richardson, D., *Atlas of the Transatlantic Slave Trade* (2010).

Hamilton, K. A. and Salmon, P. (eds), *Slavery, Diplomacy and Empire: Britain and the Suppression of the Slave Trade, 1807–1975* (2009).

Hopkins, K., *Conquerers and Slaves: Sociological Studies in Roman History* (1978).

Hochschild, A., *Bury the Chains: Prophets and Rebels in the Fight to Free an Empire's Slaves* (2005).

Hunt, P., *Slaves, Warfare and Ideology in the Greek Historians* (1998).

Hunwick, J. and Powel, E. T. (eds), *The African Diaspora in the Mediterranean Lands of Islam* (2002).

Jordan, W. D., *White over Black: American Attitudes towards the Negro, 1550–1812* (1968).

Kulikoff, A., *Tobacco and Slaves: The Development of Southern Cultures in the Chesapeake, 1680–1800* (1986).

Law, R., *The Slave Coast of West Africa, 1550–1750: The Impact of the Atlantic Slave Trade on an African Society* (1991).

Law, R. and Lovejoy, P. E., *The Biography of Mahommah Gardo Baquaqua: His Passage from Slavery to Freedom in Africa and America* (2002).

Levy, R., *The Social Structure of Islam* (1965).

Lewis, B., *Race and Slavery in the Middle East: An Historical Inquiry* (1992).

Miers, S. and Kopytoff, I. (eds), *Slavery in Africa: Historical and Anthropological Perspectives* (1977).

Morgan, E. S., *American Slavery, American Freedom: The Ordeal of Colonial Virginia* (1975).

Patterson, O., *Slavery and Social Death: A Comparative Study* (1982).

Phillips, W. D., *Slavery from Roman Times to the Early Transatlantic Trade* (1985).

Rodgers, N., *Ireland, Slavery and Anti-Slavery: 1612–1865* (2009).

Schama, S., *Rough Crossings: Britain, the Slaves and the American Revolution* (2006).

Smith, D. (ed.), *Slavery Now and Then* (2007).

Thomas, H., *The Slave Trade* (1997).

Thornton, J., *Africa and Africans in the Making of the Atlantic World* (1998).

Vaughan, A. T., *Roots of American Racism* (1995).

Walvin, J., *Atlas of Slavery* (2005).

Walvin, J., *A Short History of Slavery* (2007).

INDEX